DISCOVER Colorado

DISCOVER Colorado

Its People, Places, and Times

Second Edition

Matthew Downey and Jenny Pettit

UNIVERSITY PRESS OF COLORADO
Boulder

THE AUTHORS

Matthew Downey is a professor of history emeritus at the University of Northern Colorado. He also directed UNC's Interdisciplinary Studies Elementary Teaching major for future elementary teachers. Professor Downey has written several history textbooks as well as numerous books and articles about history education.

Jenny Pettit has taught social studies for over sixteen years in public, private, and online schools. She has developed and published curriculum for elementary, secondary, and college levels. Jenny is the social studies curriculum coordinator for the St. Vrain Valley School District.

Second Edition

Published by University Press of Colorado
5589 Arapahoe Avenue, Suite 206C
Boulder, Colorado 80303

Printed in the United States of America
First edition © 2007 by Matthew Downey and Ty Bliss, published by Pruett Publishing Company

The University Press of Colorado is a proud member of
the Association of American University Presses.

The University Press of Colorado is a cooperative publishing enterprise supported, in part, by Adams State University, Colorado State University, Fort Lewis College, Metropolitan State University of Denver, Regis University, University of Colorado, University of Northern Colorado, Utah State University, and Western State Colorado University.

∞ This paper meets the requirements of the ANSI/NISO Z39.48-1992 (Permanence of Paper).

DOI: 10.5876/9781607323587

Library of Congress Cataloging-in-Publication Data
Downey, Matthew T.
Discover Colorado : its people, places, and times / Matthew Downey and Jenny Pettit. — Second edition.
pages cm
Includes index.
ISBN 978-1-60732-357-0 (cloth) — ISBN 978-1-60732-358-7 (ebook)
1. Colorado—History—Juvenile literature. I. Pettit, Jenny. II. Title.
F776.3.D68 2015
978.8—dc23
2014042186

Design by Daniel Pratt

To this book's readers:
students setting out to discover Colorado's
fascinating people, places, and times.

Contents

DISCOVER Colorado

UNIT ONE
A Place Called Colorado

People

Millions of people live in the place we call Colorado. Different kinds of people here make their living in different ways. They also live in very different places within Colorado.

Places

Colorado is made up of different regions and life zones. Regions are large areas where the landscape looks much the same. Life zones have similar animals and plants.

Times

Colorado's landscape, plants, and animals have changed over time. Over millions of years, entire mountain ranges have come and gone. Dinosaurs once walked where cattle now graze. The land has its own history.

Geography

Before You Read

Scan this chapter. Look at the section headings, photos, captions, and the bold printed words. Then write in your notebook two or three sentences that explain how you think geography will help you learn about Colorado.

KEY-WORDS

- capital cities
- landscape
- location
- place
- scales
- spatially
- longitude
- latitude

WHAT IS GEOGRAPHY?

Geography is the study of places and people and how they interact. Places include not only states and **capital cities** but river valleys, grasslands, and farming country. Geography is about why people move from one place to another and how they make use of its resources. It is also the study of how people change the **landscape** and animal and plant life of a place and how these environments change them. Geography is a way of thinking about how things are related in space. It is a way to view the world in which we live.

Focus Your Reading

- What is geography?
- What tools do geographers use?
- What do geographic thinkers want to know about?

ASKING GEOGRAPHIC QUESTIONS

The study of geography begins by asking geographic questions. For example, pretend that you have a new on-line friend from a foreign country. It was your teacher's idea. She thought that having an on-line friend (they used to be called "pen pals") would help you learn about other people and distant places. She also thought it would be a good way

for you to learn more about where you live. Your friend may know little about this part of the world and may have many questions that you will need to answer. So what was the first question your new friend asked?

"Where is Colorado?"

Where a place is located is a geographic question. Geographers, people who make a living studying geography, often ask that question. So do ordinary people, including students like you, when they think geographically. Thinking geographically begins by asking questions about **location** and **place**. We will start with these and move on to other questions later.

While You Read

List in your notebook three tools geographers use.

GEOGRAPHIC TOOLS

Geographers have created tools to help us answer questions about location and place. These tools include globes and maps. Globes provide an overview of the world. They help us answer really big questions about where continents and oceans are located and how they are **spatially** related. Maps are better for smaller questions, such as the distance between cities. Not all maps are the same, as they are drawn to different **scales**. By *scale* we mean how many miles equals one inch on a map. Using the maps on page 5, write a response to your new friend that explains where Colorado is located.

Maps provide different kinds of information to help us locate places. Road maps (see Colorado road map on page 6) show the distance or miles between towns and cities. Some maps include **longitude** and **latitude** lines (see Reading a Map section page 8). These lines divide the world into the parts of a circle called "degrees," indicated by the symbol ° next to the number. The latitude lines that run north and south show distance from the Equator to the North or South Pole, which is 90 degrees of a circle. The east and west longitude lines show distance from the 0° line, or

Where is Colorado?

Our world is the planet
Earth.

Our continent is
North America.

Our country is the
United States of America.

Our state is
Colorado.

Colorado roads

Prime Meridian, which is a complete circle of 360 degrees. Maps are not the only tools we use to locate places. We can locate our school or home by a satellite photograph, such as the one on page 7. Global Positioning Systems use communication satellites to show us where places are located and how to get there.

GEOGRAPHIC THINKING

Geographic thinking begins with asking questions about where places are located. But it does not stop there. Geographic thinkers also want to know about those places. They especially want to know how the location of a place

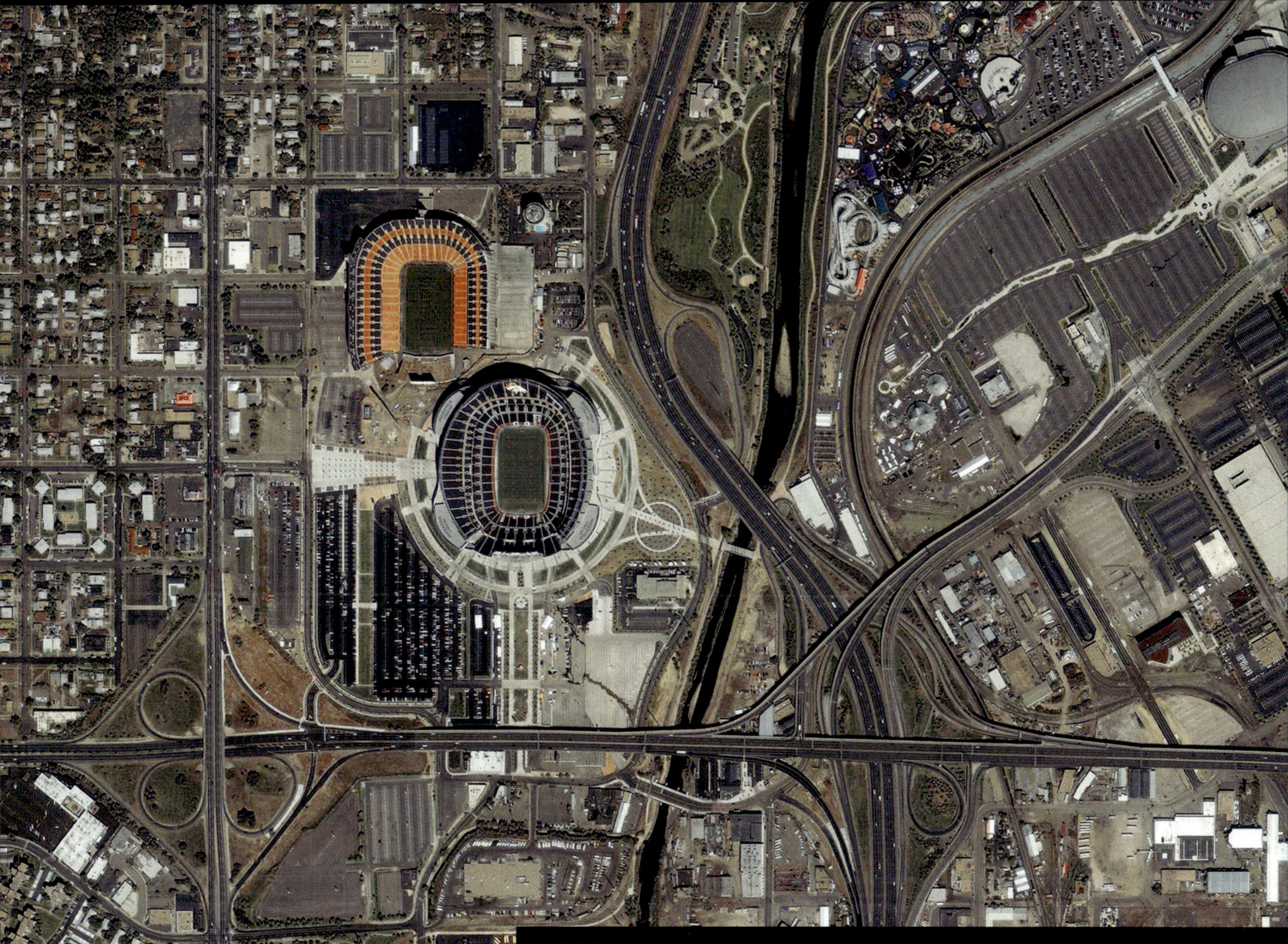

IKONOS satellite image © DigitalGlobe. Image courtesy of Satellite Imaging Corporation

Satellite photograph of Denver

affects the people who live there. Finding out more about a place involves asking other kinds of geographic questions. Some geographic questions about places in Colorado are:

- Why is Denver located where it is?
- Why have so many people moved there?
- How does Colorado Springs's location affect what people do there?
- How did people in mining areas change the physical environment (landscape)?
- How did people on the Eastern Plains change the natural environment (plants and animals)?
- What kinds of problems do people who live in the mountains face?

While You Read

With a partner or small group, create three questions about how the location of your community affects the people who live there.

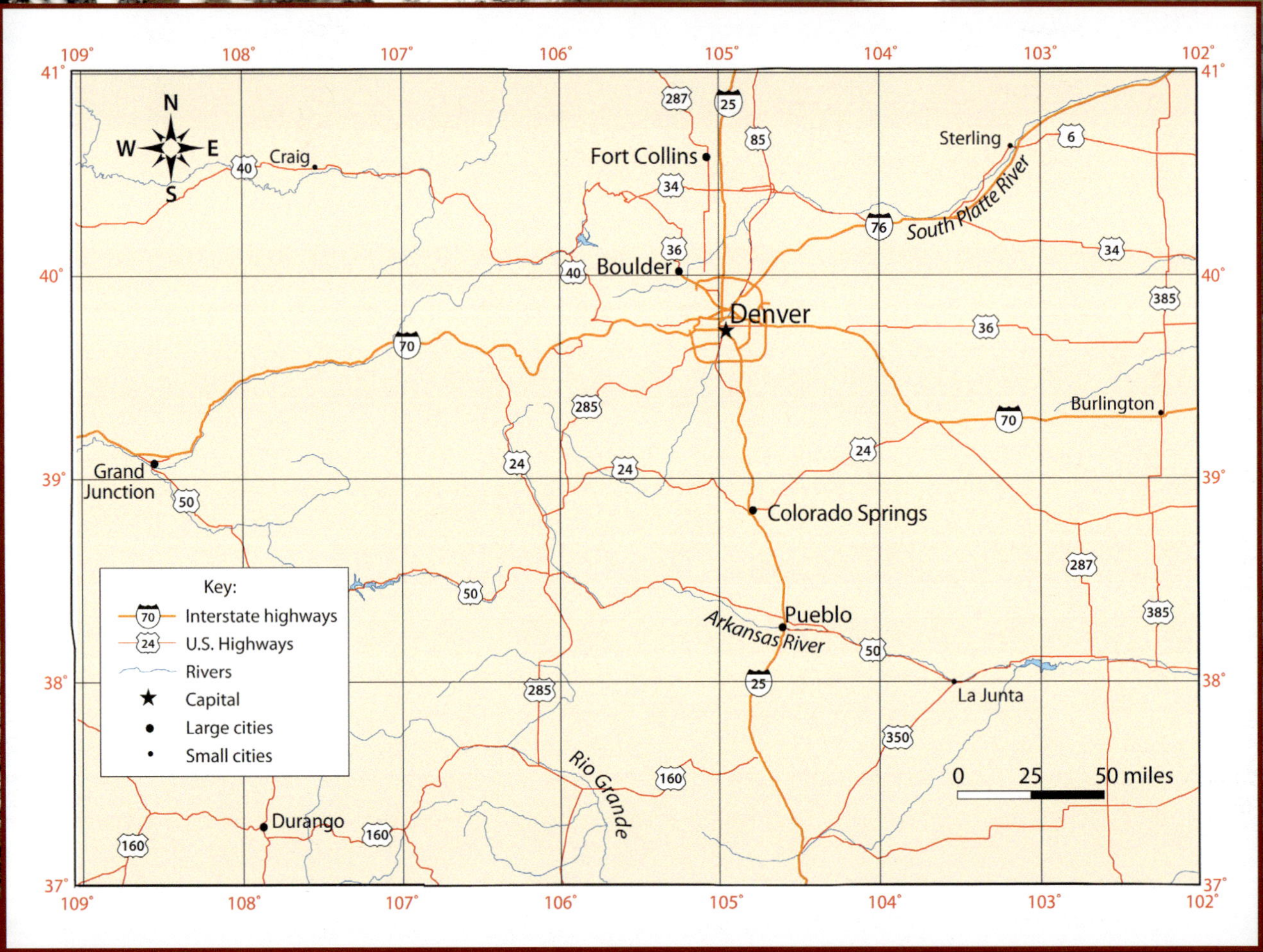

Reading a Map

Maps are geography's most powerful tools. They contain useful information for those who know how to read. Reading a map is different than reading a book. Maps have words, such as the names of places, but they also include other kinds of information.

Most maps include:

- **A Compass Rose:** It shows cardinal directions (North, South, East, West) and the intermediate points between them (Northeast, Northwest, Southeast, Southwest).
- **Scale of Miles:** It shows how distance is represented on a map.
- **A Key:** It explains what the symbols or graphics stand for.
- **A Grid:** It consists of horizontal and vertical lines that help the reader locate places on a map.

Geographic thinkers also want to know about connections between places. So they ask such questions as:

- What do mountain communities have in common?
- How are places in the San Luis Valley connected to each other?

Geographic thinkers want to know how people use technology to get what they need from the physical environment. They ask questions like these:

- What technology do farmers use to irrigate their fields?
- What tools and machines do coal miners use?

Geographic thinkers are also interested in how the physical environment of a place was shaped. These are some good physical environment questions:

- How did the Rocky Mountains take shape?
- How was the Black Canyon of the Gunnison River carved into the earth?

While You Read

What makes the community in which you live special?

COLORADO AND ITS NEIGHBORS

Let's go back to the pretend e-mail you received. You also need to answer your new friend's second question:

"What makes Colorado special?"

Being special can mean different things. It can mean what makes a place different from others, including its nearby neighbors.

While Colorado is like some other states, it is also different in many ways. It is very different from distant states on the East Coast or in the South or Midwest. It has a drier climate, milder weather, and a very different landscape. Colorado has more in common with other states in the Rocky Mountain and Great Plains regions. Eastern Colorado is a lot like the plains states that are its neighbors to the east. The mountain areas of Colorado are like the mountain areas in states to the north and south. Western Colorado is a lot like eastern Utah, its neighbor on the west. Colorado is different from any of these states in the way it combines different kinds of climates and geographic features. Using the information in this chapter, point out to your new friend two or three ways in which Colorado is different.

A special place may also be a particular place that people enjoy visiting. Colorado has many such places. These include state and national parks, recreation areas, and lakes and rivers. In your response to your friend, describe one place in Colorado that you think is very special. Locate it on the road map on page 6. Then explain how you get there from your home. Draw a map showing the route you take, or write out the directions.

After You Read

Reread the sentences you wrote for "Before You Read." What can you add to these based on what you have read since then?

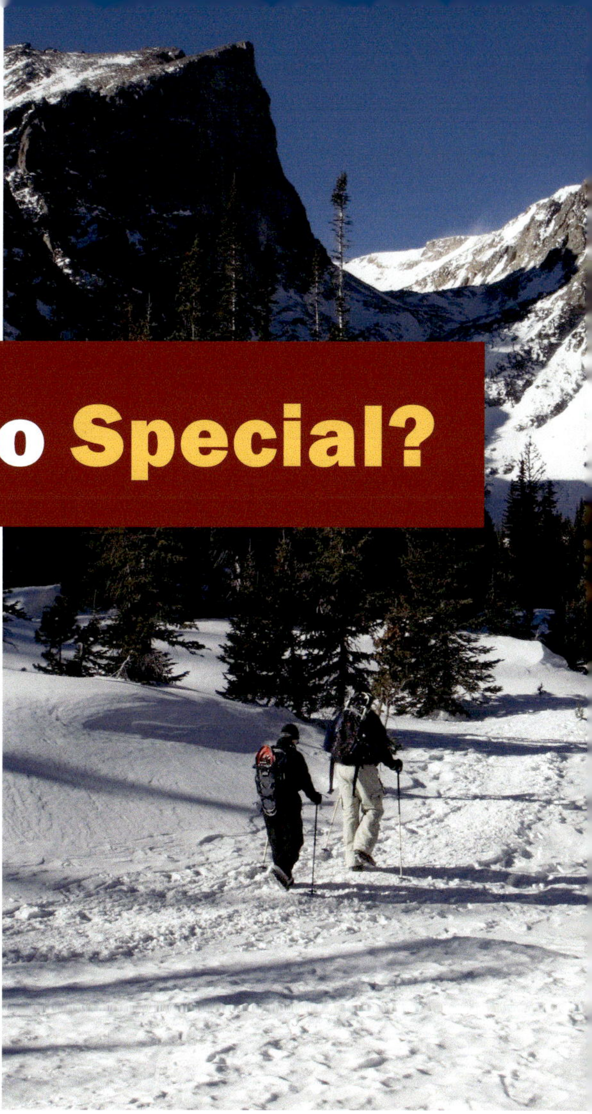

What Makes Colorado Special?

CHAPTER 1

Regions of Colorado

FOCUS QUESTION

How are Colorado's regions different from one another?

Before You Read

Copy these four statements into your notebook, and say whether you agree or disagree with each statement. After you finish reading this chapter, come back to your answers and change them if necessary.

1. The plains of Colorado are level and flat, from Kansas to the Rocky Mountains.
2. All of Colorado's Rocky Mountains were formed by erupting volcanoes.
3. The Colorado River begins high in the Rocky Mountains and flows east to the Atlantic Ocean.
4. Plateaus are deep valleys.

KEY WORDS

- **mesas**
- **region**
- **piedmont**
- **plateau**
- **high plains**
- **sea level**
- **climate**
- **urban corridor**
- **altitude**

Imagine that you are flying on a jet plane. The pilot says on the intercom that you have entered Colorado. Out the window you see a flat landscape marked with the straight lines of roads. Here and there are the tiny shapes of barns and houses. Half an hour later, you look out again. Now you see hills and valleys. Next to the foothills are towns and cities. Cars that look like tiny specks crawl along the roads. The next time you look, the scene has changed again. You see rugged mountains with snow-covered peaks. Green trees cover the mountainsides.

You take a last look when the pilot says you are about to enter Utah. Again the scene has changed. Deep canyons and flat-topped **mesas** stretch as far as you can see. The red and yellow sandstone glows in the sun.

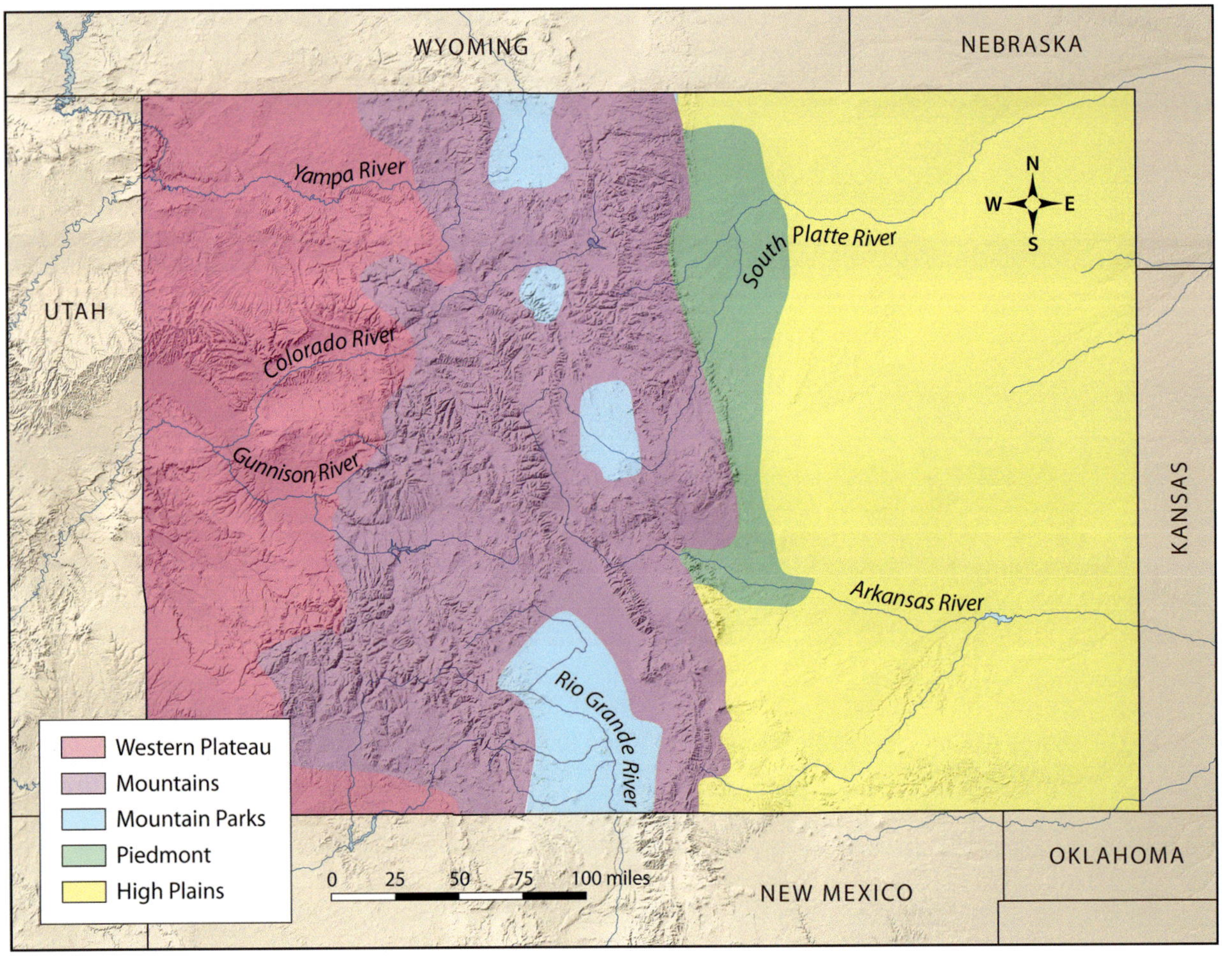

Regions of Colorado

What Are Regions?

Such a flight would teach you that Colorado has different regions. A **region** is made up of places that have things in common. The Ute Indians used to say that Colorado has three regions. They called the low areas "Lower Earth." The mountain valleys were "Middle Earth." They named the high ridges and peaks "Upper Earth." Geographers now divide Colorado into four regions: the plains, the **piedmont**, the mountains and parks, and the western **plateaus**. In this chapter, we will look at how these regions differ.

THE HIGH PLAINS

The **high plains** are located in eastern Colorado. This region is part of the Great Plains. The Great Plains are grasslands that extend from Canada south to the Gulf of Mexico.

Skills and Tools for Learning

A Regional Map

Geographers make and use different kinds of maps. Some are physical maps that show rivers and other natural features. Others include the boundaries of nations, states, and counties. These are called political maps. Still others divide up the land into areas or regions that have certain things in common. The map on the opposite page is a map of the regions of Colorado.

The map on the opposite page divides Colorado into four regions: Western Plateau, Mountains, Piedmont, and High Plains, with places called Mountain Parks included in the Mountains region. The Mountain Parks are not a separate region because they are not joined together. This regions map also includes physical features including mountains, plateaus, and rivers.

- A region is made up of places that have things in common. Can you think of other ways to divide Colorado into regions?
- In which region do all of Colorado's rivers begin? Can you explain why rivers begin in that region?
- Can you find the region that you live in? What do many places within your region have in common?
- Can you think of one thing that any of the other regions have in common?

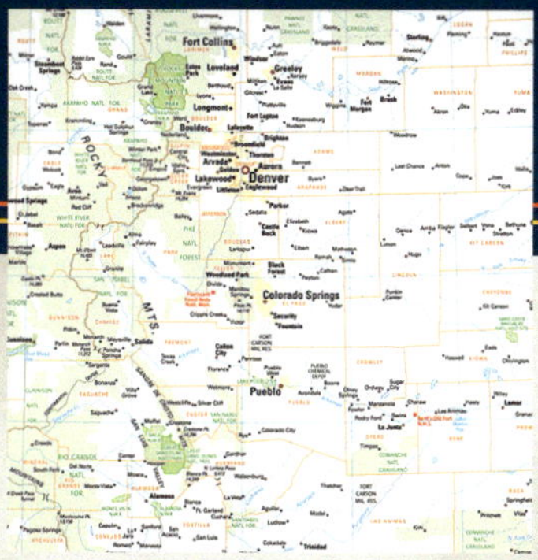

Map of cities

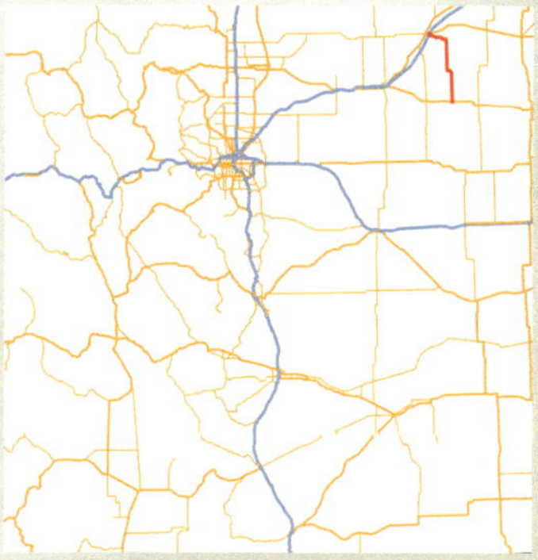

Map of highways

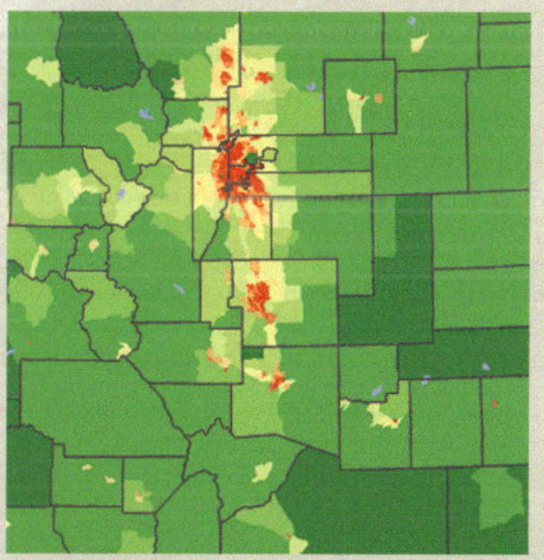

Population map

Topographic map

Pawnee National Grassland

Pawnee National Grassland provides visitors with a sweeping view of the high plains of eastern Colorado. This 193,000-acre tract of plains grassland has been preserved as public land. It includes Pawnee Buttes, a rock formation that rises 300 feet above the plains. Pawnee National Grassland is known worldwide as a site for watching native predator birds. It is located about thirty miles east of Fort Collins.

Pawnee National Grassland in Colorado

Focus Your Reading

- What physical features best describe the plains?
- Where are the Great Plains located?
- What is the climate of the plains?

While You Read

Look for the major characteristics of the high plains as you read this section. Compare your answers with a partner's when you finish.

The high plains are the flattest part of the state. From the window of a plane, the land looks flat. In fact, it is gently rolling. You will notice the dips and rises if you drive across the plains in a car. The plains also tilt upward as you drive west. The plains near Denver are 2,000 feet higher above **sea level** than they are at the Kansas state boundary.

The Plains' Climate

The high plains have an arid, or dry, **climate**. Summers are hot and dry; winters are cold and dry. Less than fifteen inches of rain falls each year. That makes the region too dry to raise most farm crops. Most of the rain falls during the spring. The high plains also get moisture from snowstorms. The worst storms are called blizzards. Blizzard winds drive the snow into huge drifts that block roads and pile up against the sides of houses. Blizzards can wipe out entire herds of cattle.

THE PIEDMONT

The piedmont region lies between the plains and the Rocky Mountains. *Piedmont* means "foot of the mountains." It includes hills and river valleys.

The piedmont was carved out millions of years ago. Floodwater rushed down from the mountains to cut valleys into the high plains. The widest part is the South Platte River Valley north and east of Denver. This valley is fifty miles wide in places. The river is up to 800 feet lower than the plains. The low land along the Arkansas River is not as wide, nor is it cut as deep.

Towns and Cities

Most of the people in the state live in the piedmont. The Front Range **urban corridor** is located there. The urban corridor is a broad strip of land that extends from Fort Collins to Pueblo. It contains most of Colorado's large towns and cities. More than 80 percent of the state's people live there.

Denver, the state capital, lies in the valley of the South Platte River. It is called the Mile High City, as it is 5,280 feet above sea level. Although it is a mile high, Denver is lower than the plains east of the city. The freeway east of Denver climbs for thirty miles before it reaches the high plains.

The climate is similar to that of the plains. Summers in the river valleys are hot and dry. Winters are cold and dry. The hills along the base of the mountains get a little more rain than the plains. Summer days are not as hot because of the hills' higher elevation.

Focus Your Reading

- Where is the piedmont region located?
- How was this region created?
- What is the climate like?

While You Read

Write down all the words and phrases you find that define and describe the piedmont. If you had to eliminate all but the three most important, which three would remain?

Front Range urban corridor

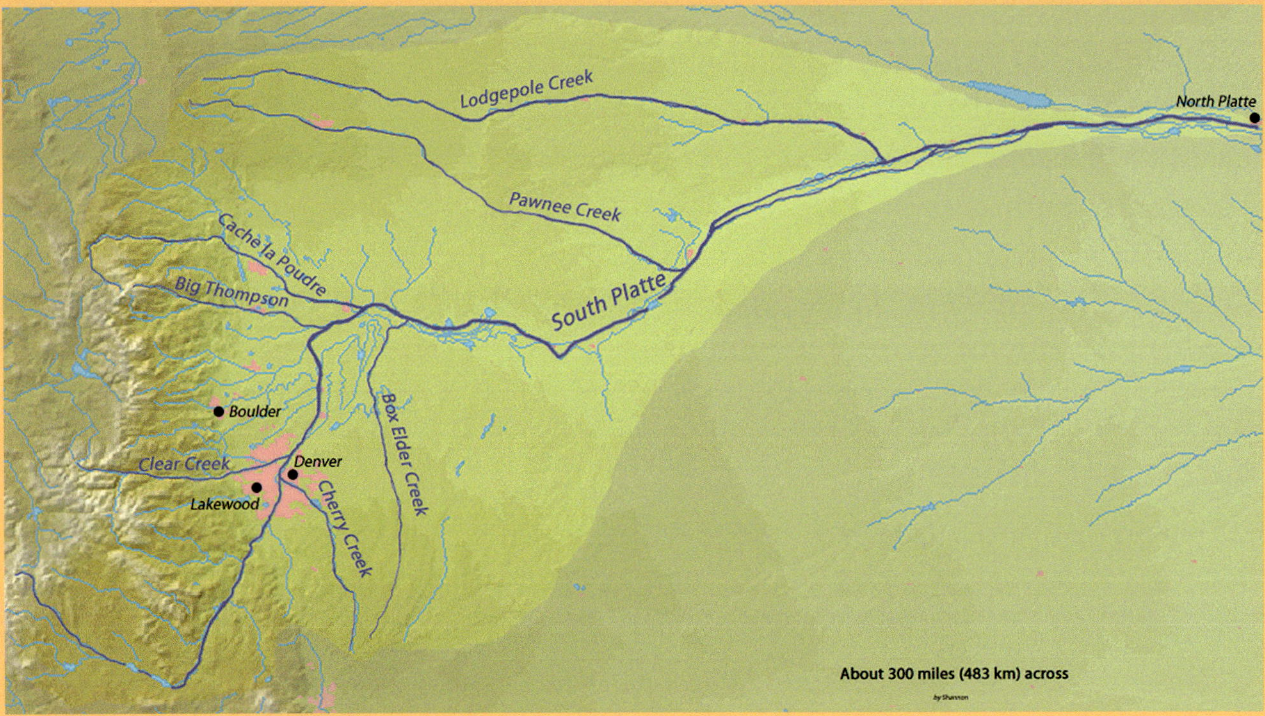

South Platte River Valley

The northern part of the piedmont region has many rivers and creeks. They flow into the South Platte. The major rivers are the Cache la Poudre and the Big Thompson. Can you find them on this map of the South Platte River Valley?

Focus Your Reading

- Where are the Rocky Mountains located in Colorado?
- Why do the mountains receive more rain and snow than other regions?
- Why are the mountains an important resource for Colorado?

MOUNTAINS AND PARKS

The Rocky Mountains make up two-fifths of the state's land area. They extend north and south through the middle of the state. The Rockies are part of a chain of mountains that extends from Alaska to New Mexico. Colorado's mountains are the highest part of the Rockies. The state has fifty-three peaks higher than 14,000 feet. Colorado is the second-highest state (after Alaska) in the United States. It has an average **altitude** of 6,800 feet.

Mountain Ranges

In this state, the Rockies are made up of two sets of mountain ranges. They run north to south. On the east, the Front Range includes Pikes Peak, Mount Evans, and Longs Peak. The Park Range lies farther west. It includes the Sawatch Range and the San Juan Mountains.

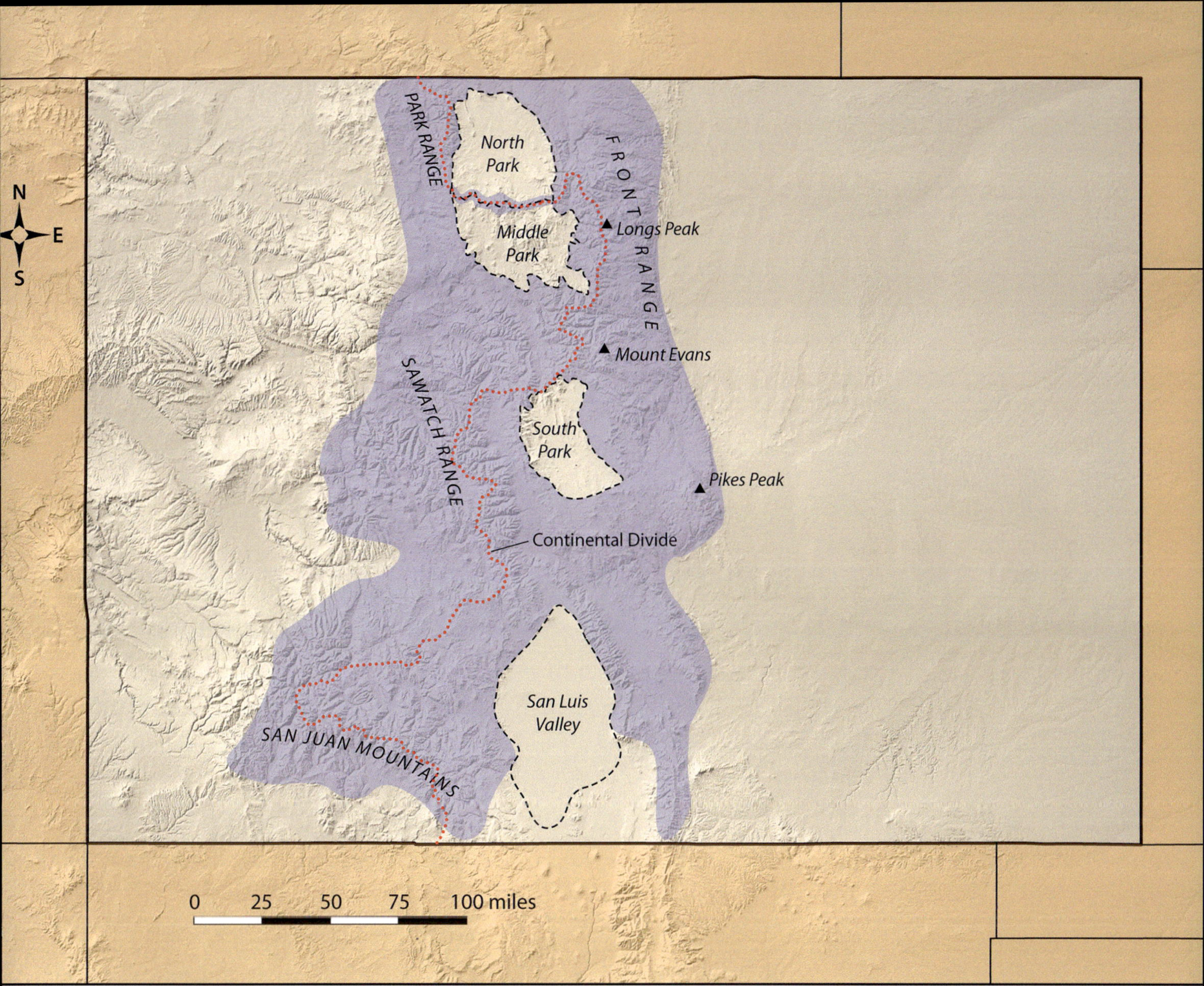

Colorado's mountain parks, mountain ranges, and major peaks

The Rocky Mountains are "young mountains." They are about 60 million years old. ("Old mountains" are hundreds of millions of years old.) The Rockies were formed when two landmasses drifted together. They pushed up huge blocks of rock. Over time, glaciers carved ridges and U-shaped valleys. This gave the Rocky Mountains their rugged look.

While You Read

As you read, look at a map of Colorado. See if you can locate Colorado's Front Range and the three mountain peaks mentioned in this section. Then, look for the four mountain parks that you read about.

Mountain Peaks

Between the Front Range and the ranges to the west are meadows called mountain parks. At one time, great herds

Mountains tower over the San Luis Valley.

San Luis Valley

The San Luis Valley is the only park area in which food crops are grown. They include potatoes, barley, and lettuce. Colorado's other three mountain parks are meadowland used for grazing cattle and cutting hay.

of bison, deer, and elk grazed in these meadows. Early French fur traders called them *parcs*, after the wild game parks or preserves in France. They are now called North Park, Middle Park, South Park, and the San Luis Valley (once known as San Luis Park).

Rain and Snow

Of all of Colorado's regions, the Rocky Mountains get the most rain. The lower slopes get from twenty-five to thirty inches of rain and snow each year. The high peaks receive fifty or more inches per year. The rain and snow come from storm clouds that move across Colorado from west to east. When the clouds reach the mountains, air currents sweep them up into colder air. The cold air turns some of the clouds' water vapor into liquid. It falls to Earth as rain or snow.

The mountains are the source of the state's major rivers. Runoff from rain and snow forms streams high up in the

Meadow in North Park with stacks of hay

Rockies. Streams on the east side of the Continental Divide flow into the North Platte, South Platte, and Arkansas Rivers. Some of this water makes its way to the Gulf of Mexico. Runoff from the west side of the Continental Divide flows into the Colorado River. It ends up in the Pacific Ocean.

Mountain Resources

The mountains have been a major resource for the people of this state. The Indians and white settlers went there to hunt and to cut lodge poles for homes. Fur traders trapped beaver in mountain streams. Miners found gold and silver there. The mountains now lure skiers from all over the world. In summer, people come to hike mountain trails.

The mountains are the state's best-known landmarks. People arriving by car can see Pikes Peak from 130 miles away. The view from the top of Pikes Peak led Katharine Lee Bates to write the words for "America the Beautiful." It goes, in part:

O beautiful for spacious skies,
For amber waves of grain,
For purple mountain majesties,
Above the fruited plain!

Pikes Peak

Focus Your Reading

- What landforms are typical of the plateau country?
- Why are rivers important to this region?
- What national monuments can you visit there?

THE WESTERN PLATEAUS

The plateau country is Colorado's fourth region. It extends west from the slopes of the Rocky Mountains to the Utah state boundary. Plateaus are nearly level highlands. Over the years, floods from the mountains cut deep canyons. But they failed to wear away the hardest rock on top. This left the high, flat-topped mesas we see today. This region is also called the Western Slope.

The plateau country is a land of bold shapes. The high mesas extend as far as the eye can see. In summer, the valleys are cut up into squares of many shades of green. These are fields and fruit orchards. In winter, the land wears desert colors of red sandstone, brown grass, and gray sagebrush.

A Dry Climate

The plateau region has a dry climate. It gets about ten to fifteen inches of rain and snow per year. That is too dry for farming, except along the rivers. There, farmers irrigate their fields. Parts of the plateau country are deserts that get less than ten inches of rain each year.

The Roan Plateau

Grand Mesa in Colorado's plateau country

Rivers and Cities

This region has many rivers. The largest is the Colorado River. It begins as a brook in the mountains where pine trees are green all year long. The Colorado River leaves the state in a desert in which few plants can survive. The Uncompahgre and Gunnison are other major rivers.

The largest towns and cities in the region were built along rivers. They include Montrose (Uncompahgre River), Delta (Gunnison River), and Grand Junction. The city of Grand Junction was built at the junction of the Grand and Gunnison Rivers. The Grand River is now called the Colorado River.

While You Read

Study the photo of the Grand Mesa on this page. Do a quick sketch in your notebook of the mesa and one of Pikes Peak on page 21. Compare the two. How are the Grand Mesa and Pikes Peak the same? How are they different?

After You Read

1. Turn to the "Before You Read" activity in your notebook. Read the four statements and change your answers if you need to.
2. If you could choose to live in any of the four regions of Colorado, which would it be, and why? Write a descriptive paragraph explaining your choice.

Colorado National Monument

The Colorado National Monument features spectacular views of the plateau and canyon country. It includes thirty-two square miles of sheer walls, deep canyons, and scenic overlooks. One freestanding tower of rock called Independence Monument rises 450 feet from the canyon floor. Each year, about 275,000 people visit Colorado National Monument, which is located between Fruita and Grand Junction.

"I came here and found these canyons, and they feel like the heart of the world to me. I'm going to stay and build trails and promote this place, because it should be a national park."

—John Otto (first Park Custodian at Colorado National Monument), 1907

Thinking about Colorado Water

Do you know . . .

why people in Colorado think so much about water?

People in Colorado think about water a lot. Every month people from each region hold "roundtable" meetings to discuss their water needs. The state has a water plan for putting water to better use. Cities urge homeowners to use water wisely. Farmers look for better ways to irrigate their fields. Newspapers report on the state's water problems.

Have you ever wondered why people in Colorado are so concerned about water?

Water is Colorado's most important resource. Everyone needs it. In many places, there is not enough water to meet everyone's needs. Cities need more water because more people are moving to Colorado to live. Sometimes there is too much water, when floods wash out roads and bridges. Water quality is another concern. Minerals leaking from old mines pollute many of Colorado's rivers and mountain streams.

- What water issues does your region face?
- How does your city keep your water safe to drink?
- What about water most concerns you?

Asking Geographic Questions
Your Response

This chapter began with this question:

How are Colorado's regions different from one another?

1. **Review**
   Review the information in your notes and in this chapter about each region.
2. **Reflect**
   With a partner or in a small group, discuss how the regions are different.
3. **Respond**
   In your notebook, explain how Colorado's regions are different.

CHAPTER 2

Colorado Life Zones

FOCUS QUESTION

How are plants and animals different from one Colorado life zone to another?

Before You Read

Make a five-column chart in your notebook. Label the columns "Grasslands," "Shrub and Woodland," "Montane Forest," "Subalpine Forest," and "Alpine Tundra." Fill in the columns as you read about the **location**, **common plants**, and **animals** of each of these zones.

KEY WORDS

- **tundra**
- **elevation**
- **precipitation**
- **droughts**
- **irrigate**
- **coniferous**

Take another trip across Colorado, this time by car. Make it a trip from your home on the plains to Pikes Peak. The plains grass has already turned brown, as it is a hot day in June. In the fields, prairie dogs sit beside their holes. Nearer to Colorado Springs, you see more green plant life. The hills behind the city are covered with shrubs and piñons. As you drive into the mountains, you see more trees. Ponderosa pines cover the slopes along the road. Magpies and jays perch on the limbs. After you turn off toward Pikes Peak, the road is much steeper. The ponderosas give way to lodgepole pines and aspen trees. Hawks circle above. Maybe you will see a bald eagle. Finally, you reach tree line. Beyond is the **tundra**, with tiny plants that hug the ground. Ground squirrels run for cover. You step out of the car and wonder why you forgot to bring a jacket. The air is quite cool.

A bald eagle

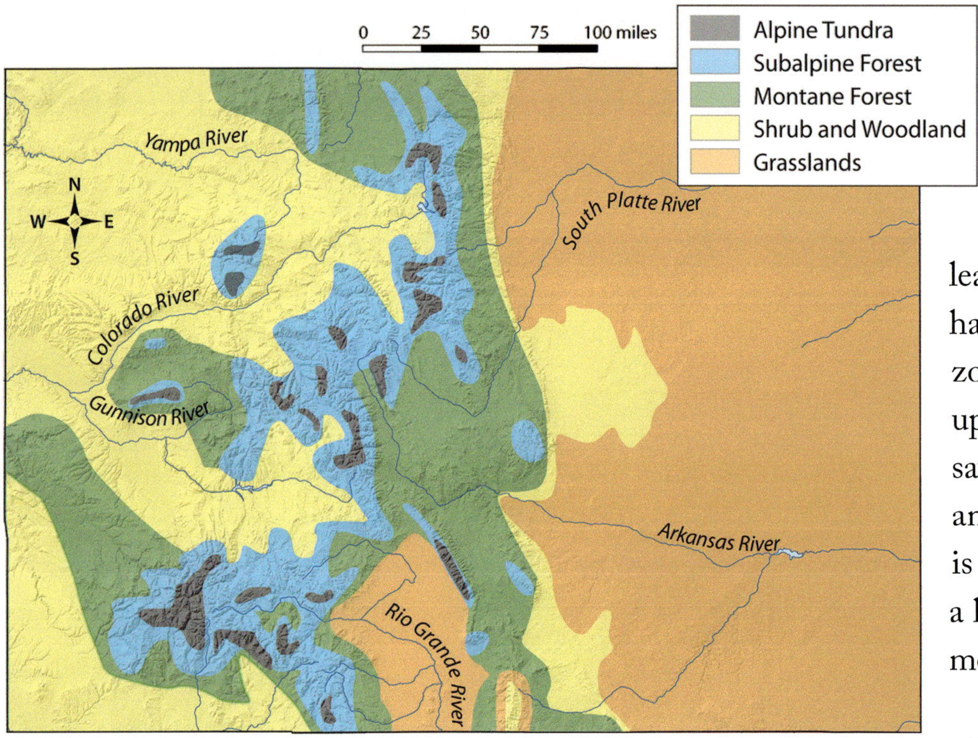

Colorado's five life zones

Different Life Zones

What would you learn from such a trip? You would learn that Colorado has different life zones. As you went up in elevation, you saw different plants and animals. That is because places at a high **elevation** get more moisture.

The mountain city of Leadville receives more than forty inches of **precipitation** (rain plus snow) each year. The town of Mack on the Utah border gets less than ten inches per year. Pine trees need moisture. They can grow at Leadville but not at Mack. They also cannot grow at the top of Pikes Peak. The climate is too cold there. The temperature drops 3.3 degrees for every 1,000 feet above sea level. On a drive from Lamar (3,615 feet) to the top of Pikes Peak (14,110 feet), it drops about 35 degrees. The temperature would drop about that much if you sailed from Florida to Iceland. Colorado has different life zones because of wide ranges in rainfall and temperature from place to place.

Focus Your Reading

- How many life zones does Colorado have?
- What are the names of these zones?
- How are life zones determined?

LIFE ZONES

What is a life zone?

Life zones are areas that have similar plants and animals. They are usually defined by plant life. Many animals wander from one zone to another. When food is scarce in the mountains, bears come down to raid garbage cans in the foothills. Elk and mountain lions live in two or three zones during the course of a year. Mule deer, coyotes, hawks, and owls are found nearly everywhere in Colorado. It is easier to define life zones by the plants than by the animals, in part because plants tend to stay put.

The Five Life Zones

Colorado has five life zones. They are different mainly in how high they are above sea level and in the plants that live there. The lowest life zone is the grasslands zone. The largest grasslands is the plains of eastern Colorado. It gets too little rain for trees to grow, except along the banks of streams. Tall plants and low trees grow in the higher shrub and woodland zone. This zone extends along the Front Range. The plateau country of western Colorado is also in this zone. Higher up is the montane zone. It includes the lower mountains and the mountain parks. It has enough rainfall for ponderosa pines and Douglas fir trees to grow. Above it is the subalpine forest zone, a second zone of evergreens. This zone gets the heavy rainfall that Engelmann spruce and fir trees need. Highest of all is the alpine tundra zone, which is above tree line. It is high and cold, and the wind never stops blowing. Small, ground-hugging plants are all that can survive there.

THE GRASSLANDS LIFE ZONE

The grasslands life zone includes the plains region of eastern Colorado. It extends from about 3,500 feet to about 5,000 feet above sea level. The grasslands have an arid, or dry, climate. This area gets less rainfall than almost any other region in Colorado. The grasslands sometimes have **droughts**, or several very dry years in a row. During a drought, the hot, dry air sucks moisture out of the soil. Wind blowing across the parched ground creates dust storms. Brown clouds of dust can darken the midday sky. Only the driest areas of the western plateaus get less rainfall than the grasslands life zone.

Focus Your Reading

- Where is this life zone located? (See map on page 30.)
- What plants are most common?
- What animals live here?

The grasslands life zone

Alpine Tundra
above 11,000 ft.

Mat and cushion plants

Subalpine Forests
9,000 to 11,000 ft.

*Engelmann spruce and fir,
huckleberry and elderberry bushes*

Shrub and Woodland
5,000 to 6,500 ft.

Grass, low trees, woody plants

Semi-desert Shrublands
below 5,000 ft.

Big sagebrush, bitterbrush

Colorado s Life Zones

shown from the lowest to the highest in elevation

Tree Line

11,000 to 12,000 ft.

Montane Forests

6,500 to 9,000 ft.

Ponderosa pine, lodgepole pine, aspen

Plains Grasslands

below 5,000 ft.

Blue grama, buffalo grass

Birds without Trees

Where do birds build their nests on the grasslands where few trees grow? The lark bunting makes its nest on the ground. To hide its eggs from predators, it covers the nest with dry grass. The lark bunting is an expert at camouflage.

Lark bunting

While You Read

Write words and phrases in the "Grasslands" column on your chart that describe this zone's location, plants, and animals.

Grass and Food Crops

Grass has adapted to the climate of the plains better than other plants. Short grasses, such as blue grama (Colorado's state grass) and buffalo grass, need less moisture than tall plants. They grow in clumps several inches apart. This allows room for the plants to send roots out in search of moisture. Grass grows and produces seeds during the short wet periods. It stops growing after the hot days of summer arrive. Although the grass turns brown, the roots are still alive. During a drought, plains grass can stay dormant for two or three years. When rain finally comes, the roots send up new shoots. The grass is green again.

The grasslands produce some food crops. Farmers grow wheat using dryland farming methods. That is, they plant winter wheat that comes up early in the spring. Winter snow and spring rains provide the moisture the plants need. The wheat is harvested before the hot summer sun sucks up the moisture. Plains farmers also **irrigate** their crops. They get water from the South Platte, Arkansas, and Colorado Rivers and from deep wells. Sprinklers fitted to long pipes extend out from the wells. They create green circles of crops in the brown grasslands.

Few trees grow on the grasslands. The most common are cottonwoods and willows. They grow along the banks of creeks and in low-lying areas that collect moisture.

Pronghorn antelope

Grassland Animals

The grasslands provide food for many animals. Large herds of bison once grazed there. In modern times, herds of cattle have replaced the bison. Many kinds of wild animals live on the grasslands. They include pronghorn antelope, coyotes, prairie dogs, ground squirrels, and gophers. The pronghorns feed on the grasslands' short-stemmed grasses. Prairie dogs, jackrabbits, and other small animals eat seeds and small plants. They, in turn, provide food for predators, such as coyotes. The Colorado state bird, the lark bunting, and other birds live on the grasslands.

Cattle grazing on the Eastern Plains

Skills and Tools for Learning

People and the Environment

Unlike plants and animals, people can live in any of Colorado's life zones. Many farmers and ranchers live in the grasslands. Most people work in the shrub and woodland zone. That is where most of Colorado's cities are located. People ski in the winter in the montane forests. In the summer, hikers visit the subalpine forests and climb mountains in the tundra.

People are better able than plants and trees to adapt to more than one environment. They have learned how to survive in climates that are cold or hot and humid or dry. People can also modify or change the environment. With irrigation, farmers can make crops grow in places where it seldom rains. Ski areas spray water on the slopes to make artificial snow. Road builders make tunnels through the mountains.

Describe the life zone in which you live and how people interact with it. What native plants still grow there? What native animals live there? List three ways you and your family have adapted to that environment. List at least one way you have modified it.

Tunnel through mountain

How do these photos show that people can modify the environment?

Green landscapes next to arid grasslands

Lake Pueblo dam

A river otter

A gray wolf

Change over Time

A life zone's plants and animals change over time. People cause many changes. Weeds and grasses brought in by early settlers in Colorado crowded out native grasses. Hunters and farmers killed off native animals such as bison, wolves, and otters.

THE SHRUB AND WOODLAND LIFE ZONE

The shrub and woodland life zone is the next highest in elevation. It extends from 5,000 feet to about 6,500 feet above sea level. In eastern Colorado, it includes the foothills of the Rocky Mountains. The shrub and woodland areas of western Colorado and the San Luis Valley are also in this zone. In western Colorado, semi-desert shrubland takes the place of grassland at the lowest elevation.

Focus Your Reading

- Where is this life zone located?
- What plants are most common?
- What animals live here?

Plant Life

The zone's plant life includes grass, shrubs, and low trees. Shrubs are woody plants and bushes that grow close to the ground. Southern Colorado shrubs include piñons and junipers. Scrub oak and mountain mahogany are more common along the Front Range and on the Western Slope. The shrubs of northwestern Colorado include grayish green sagebrush. All of these areas also include small groves of trees.

Woody plants do well in this zone. They require more moisture than plains grass but less than trees. This zone receives fifteen to twenty inches of precipitation per year. In summer, the temperature is cooler than on the plains.

While You Read

Write words and phrases in the "Shrub and Woodland" column on your chart that describe this zone's location, plants, and animals.

Piñon and juniper shrubs

Mule deer

Shrub and Woodland Animals

The shrubs provide food and protection for many kinds of animals, including the mule deer. They are browsers rather than grass eaters. Deer like to eat the leaves and tender branches of shrubs. Cottontail rabbits, chipmunks, ground squirrels, and mice also live in this zone. The low bushes protect them from predators, such as coyotes, gray foxes, bobcats, and mountain lions. The most common birds are piñon jays, brown towhees, and sage grouse.

Shrubs

Shrubs are useful plants. Native Americans made bows from the tough wood of Rocky Mountain junipers. They ground up juniper leaves and berries to flavor food and to use as medicine. The branches of Rocky Mountain maple shrubs made fine arrows and snowshoes. White settlers made juniper berry tea to treat stomach problems.

Juniper berries

THE MONTANE FOREST LIFE ZONE

The next highest life zone is the montane forest zone. It extends from 6,500 feet to 9,000 feet in elevation. This zone rises above the foothills and shrub-covered mesas. Much of it is covered with forests.

Focus Your Reading

- Where is this life zone located?
- What plants are most common?
- What animals live here?

Many Kinds of Trees

The most common trees are ponderosa pines, lodgepole pines, and aspens. All but the aspens are **coniferous** trees. That is, they produce cones and remain green year-round. In the fall, aspen leaves turn yellow and drop off. Ponderosas are spaced wide apart. They need room to spread their limbs. Lodgepole pines grow close together in thick stands. They have very few limbs. That made them easy to use for tepee poles and logs for cabins. They are called lodgepole pines for that reason.

Douglas firs, blue spruce trees (Colorado's state tree), and other coniferous trees also grow in this zone. Douglas firs are most often found on shaded slopes that retain moisture. Ponderosa pines do well on sunny mountainsides. Aspens grow on both shaded and sunny mountainsides. Blue spruce trees grow north of Pikes Peak. They need the northern mountains' wet and cool climate.

While You Read

Write words and phrases in the "Montane Forest" column on your chart that describe this zone's location, plants, and animals.

The montane forests are not solid walls of trees. The drier, south-facing mountain slopes usually have thin stands of trees. Wildflowers, such as the columbine (Colorado's state flower), and shrubs fill in the open spaces. The shrubs include juniper bushes, wild strawberries, and wood lilies.

This Zone's Many Animals

The forests provide food for mule deer, black bears, porcupines, and other animals. Elk and bighorn sheep (Colorado's state animal) graze in the mountain meadows. Many kinds of small animals also live there. They include beavers, chipmunks, and squirrels. Beavers build their homes in mountain streams and ponds. Their predators, weasels and martens, also live there. The rocky streambeds provide shelter for fish, including the greenback cutthroat trout (Colorado's state fish). Many kinds of birds make their nests in the forests' tall trees. They include finches, jays, magpies, and water pipits.

Colorado bear

Aspen leaves turning yellow in the fall

THE SUBALPINE FOREST LIFE ZONE

The subalpine forest is the most rugged zone in Colorado. It is known for its tall trees, plunging waterfalls, and soaring eagles. The word *alpine* means "high mountains." The subalpine zone is the forest area just below the high mountain peaks. In Colorado, it extends from 9,000 feet to 11,000 feet above sea level.

This zone is covered with dense forests. Most of the trees are Engelmann spruce and fir. These tall, thin trees rise up like church spires. They grow to a height of 80 feet to 100 feet. Their short, stubby branches make them seem even taller. Because these trees grow in dense stands, the sunlight seldom reaches the ground.

Focus Your Reading

- Where is this life zone located?
- What kinds of trees and plants grow here?
- What animals live here?

A Cold Climate

The subalpine forests have a cool, wet climate. Heavy snows and summer rains produce forty to fifty inches of precipitation per year. In the shade under the trees, the ground is damp, and the air is cool most of the year. Huckleberry and elderberry bushes and moss cover the

Subalpine meadow

While You Read

Write words and phrases in the "Subalpine Forest" column on your chart that describe this zone's location, plants, and animals.

ground. The ground is also littered with the trunks of dead trees that have fallen over the years.

The cold air at the upper edge of this zone stunts the growth of trees. Some trees that are less than a foot tall may be hundreds of years old. These forests of dwarf trees are called elfin forests.

Animals of the Subalpine Zone

Several kinds of animals like the cool, wet climate of the subalpine zone. It was once the home of the grizzly bear, as grizzlies no longer live in Colorado. Rocky Mountain bighorn sheep live in this zone. During the summer, elk graze in the subalpine meadows. Smaller animals also live in this zone, including chipmunks, ground squirrels, and packrats. Birds of the subalpine zone include nutcrackers, hummingbirds, and the American dipper. The dipper dives into fast-flowing mountain streams to feed on insects.

Pine trees in winter

Pine Trees

Colorado's Native Americans had many uses for pine trees. They made tepee poles from the slender trunks of lodgepole pines. The Utes ground up the sweet-scented needles of fir trees to make baby powder. They also burned fir needles to freshen the air in wickiups and tepees. In springtime, Indian children ate the sweet inner bark of ponderosa pines like candy. The sap rising in the trees contained natural sugars.

Lodgepole pines

Alpine tundra

THE ALPINE TUNDRA LIFE ZONE

The highest zone is the alpine tundra life zone. It lies above tree line. Trees cannot grow at an elevation higher than 11,000 feet to 12,000 feet above sea level because of the cold air. Higher than that, only low-growing plants and grasses can survive. The earth beneath the surface of the tundra is frozen year-round.

Focus Your Reading

- Where is this life zone located?
- What kinds of plants grow here?
- What animals live in or visit this zone?

Plants of the Tundra

In midsummer, the tundra is covered with tiny plants. They include blue forget-me-nots, pink moss, and yellow rydbergia. These plants hug the ground and hide behind rocks to escape the fierce winds at this elevation. Otherwise, the wind would rob them of the moisture they need to survive. Tundra plants also remain small because they have so little time to grow each year. The summers are short; the winters are long and cold.

Banner Trees

Trees at timberline are faced with fierce winds. Some grow branches only on the side opposite from the wind. These lopsided trees are called "banner" trees. Their branches look like banners flying in the wind.

While You Read

Write words and phrases in the "Alpine Tundra" column on your chart that describe this zone's location, plants, and animals.

Tundra Animals

Most of the animals of the tundra are summer visitors. Chipmunks, ground squirrels, and marmots come up from the forest zones below to feed on the alpine plants. So do elk and Rocky Mountain bighorn sheep. The only year-round animals are the tiny pikas. They spend the winters in underground burrows.

White-tailed birds called ptarmigan also live on the tundra year-round. To blend with the landscape, the

Ptarmigan in winter

Pika

The Pika

The pika is the only mammal that is native to the alpine tundra. These small, tailless creatures scamper over the tundra collecting grass. They place the grass in little piles on sun-warmed rocks. When the grass has dried, they store it away for winter food.

ptarmigan shed their feathers three times each year. They change colors from gray to speckled gray to white. They survive the harsh winter by digging burrows into the snow. Twigs, leaves, and seeds of tundra plants provide them with food.

Rocky Mountain National Park is one of the best places in Colorado to view the tundra. Trail Ridge Road, the main road through the park, crosses this zone.

After You Read

1. Review your completed life zones chart. Compare yours with that of a partner. Discuss the differences. What could you add? What would you change?
2. Use this chapter's "Key Words" in a paragraph to summarize what you have learned about Colorado's life zones. Work with a partner to write a first draft. Meet in a small group with other students to compare your drafts. Would you add anything? Would you change anything?

Thinking about Colorado Water

Do you know . . . why Colorado is called the Mother of Rivers?

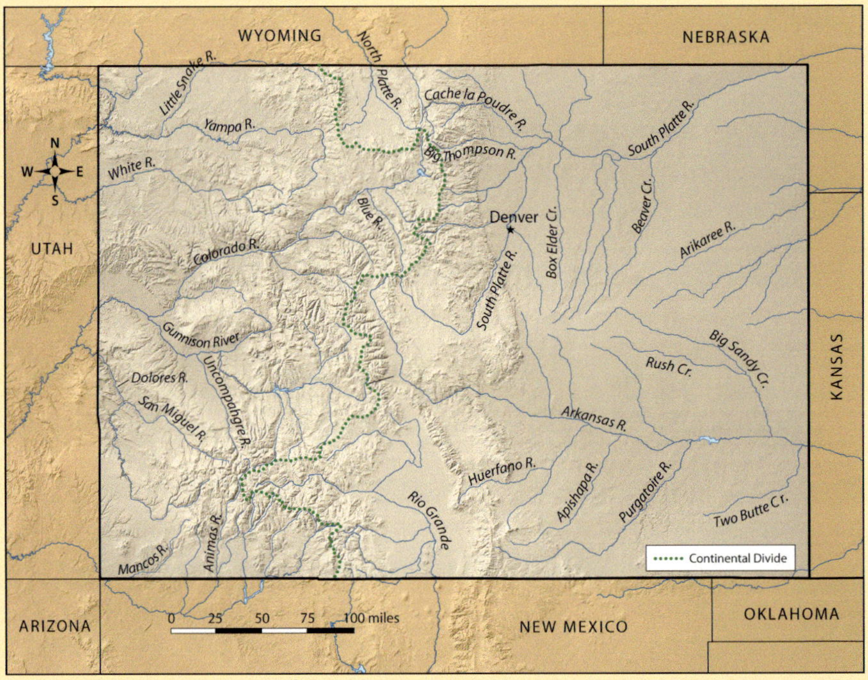

Colorado has four large rivers, with many smaller rivers flowing into them. Each of these rivers begins in Colorado and flows into other states. Because so many begin here, people call Colorado the "Mother of Rivers."

Have you ever wondered why so many rivers begin in Colorado?

To find an answer, look at Colorado's river systems. A river and its tributaries make up a river system. A tributary is a stream or river that flows into a larger one. Colorado's largest rivers are the Colorado River, the Arkansas River, the South Platte River, and the Rio Grande River. Can you find these rivers on the Colorado river map on this page?

Look closely at the river system that is closest to your home.

- Where does it begin?
- Which direction does it flow?
- What other rivers flow into it?
- Where does it leave the state?

Have you noticed that Colorado's river systems begin in only one of Colorado's regions? It is the region that gets the most rain and snowfall. Do you know the answers to these questions?

- Which region is the "mother" of Colorado's rivers?
- Why do rivers begin there?
- How is the Continental Divide related to the direction in which the major rivers flow?

Asking Historical Questions
Your Response

This chapter began with this question:

How are plants and animals different from one Colorado life zone to another?

1. **Review**
   Review the information in your notes and in this chapter about the plant and animal life of each life zone.
2. **Reflect**
   With a partner or in a small group, discuss how the plant and animal life of each zone is different.
3. **Respond**
   In your notebook, explain how the plant and animal life differ from one zone to another.

UNIT TWO
Colorado's People in Prehistoric Times

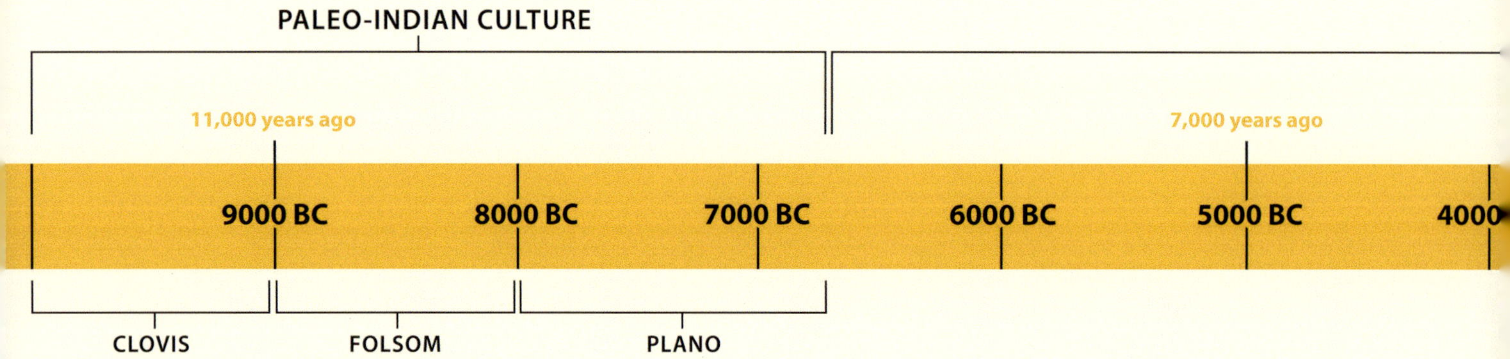

People

Colorado's first people arrived in prehistoric times. That was before people kept written records or wrote history. We know about these people from other kinds of evidence they left behind.

Places

The prehistoric people lived in most regions of Colorado. They hunted wild animals on the Eastern Plains. Some went into the mountains to find stone for spear points. Others hunted and gathered plants in the western plateau country.

Times

The lives of prehistoric people changed over time. That is why prehistoric time is divided into different periods. The people of each period hunted different animals. They used different weapons and tools.

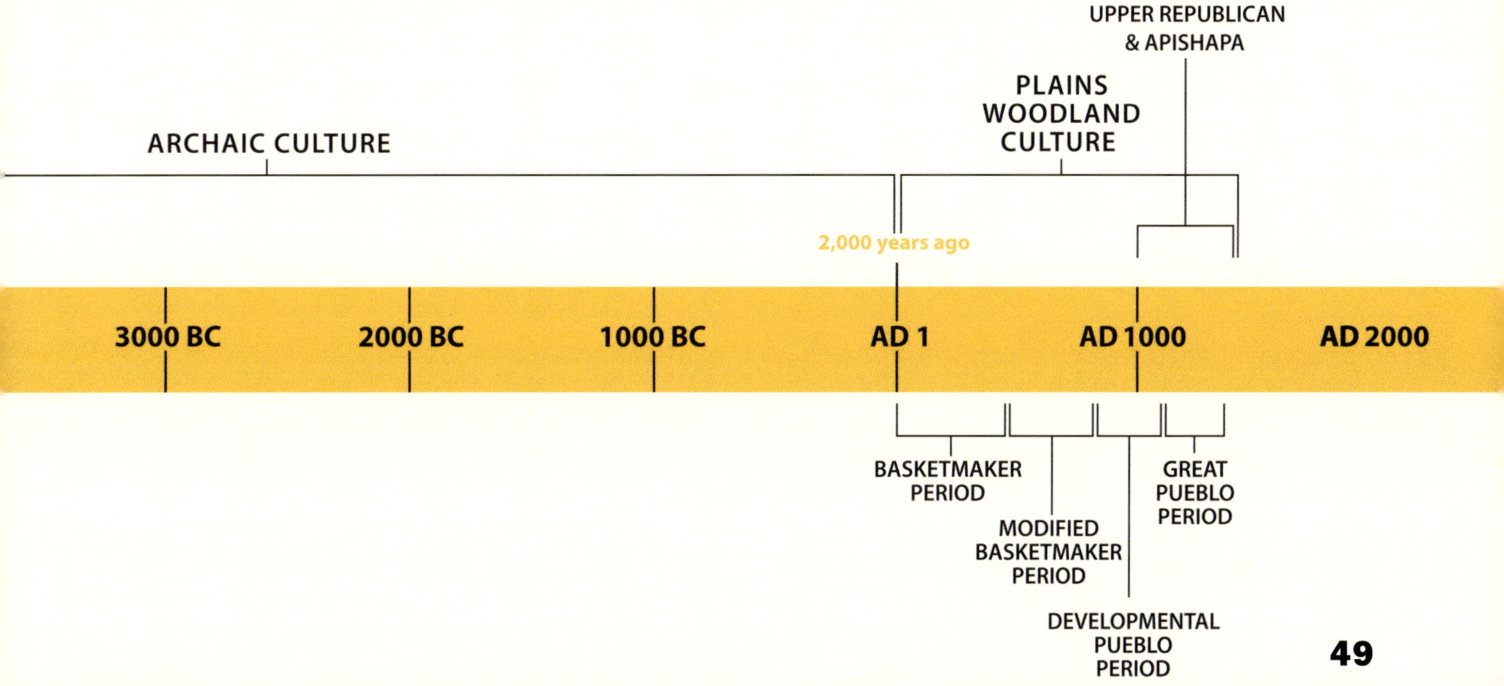

CHAPTER 3

Early Hunters of Colorado

FOCUS QUESTION

How did hunter-gatherers respond to changes in the environment?

Before You Read

In your notebook, draw a graphic organizer with four columns and these headings:

- Paleo-Indian
- Archaic
- Plains Woodland
- Upper Republican and Apishapa

Then, skim this chapter to see how it is organized. Get ready to take notes while you read.

KEY WORDS

- **archaeologists**
- **extinct**
- **cultures**
- **artifacts**
- **gatherers**
- **pottery**

In the summer of 1926, J. D. Figgins received a box from New Mexico. He was the director of the natural history museum in Denver. The box contained a chunk of earth. Lying in the dirt were bison bones and a spear point. George McJunkin, an African American cowboy, had found bison bones near the town of Folsom, New Mexico. **Archaeologists** found the spear point next to the bones they sent to Denver. A hunter must have thrust this spear into the bison's ribs.

Clovis point

AN EXTINCT BISON

Figgins was amazed when he opened the box. The bones came from an **extinct** bison. The spear point next to it,

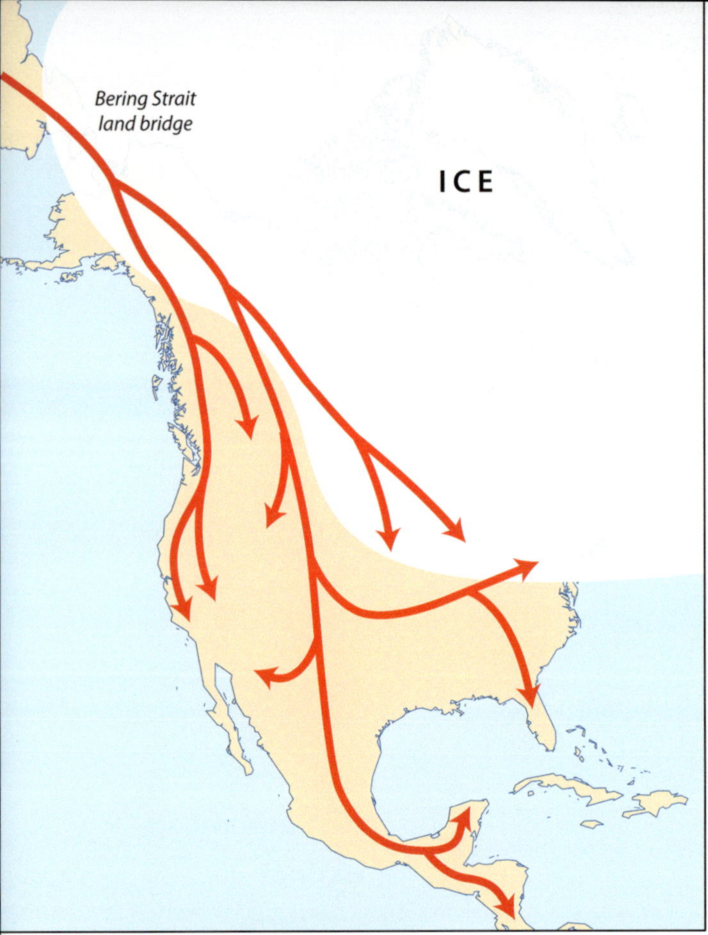

Route followed by Paleo-Indian hunters over the Bering Strait land bridge

although broken, was well made, with finely chipped edges. Long grooves ran down each side. Figgins had never seen a spear point like it. But the most amazing thing was the age of the bison. It had been extinct for about 10,000 years. That placed humans in New Mexico much longer ago than anyone had imagined. The spear point was given the name "Folsom point," after the town of Folsom, New Mexico.

The study of early people in North America began with this find. It sent archaeologists out in search of early bison hunters. They found Folsom points in Colorado and other places in North America.

THE PALEO-INDIANS (12,000 BC TO 5000 BC)

The first people who lived in North America are called Paleo-Indians. The word *paleo* means "very old." These people arrived from Siberia about 18,000 to 20,000 years ago. They crossed the Bering Strait, a waterway between Siberia and Alaska. During the last Ice Age, the strait was a land bridge. Ancient hunters used it to follow herds of animals into North America.

The Paleo-Indians hunted mammoths, camels, and bison. They killed them with spears that had sharp stone points. There were three different Paleo-Indian **cultures**: Clovis, Folsom, and Plano. The people of each culture used a different kind of spear point.

Focus Your Reading

- When did Folsom people live in Colorado?
- How were Clovis and Folsom points alike?
- How did Plano people hunt bison?

Clovis Culture

In 1932, J. D. Figgins visited a Paleo-Indian site near Dent, Colorado. (An archaeological site is any place where

artifacts, or objects made by humans, are found.) A railroad worker had found a pile of bones washed out of a ravine. Mixed with the bones were spear points. The bones and stone points were different from those found at Folsom, New Mexico. These points were larger and heavier and were not as well made. The bones were those of a Columbian mammoth, an extinct elephant. These huge animals had died out at least 11,000 years ago. Figgins concluded that the spear points at Dent were even older than the Folsom points.

Folsom point found next to bison bones

Who Made the Clovis Point?

The points found at Dent are now called Clovis points. They were named for similar points found near Clovis, New Mexico. The way of life of the people who made them is called the Clovis culture.

Archaeologists have found Clovis points elsewhere in Colorado. They also found stone blades, probably used to scrape hides. The heavy points and scrapers tell us that Clovis people hunted big animals and likely wore hide clothing. They may have overhunted the mammoth. These big animals soon became extinct. What did these people look like? What kinds of shelters did they build? No one knows. A few stone tools are the only Clovis artifacts that have survived.

While You Read

Look for clues in the three sections about Paleo-Indian culture that will answer the questions: *Who are we reading about—Folsom, Clovis, or Plano*? and *What do we know about them*? Write the answers to these questions in the first column of your organizer.

Folsom Culture

After finding Folsom points in New Mexico, archaeologists looked for them elsewhere. They found the grooved points in dozens of places in the United States. Colorado alone has eleven Folsom sites. Some are kill sites, where bison were

The Case of the Missing Bones

The tailbones were missing from the skeletons of the ancient bison found at Folsom, New Mexico. The missing bones provided additional evidence that humans had killed the bison. When the hunters skinned the animals, they removed the tail with the hide. They took the tailbones with them.

slaughtered. Others are campsites where hunters stopped for a while. Campsites usually contain the most artifacts.

A Folsom Campsite

We know a great deal about Folsom culture from a campsite near Fort Collins. In the camp, archaeologists found Folsom points in various stages of manufacture. These helped them understand how the points were made. The archaeologists also found stone scrapers and bone needles, probably used to make clothing. They found engraved bones that may have been used like dice, as game pieces. Folsom people did not just hunt bison. The bones included those from pronghorn antelopes, rabbits, foxes, wolves, and coyotes.

Plano Culture

In 1957, a dust storm on the plains exposed still more ancient bones. The wind uncovered the top layer of a ravine filled with bison bones. Joe Ben Wheat, an archaeologist, dug up the rest. Altogether, he found the bones of 190 ancient bison. Most were from fully grown bulls and cows. Some were from calves only a few days old. Mixed with the bones were dozens of human artifacts.

A Plano Bison Hunt

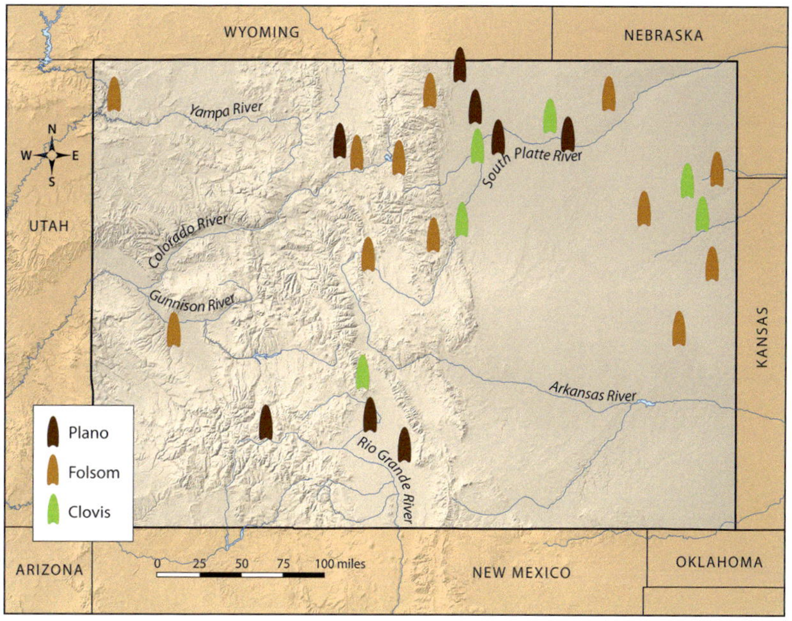

Folsom, Clovis, and Plano archaeological sites in Colorado

From this evidence, Joe Ben Wheat pieced together the following story. One day about 6500 BC, hunters came upon a herd of bison. Coming in quietly from three sides, the hunters surrounded the herd. On the fourth side was a dry ravine. At a signal from the leader, the hunters must have rushed at the herd, shouting and yelling.

The bison stampeded toward the ravine. The lead animals probably jumped across the six-foot-wide ditch. Others tripped and fell. The rest of the herd tumbled over them into the ravine. As the bison piled on top of one another, the hunters rushed in with spears. Within a few minutes, they had killed nearly 200 bison.

The way the bones were placed told Joe Ben Wheat what the hunters did next. He found leg and rib bones with cut marks heaped together in separate piles. The hunters had cut off the legs and ribs of the animals lying on top. They had moved these pieces aside and sliced off the meat. At the bottom of the ravine, Wheat found complete skeletons. These animals were buried under the bison on top of them. The hunters had not bothered to remove the meat from these animals. The bison on top provided all the meat they could use.

A bison skull

Plano Points

Among the bones, Wheat found scrapers and stone spear points. Some of the scrapers were worn down or broken. The hunters must have worn them out scraping the hides. The spear points were narrower and lighter than Clovis

Paleo-Indian mammoth hunters in Colorado

or Folsom points. They were very finely chipped but did not have grooves on the side. They are called Plano points. The way of life of these hunters is called the Plano culture.

The Plano people lived in Colorado after the Clovis and Folsom hunters. Plano sites date from about 8000 BC to 5000 BC. They, too, hunted a bison that is now extinct. This animal, *Bison occidentalis*, was larger than present-day bison but smaller than those of Clovis and Folsom times. Plano people lived in larger groups than the earlier hunters. The hunters at the site Joe Ben Wheat uncovered had cut off enough meat to feed 150 people for a month. Plano hunting bands must have been about that large.

A Wet and Cool Climate

The environment during Clovis and Folsom times was wetter and cooler than today. Larger plants and taller grasses grew on the plains of eastern Colorado. Huge mastodons and mammoths found more than enough food. Later on, the climate changed, becoming warmer and drier. How would that affect plant and animal life? How would humans adjust to climate change?

Skills and Tools for Learning

Identifying and Interpreting Artifacts

Imagine that you are an archaeologist who has uncovered an Archaic Period campsite in Colorado. You have carefully removed most of the soil from around the artifacts you have found. Before removing them, you decide to make a list identifying what you have found. Study the graphic carefully. Some of the items are human-made; others are objects found in nature.

Write this list on a sheet of paper, with plenty of space after each term.

- Spear point
- Bone tool (awl)
- Stone scraper
- Grinding stone
- Pottery shard

Identifying the Artifacts

Now draw a picture of the artifact next to the term it represents. Exchange artifact sheets with a partner, and discuss any differences you may find.

Interpreting the Artifacts

Using the artifacts you have identified, answer each of these questions. Be sure to explain how the artifacts helped you answer the question:

- Did they farm for a living? How do you know?
- Did they hunt mastodons or other big animals? How do you know?
- Did they include seeds and wild grain in their diet? How do you know?
- Did they probably use animal hides? How do you know?

Using an atlatl

Focus Your Reading

- How did hunting change during the Archaic Period?
- How did weapons change?
- What kind of shelter did these people use?

While You Read

In the second column of your organizer, list all the things you have read about the Archaic Period people that make them **different** from the Paleo-Indians.

THE ARCHAIC PERIOD (5000 BC TO AD 1)

Between 5000 BC and AD 1, the hunters' way of life changed. They developed a new spear point, used their weapons in new ways, and changed their diet. Archaeologists call this the Archaic Period. Archaic means "ancient."

Hunters in Colorado began to use a new spear point about 5000 BC. These were smaller than Plano points and had notches in the sides. They probably needed smaller points because they hunted smaller animals. Campsites of this period are littered with the bones of deer, jackrabbits, cottontails, and prairie dogs. The sites include few bison bones. The notched sides or corners probably helped the hunters tie the points onto their spear shafts.

These hunters used their spears in a new way. Earlier hunters killed most animals close up. They rushed up to a mammoth or bison and jabbed it with their spears. Hunters of the Archaic Period threw their spears. They used an atlatl to throw them farther and with greater force. An atlatl is a stick with a hook attached to one end. The hook fits into the butt end of the spear. In effect, this tool lengthens the thrower's arm.

Learning from Primary Sources

Rock Art

We also know about the early hunters and gatherers through the drawings they made on rock formations. Archaeologists have found Archaic Period images on the walls of shallow caves, under rock overhangs, and on the smooth sides of canyons. Some are pictographs, which are images painted on the stone walls. Others, called petroglyphs, were pecked into the walls with stones. *Petro* means stone; *glyphs* are marks used in writing. Still others combine the two forms, with lines and symbols pecked onto the surface of painted figures.

These early artists created a variety of images. Most are outline drawings of people and animals, including deer, bears, and birds. Petroglyphs of animal paw prints are also common, especially bear paws. The images remind us of the importance of animals in the lives of these people. However, archaeologists do not know why they created these images. Were they records of hunts? Were they attempts to communicate with the spirits of animals before a hunt? Did they have a religious purpose? No one knows for certain.

- **What do you think the pictograph below represents?**
- **Why would someone have created it?**

A pictograph

Rock Shelter Clues

Rock shelters provide the best evidence about life in Colorado during the Archaic Period. South-facing rock overhangs were cool in summer and warm in winter. They protected hunters from wind, rain, and snow. People used them as long as there was food nearby. The shelters also protected the human artifacts, or clues, that tell archaeologists about these people.

A Warmer Climate

The people of the Archaic Period lived during a time of climate change. The lower elevations became hotter and drier. Plant and animal life changed as well. People had to adjust to environmental change. How did it affect their way of life?

People then not only ate smaller animals than earlier hunters, but they probably ate less meat and more seeds and roots. Archaeologists have found large numbers of grinding stones at these sites. The people used these hand stones and grinding stones, which were flat rocks, to grind up seeds into flour. By mixing water with the flour, they could make mush or patties to be baked over hot coals.

More Permanent Homes

The hunters and **gatherers** of the Archaic Period also had more permanent homes. Archaeologists have found Archaic spear points and grinding stones under south-facing, overhanging rock ledges. Hunting bands must have gathered under the overhangs during the winter for protection from snow and wind. In 1981, archaeologists digging near the town of Granby found the remains of an Archaic Period hut. It had been made of poles and twigs and plastered over with mud. How could anything be left of a 4,000-year-old mud shelter? The hut had burned down, leaving behind chunks of fire-hardened clay. The shapes of the upright poles from the walls were imprinted in the clay.

THE PLAINS WOODLAND CULTURE (AD 1 TO AD 1300)

For the hunters on the plains of eastern Colorado, even larger changes were in store. About AD 1 they probably used bows and arrows for hunting. They also made clay **pottery** for cooking and storing food. They borrowed these new ideas from people living in Kansas and Nebraska. Those people, in turn, got the ideas from the Eastern Woodland people who lived east of the Mississippi River. This new way of doing things was called the Plains Woodland culture.

These plains people used different kinds of stone points. Some were spear points. The smaller points look like arrowheads. Archaeologists have not found bows or arrow shafts. Wooden weapons from that long ago would not have survived. But few doubt that Plains Woodland people hunted with bows and arrows.

Focus Your Reading

- What ideas did the Plains Woodland people borrow?
- What do the terms *grand circuit* and *rotary engine* mean?
- What kind of pottery did Plains Woodland people make?

Bison Drives

These plains hunters killed bison by driving them over cliffs. They laid out lanes with boulders leading toward the cliffs. Along the lanes they built rock piles large enough to hide a person. As hunters chased a bison herd into the lane, others shot arrows from behind the rock piles. The herd stampeded toward the cliff, trying to escape. Those not brought down by the hunters were killed in the fall.

Some Plains Woodland hunters covered large areas in search of food. Those who spent winters along the Front Range set out each spring on a huge circular trip. Archaeologists call this yearly trip "the grand circuit," or "the rotary engine." The hunters moved north along the Front

While You Read

Look for the main idea in each of the paragraphs in this section. These ideas help us understand how the Plains Woodland people of eastern Colorado lived. Write the main ideas in the third column of your organizer.

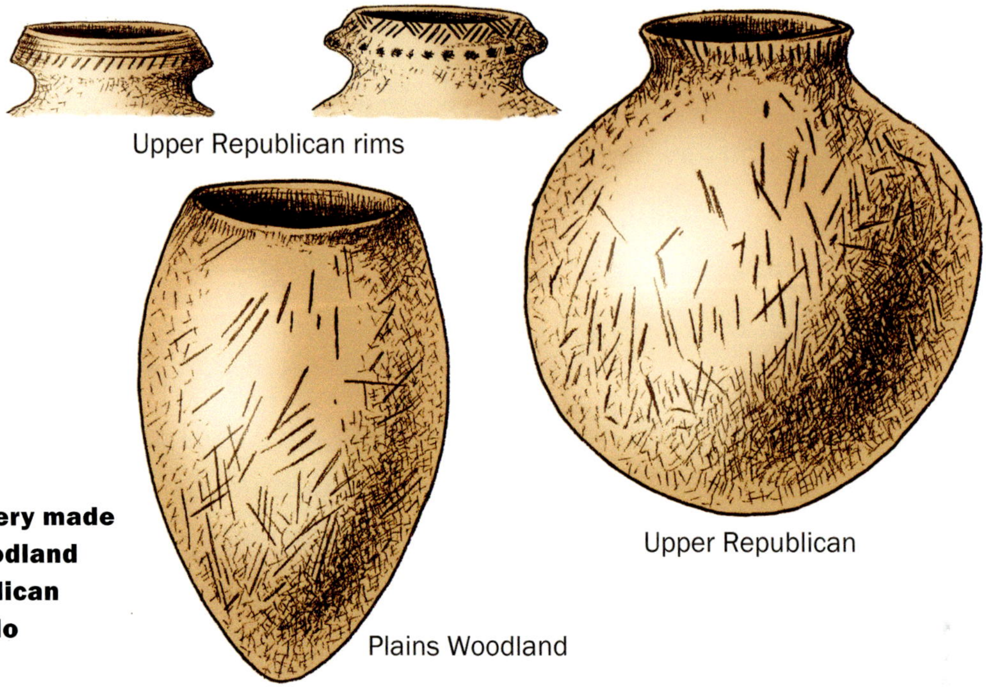

Examples of pottery made by the Plains Woodland and Upper Republican people in Colorado

Range during the spring. In Wyoming they used snow-free passes to cross the Continental Divide. Turning south, they spent the summer hunting bison and elk in North Park and Middle Park. In late fall, they climbed back up the Continental Divide to hunt bighorn sheep. Along the way, they made new stone points from rocks called jasper and chert found in the mountains. They also collected nuts and other plants. In the fall, they returned to the plains. The nuts, seeds, and dried meat they brought back would last them through the next winter.

Bull elk

Rocky Mountain bighorn sheep

Using Clay Pots

The Plains Woodland people were the first plains people to use fired clay pots for cooking and storing food. Their pots are easy to recognize. They have a wide mouth and a pointed bottom. Such pots had to be set in holes in the ground to keep them upright. The pots also have distinctive cord markings on the outside. The pottery makers used paddles wrapped with cords to help mold the fresh clay. The plains people did not give up using baskets. They still used them for gathering seeds and roots.

The Plains Woodland people probably lived in low huts covered with animal skins. Archaeologists have found circles outlined with stones that date from this period. The stones were probably used to hold down the skin covers of huts.

Apishapa shelter with walls made from upright stone slabs

Focus Your Reading

- How did the Upper Republican people get food?
- How was their pottery different from Plains Woodland pottery?
- What kinds of shelters did the Apishapa people build?

While You Read

In the fourth column of your organizer, write about the differences between the Upper Republican and the Apishapa peoples. Then, sketch a picture of their shelters.

THE UPPER REPUBLICAN AND APISHAPA CULTURES (AD 1000 TO AD 1300)

Late in the Plains Woodland Period, two other cultures appeared on the Eastern Plains. About AD 1000, hunters from Kansas and Nebraska moved into the northeastern corner of what is now Colorado. They lived in small hunting camps along the upper Republican River. Their way of life is called the Upper Republican culture. People from Oklahoma and Texas also built camps in what is now southern Colorado along the Arkansas River. Their way of life is known as the Apishapa culture.

Upper Republican People

The Upper Republican culture was much like the Plains Woodland way of life. These people were hunters and gatherers. They probably lived in skin-covered huts. They also used pottery. Their pots were cord marked, like other plains pots. However, they were round in shape. Some pots had handles.

Apishapa People

The Apishapa people were also hunters and gatherers. They, too, made round-shaped, cord-marked pottery. But their shelters were different from those of the Upper Republican and Plains Woodland peoples.

The Apishapa built shelters on the high rims of canyons in what is now southern Colorado. They overlooked the river valley below. Some shelters had as many as twenty-five rooms. The walls were made of upright stone slabs. Stone posts held up the roofs. The first white settlers called them "forts." The Apishapa people may have been guarding against possible attacks. They certainly used the slabs of stone they found in that area in a creative way.

After You Read

1. Use the notes you've written on your graphic organizer to help you as your class discusses the ways the four cultures of big-animal hunters were the same and the ways they were different.
2. Which of the big-animal hunter cultures do you think archaeologists know the most about? Why do you think this is so? Write about it in your notebook.

Thinking about Colorado Water

Do you know . . .
how water connects us to prehistoric times?

Some of the water that we use in Colorado is called groundwater. It is water from underground that is brought to the surface by pumps. Many towns and small cities rely on groundwater for drinking. Farmers on the eastern plains use it to irrigate their crops.

Have you ever wondered why there is water underground?

Groundwater is rain or snow that collects underground in layers of rock. These layers are called aquifers. Some of this water fell as rain in recent times or seeped into the earth from nearby rivers or streams. Water in the deepest aquifers is the oldest. It collected there in prehistoric times. This water is also called "fossil water" because some of it is as old as plant and animal fossils.

Some wells in Colorado are hundreds of feet deep. Water from deep wells fell as rain or snow thousands or perhaps millions of years ago.

- Do you live in a city that depends on groundwater?
- Have you eaten food grown in eastern Colorado?
- Could it have been grown with water that fell as rain or snow when prehistoric people lived in Colorado?

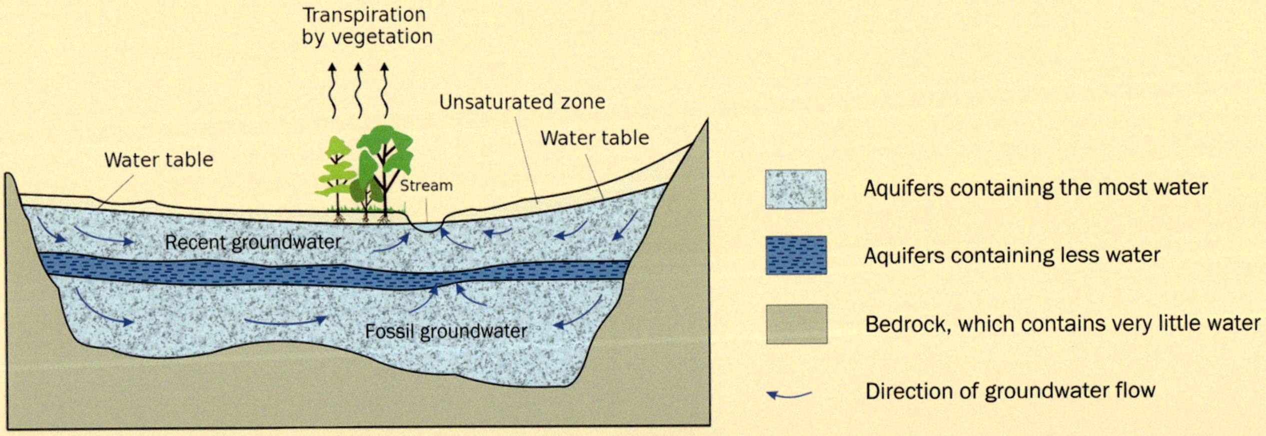

Asking Historical Questions
Your Response

This chapter began with this question:

How did hunter-gatherers respond to changes in the environment?

1. **Review**

   Review the information in your notes and in this chapter about how hunter-gatherers responded to changes in the environment.

2. **Reflect**

   With a partner or in a small group, discuss how hunter-gatherers responded to changes in the environment.

3. **Respond**

   In your notebook, explain how hunter-gatherers responded to changes in the environment.

CHAPTER 4

Basketmakers and Pueblo Dwellers

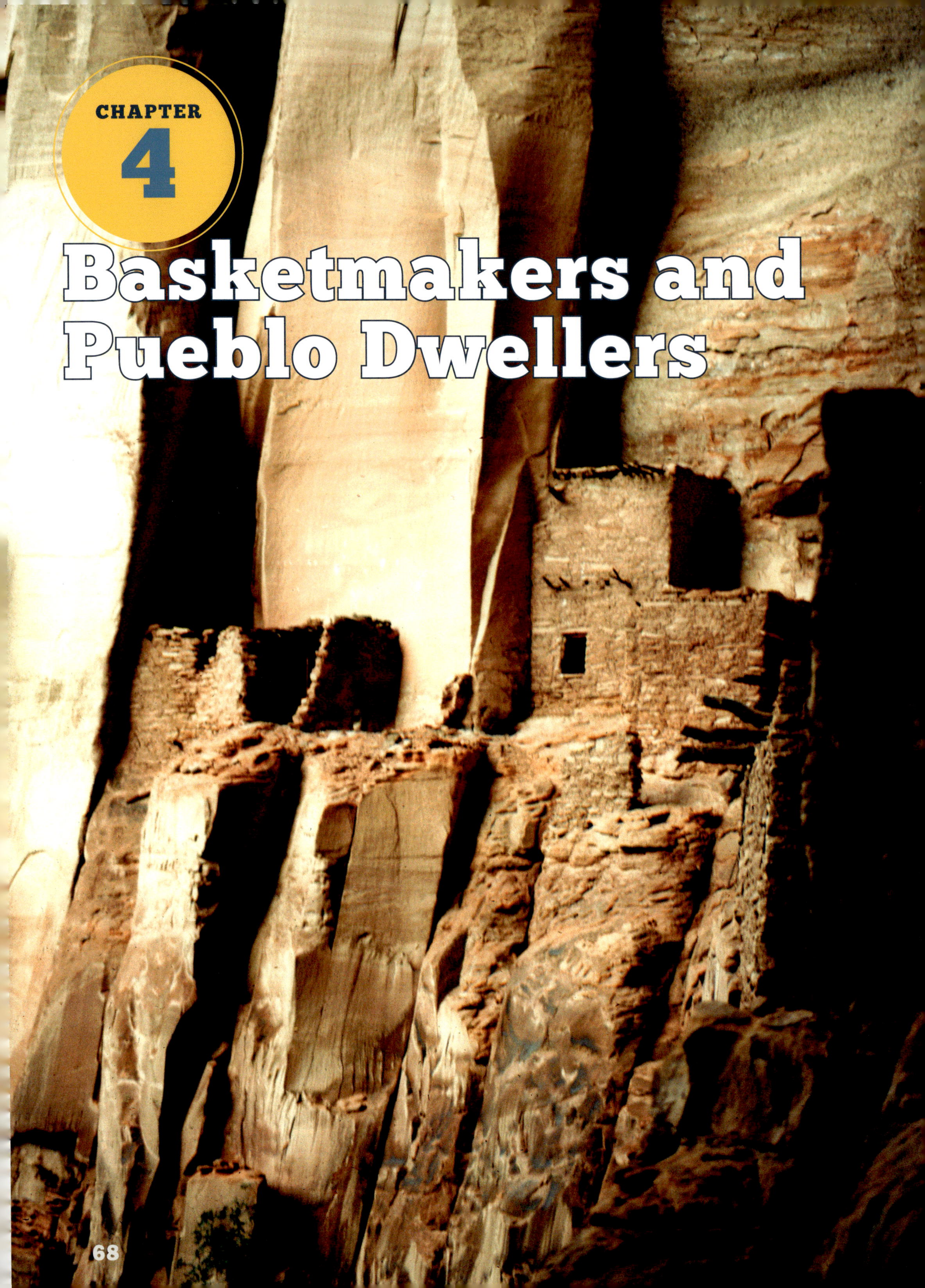

FOCUS QUESTION

How was the Pueblo Dwellers' way of life different from that of the hunter-gatherers?

Before You Read

Scan this chapter, paying attention to section headings, bold print, photos, captions, and drawings. Then, draw a concept map in your notebook with the main topic (Basketmakers and Pueblo Dwellers) in the center circle. Brainstorm words and ideas you think are related to this topic, and arrange them on lines connected to the circle. Talk with a partner or in a small group about why you have chosen these words and ideas.

KEY WORDS

- **Anasazi**
- **ancestors**
- **Pueblo Indians**
- **pithouses**
- **reservoir**
- **descendants**
- **native culture**

On December 18, 1888, two ranchers were looking for stray cattle. Richard Wetherill and Charlie Mason followed cattle tracks to the top of a mesa. At the top, Wetherill got off his horse and walked to the edge of a cliff. He looked out across the canyon. On the canyon wall across from him, he saw a wide opening. Inside it were the ruins of a cliff dwelling.

Wetherill had seen cliff dwellings before. But he had never seen one this large. It had dozens of rooms. Many of them were stacked one on top of another. Near the center was a tower that rose three stories high. It was as big as a palace. Wetherill named the dwelling Cliff Palace.

Cliff Palace

Focus Your Reading

- Where is Cliff Palace located?
- How long have people lived in that area?
- What are the people who once lived there called?

The two men rode to the other side of the canyon. Then they climbed down into the ruins. On the floor of the huge cave they found pottery bowls, mugs, water jars, and a stone ax. The people who lived there hundreds of years before had left most of what they owned. In the weeks to come, Wetherill and Mason found other cliff dwellings like Cliff Palace.

ANCIENT PEOPLE OF THE FOUR CORNERS

The cliff dwellings are located in the Four Corners area. The corners of four states—Colorado, New Mexico, Utah, and Arizona—meet there. The mesa Wetherill and Mason rode up is called Mesa Verde.

The cliff dwellers are known by different names. The Navajo Indians called them the **Anasazi**. That Navajo word means "ancient enemies." Perhaps the two groups of people were enemies long ago. Archaeologists today call them the Ancestral Puebloans. That means they are the **ancestors** of the modern-day **Pueblo Indians** of New Mexico and Arizona. They are also called Basketmakers and Pueblo Dwellers. The Spanish word *pueblo* means "town." The dwellings in which these people lived were like small towns.

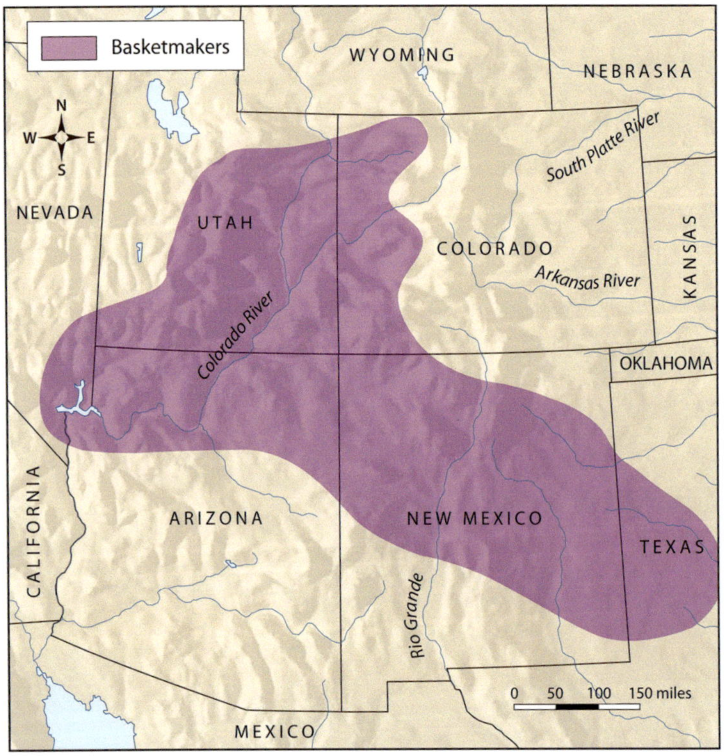

The region where the Basketmakers lived. This area later became part of the four states of Colorado, Utah, Arizona, and New Mexico.

A CHANGING WAY OF LIFE

The Basketmakers and Pueblo Dwellers lived in the Four Corners area for nearly 1,300 years. Their way of life changed over this long period. To help describe these changes,

How Mesa Verde Got Its Name

Mesa is the Spanish word for "table." *Verde* is the Spanish word for "green." Mesas are high areas that are flat on top. The mesa where Cliff Palace is located was called Mesa Verde because it was covered with green juniper trees and shrubs.

archaeologist Frank H.H. Roberts, Jr., divided this time into four periods. The first is the Basketmaker Period. Next comes the Modified Basketmaker Period. It is followed by the Developmental Pueblo Period. The last is called the Great Pueblo Period. In this chapter, we will look at each period.

BASKETMAKER PERIOD (AD 1 TO AD 450)

In 1893, Richard Wetherill made another discovery. Digging under the floor of a pueblo, he found ancient bodies buried deep in pits. They did not look like other bodies he had found at Mesa Verde. The people were taller than the Pueblo Dwellers. These people had also worn sandals that were notched in front. The Pueblo Dwellers wore rounded sandals.

Beside the bodies, Wetherill found things the people had used every day. They included baskets made of willow and yucca fibers. These people stored and cooked their food in baskets instead of pottery jars and bowls. Wetherill named these people the "basket people." Archaeologists today call them the Basketmakers.

Focus Your Reading

- How did the Basketmakers use baskets?
- What kind of clothing did they wear?
- What kinds of shelters did they build?

Decide with your partner how you will read this section about Basketmakers (chorally, trade-off, or silently) and where your stopping points will be. When you reach a stopping point, each partner needs to ask a question or state a thought or opinion about the reading.

Who Were the Basketmakers?

The Basketmakers had arrived in the Mesa Verde area about AD 1, or at least 2,000 years ago. They were the ancestors of the people who lived at Cliff Palace.

The Basketmakers spent much of the year hunting animals and gathering food. They hunted deer with spears hurled by atlatls. They caught rabbits and other small game with snares made of animal sinew. Their food included seeds, nuts, and berries.

The Basketmakers found many uses for baskets. Seeds were gathered and stored in baskets. To carry heavy loads, the Basketmakers filled large baskets and slung them over their backs. Baskets lined with pitch from pine trees made good waterproof containers. They used them to store water and for cooking. To cook food, they boiled water by dropping hot stones into cooking baskets.

Storage basket

Basketmakers making pottery and weaving baskets

Skills and Tools for Learning

Change and Continuity

Think about what life would be like if nothing ever changed. Today would be just like yesterday. Your life would be exactly like your parents' lives. You would watch the same movies and read the same books they read at your age. We are different from our parents because of change.

History is about change. Without it, there would be no history. To describe change, historians often divide the past into historical periods. The chapter you are reading is divided into four periods:

- The Basketmaker Period
- The Modified Basketmaker Period
- The Developmental Pueblo Period
- The Great Pueblo Perlod

Each period is different from the one before. It is different because of the changes that took place in how people lived.

Think of at least one big change that has taken place in your life or in your family's past.

- Think of a name to give that period of your life.
- Briefly describe the change.
- Explain why it took place.

History is also about continuity. This term comes from the word *continue*. Even when times are changing, we continue to do some things we have always done. Think of one example of continuity in your life during a time of change.

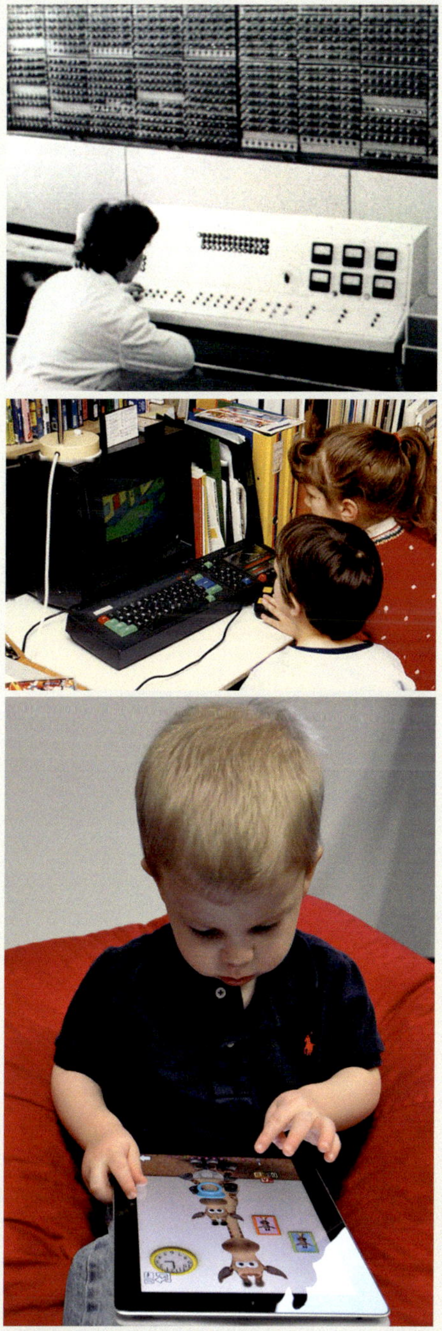

History is about change.

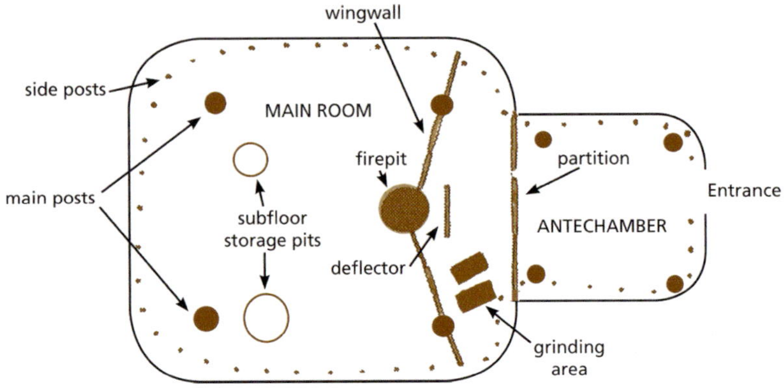

Basketmaker pithouse

Shelter and Clothing

Basketmakers found shelter in caves and under rock overhangs. For winter shelters, they built huts underneath the overhangs. The most common Basketmaker huts were one-room **pithouses**. First, they dug a pit two or three feet deep. Over it they built domelike shelters made of logs. With a fire built inside, the pithouse would stay warm even in the coldest weather.

Basketmakers wore sturdy sandals made from the tough fiber of yucca plants. These may have been their most important item of clothing. They needed good footwear to hunt and gather food in the rocky plateau country of western Colorado. Men wore a breechcloth in summer. Women wore

Basketmaker cave

Seeds of Change

Corn came to the Four Corners area from Mexico. People there had raised corn for thousands of years. The Basketmakers may have acquired corn through trade. Perhaps newcomers from the south taught the Basketmakers how to grow it. However they got it, corn changed their way of life.

a small apron. In winter, everyone wore blankets made of turkey feathers or rabbit fur.

MODIFIED BASKETMAKER PERIOD (AD 450 TO AD 750)

About AD 450 the Basketmakers' way of life began to change. That is why the next 300 years are called the Modified Basketmaker Period. The people began building pithouses with a larger and more comfortable living space. The main room had a bench that curved around the wall. The walls were made of upright poles plastered over with dried mud on the outside. The plastered walls helped keep the pithouses cool in summer and warm in winter. The new-style pithouses also had a room used as an entryway and storage area.

Focus Your Reading

- Why is this period called the Modified Basketmaker Period?
- How did pithouses change during this time?
- What clues indicate that farming became more important?

Basketmakers Settle Down

The people of this period probably spent more time raising crops and less time hunting. The improved pithouses are one indication of this. Farmers spend more time living in houses in one place than hunters and gatherers do. Archaeologists have found a large number of grinding stones in these dwellings. The people used the stones to grind corn into cornmeal.

While You Read

What clues helped archaeologists know about the changes in the Basketmakers' way of life? Write these clues in your notebook.

The Basketmakers began to make pottery as well as baskets during this period. This provides still another clue that they were settling down. Clay pots break easily. People who were always on the move used baskets instead of pottery for that reason. The Basketmakers began to use pottery for cooking and for carrying water. They also made large jars for storing food. Pottery jars were also better than baskets for keeping stored food safe from mice and rats.

Focus Your Reading

- Why are these years called the Developmental Pueblo Period?
- How were dwellings of this period different from earlier ones?
- How did people's physical appearance change?

DEVELOPMENTAL PUEBLO PERIOD (AD 750 TO AD 1100)

During this period, the people of the Four Corners began to build pueblos. They left their pithouses and moved into stone dwellings built at ground level. The new dwellings had rooms lined up in a row or in a semicircle. Six or seven families could live in the stone apartments. These one-story apartment houses were the earliest pueblos. That is why this period is called the Developmental Pueblo Period.

A pueblo from the Developmental Pueblo Period

The people used their small apartments mainly for storage and sleeping. Most of the everyday work took place in an open courtyard in front of the pueblo. It also was the center of community life. Women cooked meals there. Men sat around talking and repairing tools.

Each courtyard had at least one underground room called a kiva. The men of the pueblo used it mainly for religious ceremonies and social events. They entered the kiva by climbing down a ladder through a hole in the roof.

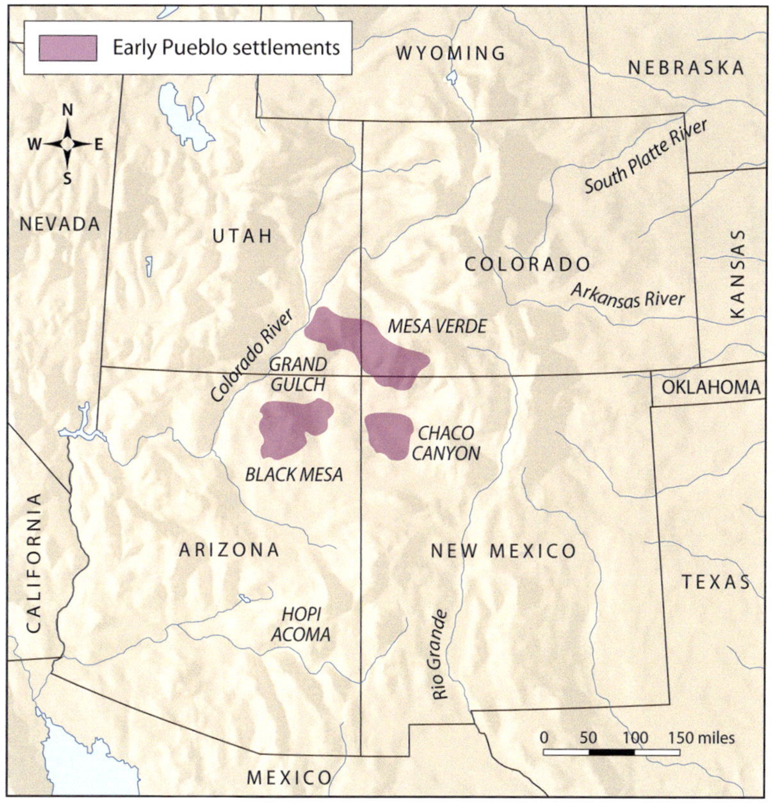

Locations of early Pueblo villages

Inside of an underground kiva used for ceremonies by Pueblo Dwellers

Farmers and Pottery Makers

The people who built the pueblos lived by farming. Each spring they planted corn, squash, and beans in their fields. They dropped the seeds in holes made with planting sticks. During the summer, they chopped weeds out of the fields with stone hoes fitted with wooden handles. That kept the weeds from using up moisture the plants needed. The farmers picked squash and fresh corn during the summer. In the fall, they harvested beans and corn to store for winter.

Modern-day corn stalk

This drawing shows how men during the Developmental Pueblo Period planted crops with a digging stick.

Beautiful cxamples of Mesa Verde pottery

During this period, the people of the Four Corners became skillful pottery makers. They made drinking mugs, pitchers, and canteens, as well as cooking pots and storage jars. They found new ways to decorate pottery. The most popular style was whitc pottery decorated with black designs.

While You Read

In your notebook, sketch a scene of what a typical pueblo community might have looked like. Pay attention to the details this section gives you about everyday pueblo life. Share your skctch with a partner.

One way the Pueblo people made pottery

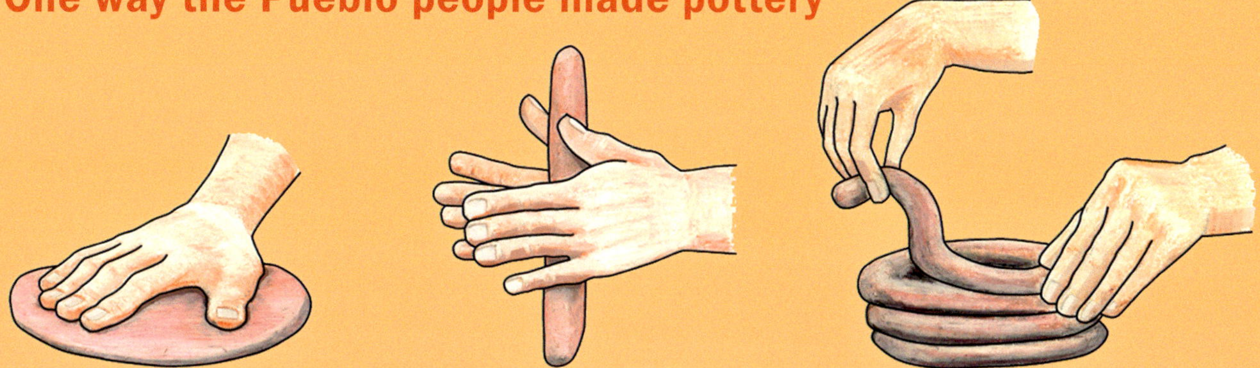

1. Make a flat pancake of clay
2. Roll more clay together to make long "ropes"
3. Lay the ropes on top of the pancake to make the sides of the clay pot

Changing Styles

Clothing styles also changed during the Developmental Pueblo Period. A new style of sandal with a square toe became the fashion. Women wore aprons made of cotton cloth instead of yucca fiber. They got the cloth through trade with Mexico and Arizona. People there had discovered how to weave cotton fibers into cloth. The Developmental Pueblo people preferred blankets woven from turkey feathers to rabbit fur blankets. Every pueblo had pens where turkeys were kept, mainly for their feathers.

The shape of people's faces and heads changed during this period. Archaeologists were surprised when they first discovered skeletons with flattened skulls. They wondered if a different people had moved into the area. Then they discovered that Pueblo mothers strapped their babies into unpadded cradleboards. The boards flattened the baby's skull, which became a permanent trait. Why did they do this? Perhaps because a flattened skull makes a person's face appear broader. People of this period must have found broad faces attractive.

Focus Your Reading

- How did the Pueblo way of life change during the Great Pueblo Period?
- What contact did the Pueblo Dwellers have with other people?
- What are some possible reasons why the Pueblo people left the Four Corners area?

GREAT PUEBLO PERIOD (AD 1100 TO AD 1300)

Beginning about AD 1100, still other changes took place in the Mesa Verde area. Among them were the larger pueblos built after that date. Instead of one-story row houses, the new pueblos were three or four stories high. They held many more people. Archaeologist Frank H.H. Roberts, Jr., called the next 200 years the Great Pueblo Period.

The people built their first big pueblos on top of the mesas. A good example is the pueblo known as Far View House. It was three stories tall and had about fifty rooms and five kivas. Located high up on Chapin Mesa, it had a stunning view of the plateaus and valleys below. The larger settlement that included Far View House also contained about a dozen smaller pueblos.

Far View House, Mesa Verde National Park

The people of the Far View settlement were farmers. They walked to nearby fields, where they grew corn, beans, squash, and melons. They could not dig ditches to irrigate their crops because no rivers or streams ran across the mesa. Just enough rain fell to provide moisture for the crops.

The Far View farmers did create a lake now called Far View Reservoir. Many archaeologists think it held rainwater and provided the settlement with drinking water for at least part of each year.

Cliff Dwellings

About AD 1200 a puzzling thing happened. Hundreds of people left the mesa tops. They built new pueblos in the giant caves that wind and water had carved out of the sandstone cliffs. Some of the new cliff dwellings were larger than the pueblos on the mesa tops. The largest was Cliff Palace. It had 151 rooms and 23 kivas.

Load-Bearing Walls

Building a three- or four-story pueblo presented the people of the Mesa Verde area with a problem. If they built rooms on top of their single-story pueblos, the walls would collapse. They solved this problem by using "rubble-core" construction. That is, they built two walls of stone blocks a foot or so apart. Then they filled the space between the walls with stones and other rubble. This made the lower wall strong enough to bear the heavy weight of the upper stories.

Cliff Palace had 151 rooms and 23 kivas. It was one of the largest cliff dwellings in the Mesa Verde area.

While You Read

Use these **codes** on sticky notes down the side margins as you read this section:

- * (I already knew this)
- + (New information)
- !! (Wow!)
- ?? (I don't understand)

Compare your text coding with your small group, and talk about the parts you do not understand. How will you get your questions answered?

Building and living in a cliff-side town was not easy. Workers had to move stones, mortar, and poles for roof supports down the steep sides of the cliffs. The people who moved there also had to climb up and down the cliff every time they worked in their fields on the mesa tops.

Why did hundreds of people move down from the mesas to homes in the cliffs? Some archaeologists believe the cliff dwellers were trying to protect their food supplies from their hungry neighbors. Food was scarce during dry years. They also may have moved to the cliffs to protect themselves from enemies. The narrow paths that led down to the cliff dwellings would have been easy to defend. Still, many people continued to live on the mesa tops. Why some people built cliff dwellings remains a mystery.

Learning from Primary Sources

Cliff Dwellings

In 1776, Francisco Domínguez and Silvestre Escalante traveled through southern Colorado searching for an easy route from New Mexico to California. Along the way, they saw two small cliff dwellings, as Escalante noted in his journal. He was the first European to leave a firsthand account of the cliff dwellings of the Four Corners area.

"**August 13:** On an elevation on the south bank of the river in ancient times there was a small settlement of the same form as those of the Indians of New Mexico [pueblo dwellings], as is shown by the ruins which we purposely examined.

"**August 23:** We halted for a siesta near a permanent stream that comes down from the sierra to a plain covered with chamise [a flowering shrub], toward the southern end of which there is a valley of good pasturage. In front of it there is a sort of ledge upon which there are ruins of a small and ancient pueblo whose houses appear to have been of stone, with which the [Ute Indians] have made a weak and crude fortification."

Fray Angelico Chavez (translator), *Diary and Itinerary by Silvestre Vélez de Escalante*

- **Where were the dwellings that Escalante found located?**
- **How were they constructed?**

Balcony House

Trading with Others

Prickly pear cactus

The Pueblo Dwellers had links to people outside the Four Corners, mainly through trade. Bands of hunters, gatherers, and part-time farmers called the Fremont people lived to the north. These people collected sunflower seeds, prickly pear cactus, and other plants. Pueblo pottery makers probably traded with them for animal skins and food. At least, archaeologists have found Mesa Verde–style pottery in ruins miles to the north of Mesa Verde.

Trade also linked the Pueblo Dwellers to people farther south. In ruins of cliff dwellings, archaeologists have found polished turquoise stones from Arizona, macaw feathers from Mexico, and abalone shell beads from the Pacific coast. The Pueblo Dwellers also may have traded with the desert people to the west. They were the ancestors of modern-day Ute Indians.

Locations of early and present-day Pueblo villages

Why Did They Leave?

When Richard Wetherill and Charlie Mason discovered Cliff Palace, it had stood empty for at least 600 years. Why did the Pueblo Dwellers leave? A long period of dry years is part of the explanation. A drought began about 725 years ago. Little rain fell for the next 23 years. But Pueblo Dwellers had survived droughts before. What other reasons caused them to leave? They had cut down most of the trees on the mesas for

Spruce Tree House was an ancient Anasazi pueblo dwelling. Its ruins are found at Mesa Verde National Park, Cortez, Colorado.

roof poles and firewood. Archaeologists estimate that Pueblo Dwellers had to travel seventy-five miles to get wood for fuel. They also may have fled from an enemy attack. Some of the abandoned pueblos contain the skeletons of people who died violent deaths.

THE PUEBLO PEOPLE OF TODAY

Where did the Pueblo Dwellers go? Most moved east toward the Rio Grande in New Mexico. Their **descendants** are the Pueblo Indians who live in the Rio Grande Valley. Others live farther west at the Acoma and Zuni pueblos and at the Hopi pueblo in Arizona.

The move to the Rio Grande Valley brought still more changes to the Pueblo people's way of life. They learned to survive droughts by living closer to a reliable source of water.

Focus Your Reading

- Where do the Pueblo people live today?
- How has Pueblo life changed since the Pueblo Dwellers left the Four Corners area?
- What aspects of Pueblo culture remain unchanged?

While You Read

Read this section with a partner. Take turns making connections to the text by finishing the sentence with "that reminds me of . . ." As you read, write your connections in your notebook.

Spanish settlers, who arrived in New Mexico in the early 1600s, introduced them to new plants, animals, and ways to do things. From the Spanish, the Pueblo people learned to grow wheat, plant fruit trees, and raise horses, goats, and sheep. During the past 200 years, American explorers, traders, settlers, and tourists have introduced the Pueblo people to other new ways to do things. The newcomers, in turn, have learned to appreciate the Pueblo people's way of life.

New and Old Ways

In modern-day pueblos, the new and the old exist side by side. Like Americans everywhere, the Pueblo people watch TV, drive cars and pickup trucks, and buy hamburgers at McDonald's. Pueblo boys and girls attend public schools and wear jeans like students elsewhere. However, the Pueblo people have kept much of their **native culture** alive. Within

Taos Pueblo, New Mexico

Modern Hopi dancers

the pueblos, boys and girls may have an "Indian" name, take part in religious dances, and wear traditional clothes on feast days. Many traditional arts and crafts have survived. Some Pueblo women, for example, still make beautiful pottery. Pueblo pottery, silver jewelry, and other crafts are sold in gift stores throughout the United States.

After You Read

1. Return to the Basketmakers and Pueblo Dwellers concept map you drew in your notebook. What would you change? What would you add after having read this chapter?
2. Suppose you could interview a Basketmaker or a Pueblo Dweller. What three thoughtful questions would you want answered? Write these questions in your notebook.

Thinking about Colorado Water

Do you know . . . why Colorado needs reservoirs?

Blue Mesa Reservoir

Far View Reservoir

Colorado has dozens of **reservoirs** in every part of the state. Reservoirs are human-made lakes.

The largest of these lakes is Blue Mesa Reservoir. It is almost 18 miles long and has 96 miles of shoreline. Constructed in 1996, it is also one of the state's newest.

Far View Reservoir at Mesa Verde is one of Colorado's smallest reservoirs. Built by the Pueblo Dwellers, it is also one of the oldest.

Have you ever wondered why Colorado has so many reservoirs?

Reservoirs store water from rain and snow that falls in the winter and spring. In the spring, water from snowmelt rushes down mountain streams, floods river valleys, and flows out of the state. By storing it, reservoirs make some of this water available in Colorado year-round. The water is used to irrigate farms, to provide cities with water, and to generate electricity.

Most archaeologists believe that Far View Reservoir was built about the year AD 950 to store spring rains over the summer for drinking water. It is now part of Mesa Verde National Park.

Can you think of other reasons to have lakes and reservoirs?

- How do people spend leisure time there?
- Which sports need large bodies of water?

Asking Historical Questions
Your Response

This chapter began with this question:

How was the Pueblo Dwellers' way of life different from that of the hunter-gatherers?

1. **Review**

   Review the information in your notes and in this chapter about the Pueblo Dwellers' way of life.

2. **Reflect**

   With a partner or in a small group, discuss how the Pueblo Dwellers' way of life was different from that of the hunter-gatherers.

3. **Respond**

   In your notebook, explain how their way of life was different.

UNIT THREE

The Indian People of Colorado

1000	1100	1200	1300	1400

1100 Utes arrive in Colorado

1400 Apaches arrive in Colorado

People

At one time, only Indians lived in Colorado. Like prehistoric people, Indians lived by hunting bison and other animals. Getting horses from Spanish settlers made hunting easier. They also gathered plants, roots, and berries.

Places

Indians lived throughout Colorado. The Utes hunted in the mountains during the summer. They spent winters in the valleys and the plateau country. The Cheyennes, Arapahos, and other tribes hunted bison on the plains.

Times

The arrival of horses brought good times to Colorado Indians. Horses could pull heavy loads. That made moving camp easier. Horses also made it easier to follow the bison herds and to kill animals for food.

- **1492** Columbus discovers the tern Hemisphere
- **1520** Cortez conquers the Aztecs in Mexico
- **1609** Spanish found Santa Fe
- **1640** Utes get horses
- **1680** Pueblo Revolt
- **1700** Comanches arrive in Colorado
- **1750** Kiowas and Kiowa-Apaches arrive in Colorado
- **1800** Arapahos and Cheyennes arrive in Colorado
- **1840** Colorado Plains Indians make peace

1500 1600 1700 1800 1900

History

125 RUNS MEDICINE. ARAPAHOE
COPYRIGHT 1899, ROSE AND HOPKINS
DENVER

Before You Read

Skim this chapter. On sticky notes, write one **big** question and three **little** questions you have about history. **Big** questions are about big ideas. **Little** questions are about details or words. Place the notes in your notebook. Try to answer them as you read.

KEY-WORDS

- **historian**
- **primary sources**
- **secondary sources**
- **change**
- **continuity**
- **cause**
- **effect**
- **consequence**
- **significance**

Focus Your Reading

- Do people in the past or people in the present make history?
- What is the difference between a primary source and a secondary source?
- What ideas do historians use to think about the past?

WHAT IS HISTORY?

History is an account of what people did in the past. It could be a book about a Colorado governor written by a **historian**. A historical account could also be a video or film by a movie director about a past event. It could be a newspaper story about something that happened in your town or city. Or it could be a history of your school written by students.

The point is that history is made by people in the present. It is not the past, which is everything that ever happened before now. History is what we make of the past. It is our version of what happened.

This is a powerful idea. It means that all of us can make history. This includes you! In fact, the best way to study history is to inquire about the past, find information about a person or a period, and construct your own version of what happened.

Write a historical question in your notebook about your family or a family you know that you would like to answer.

HISTORY AS INQUIRY

History is also an inquiry into the past. To inquire is to ask questions. Historical inquiry begins with questions about what happened, when, and where. What was the Pikes Peak Gold Rush? As you know or will find out, it was the journey in 1859 by thousands of people who crossed the plains to Colorado in search of gold. But that does not tell us much, does it?

Historical thinkers also want to know how and why events happened. Why did thousands of people think they could find enough gold to get rich? Why did the Gold Rush mainly attract young men? Why were so few women involved? These are more difficult than what, when, and where questions. To answer them, we have to look at the

Routes to the Pikes Peak mining regions

historical evidence. Then we have to interpret what the evidence means. An interpretation is a possible explanation supported by factual evidence.

To help you inquire into Colorado's past, each chapter in this book begins with a question on geography, history, or economics. Each of these questions spans the whole chapter. To respond to it, you will need to use information you learn in each part of the chapter. The parts are sections introduced by subheadings. As your inquiry moves forward, you may need to look for additional information. Ask your teacher for other sources that may provide additional evidence to help you answer your questions. Feel free to ask your own questions as well.

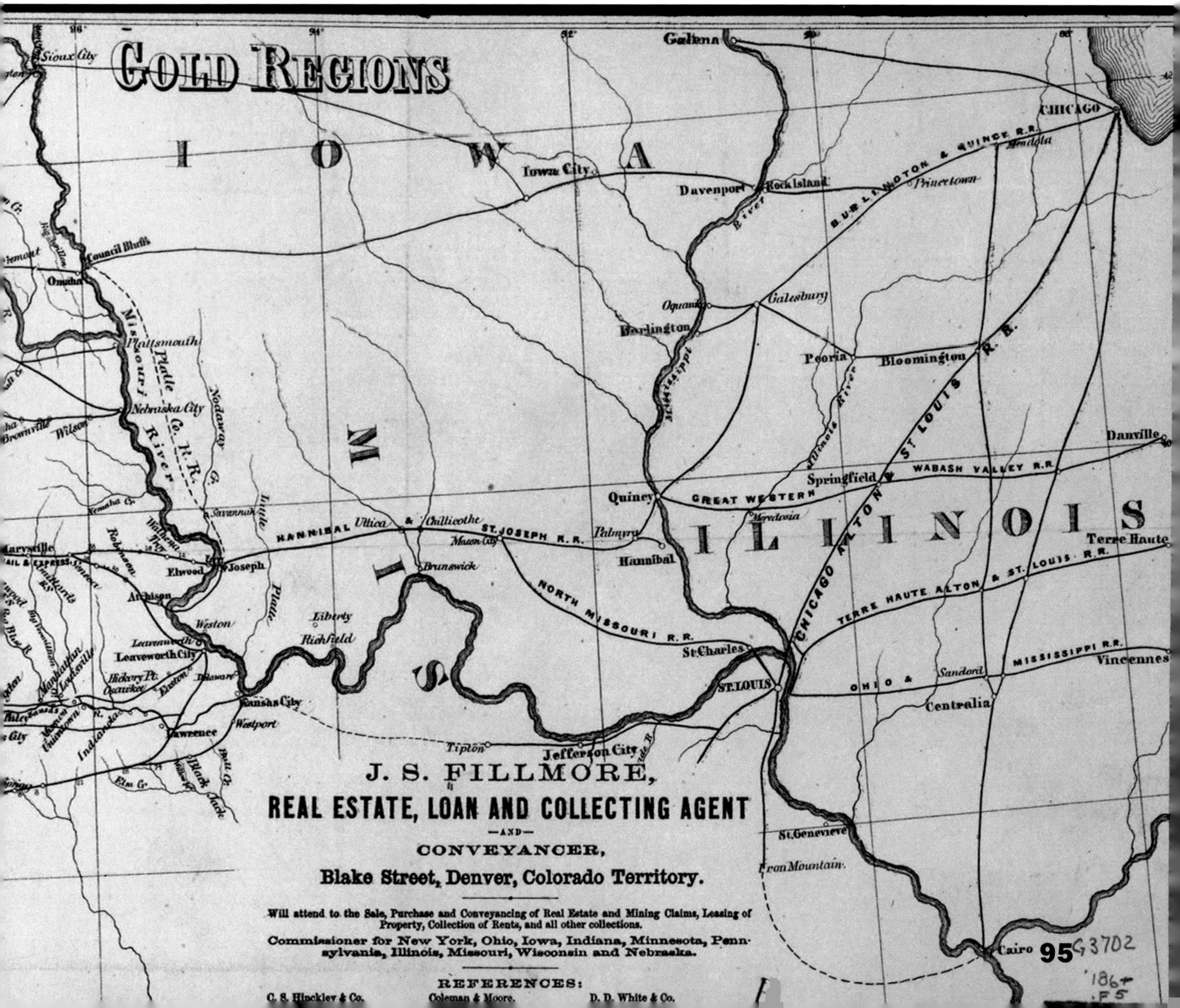

PRIMARY AND SECONDARY SOURCES

The most important evidence historians use to explain what happened and why is called **primary sources**. These are firsthand or eyewitness accounts by people who lived at the time. Diary entries, newspaper accounts, and historical photographs are commonly used primary sources. So, too, are public documents and artifacts created in the past. You will find examples of primary sources in each chapter of this book. They are included in features called "Learning from Primary Sources."

Accounts written after the event by people who were not present are called **secondary sources**. These sources are what historical thinkers produce when they write historical accounts. Historians judge each other's accounts by how well they have used evidence to explain what happened. We also call them "historical accounts." We mentioned some examples of accounts. The book you are reading now is such an account, or secondary source.

A primary source: old photographs

HISTORICAL THINKING

History is also a way of thinking. Historians use sets of ideas to think about the past. The most important set is **change** and **continuity**. Change is what history is all about, as all people and societies change over time. But not everything changes at the same time. People continue doing some things the old way. This is what we mean by continuity.

A second set of ideas historical thinkers use is **cause** and **effect** or **consequence**. We explain change by looking for the causes that brought change about. How did so many people learn about the discovery of gold in Colorado? How important were newspapers as a cause? Every change that takes place has consequences. What consequences did the Gold Rush have for Colorado's Indians? A third important

While You Read

In your notebook, make a list of five ideas historians use to think about the past. Under each idea, explain in your own words why it is important if you want to know about the past.

Primary Sources

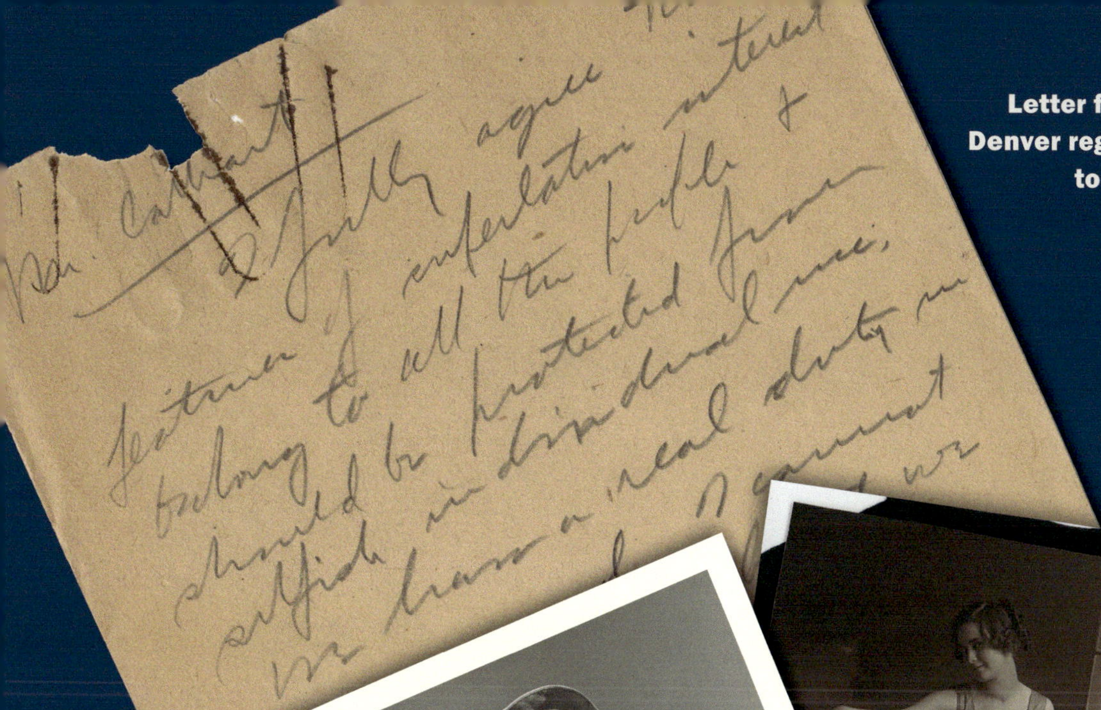

Letter from A. S. Peck, Denver regional forester, to Arthur Carhart

Caroline Bancroft high school scrapbook

Photo of a boy and lamb

Doll

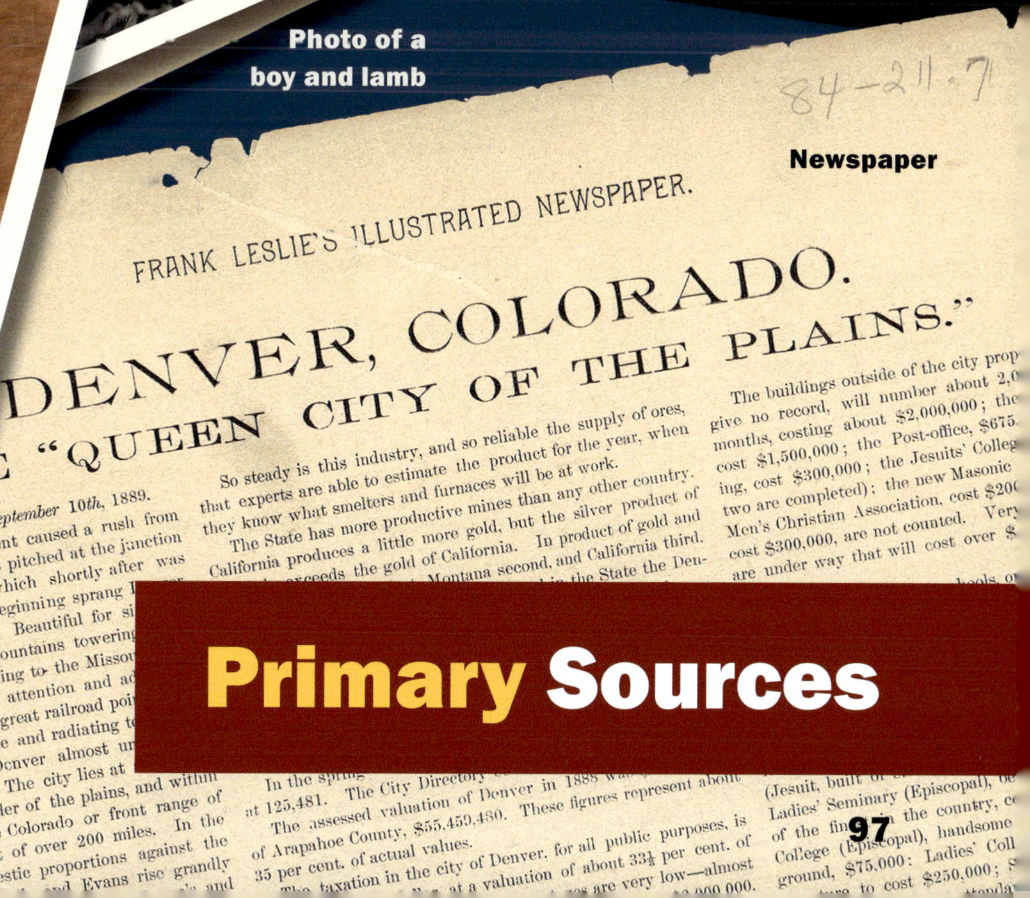

Newspaper

84-211.7

FRANK LESLIE'S ILLUSTRATED NEWSPAPER.

DENVER, COLORADO.

THE "QUEEN CITY OF THE PLAINS."

A gold miner in the Pikes Peak region

idea is **significance**, as some changes are more significant or important than others. Historians judge significance by the impact changes had on people in the past and continue to have on the present.

HISTORICAL RELATIONSHIPS

Historians also look for how events in the past are related. How are they connected to one another? The most obvious historical relationships are connections over time. These are called chronological relationships. The Gold Rush, for example, happened *after* the discovery of gold at Cherry Creek but *before* Colorado became a state. The sequence in which events happened is demonstrated by a time line. Each unit of this book begins with a time line.

Historical thinkers often divide events that are clustered together in time into periods or eras. The period 1859–67 is often referred to as the Gold Rush era. Marking off historical periods is also one way to call attention to big changes. The Gold Rush involved many different kinds of changes in the way people in Colorado lived.

While You Read

Make a time line that includes five events in your own life. Give the date for each, and arrange them in the order in which they happened.

WHY STUDY HISTORY?

We are interested in the past for many reasons. We may simply be curious. What was it like to live in a Colorado gold mining town? We may hope to learn something from the people who lived in the past. What can the Ute Indians teach us about living in harmony with nature? Knowing how people in the past dealt with change may help us live in today's rapidly changing world. We may also want to study history to learn about ourselves. To what extent are we different from people who came before us? What makes us and the times we live in different? What will historical thinkers in the future think about us?

After You Read

Share and compare your **big** and **little** questions and answers with a partner, a small group, or the whole class. Star the answers you found "right there" in the text. Put a check beside the answers you inferred or found in other resources.

CHAPTER 5

The Ute Indians

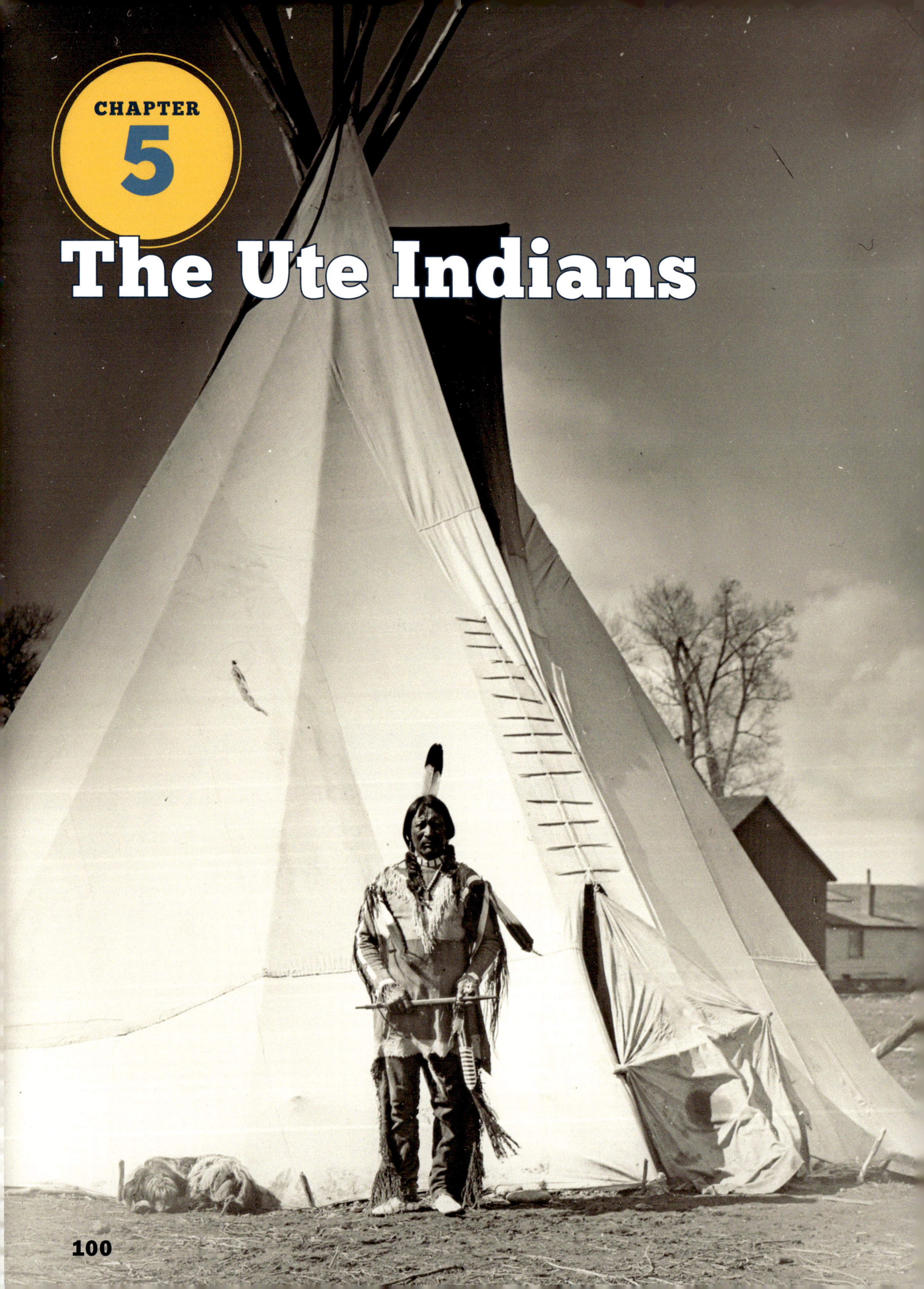

FOCUS QUESTION

How did horses change the Utes' way of life?

Before You Read

In a small group or with your whole class, skim this chapter and take turns thinking out loud by asking and answering these questions:

1. What questions will this chapter answer?
2. What questions do I have about this chapter?

In your notebook, write the questions you think are most important.

KEY WORDS

- tribe
- Navajo
- travois
- extended families
- bands
- reservations

The Utes are Colorado's longest residents. They have lived here for at least 700 years. They arrived before the Pueblo Dwellers left. The Utes were desert people. They were better able to survive a drought than the Pueblo Dwellers were.

The Utes came from the desert region of the West that includes the state of Utah. That state is named for the Utes. Desert Indians survived by eating whatever food they could find. The Paiute **tribe** of more recent times ate crickets, lizards, and ants, as well as roots and berries. Paiutes were cousins of the Utes.

The Utes once occupied much of Colorado. They hunted from the plateaus of the Western Slope to the Eastern Plains. In the winter, they camped in the southern part of the state. The Utes spent most of the year in the mountains. That is why they are called the Mountain People.

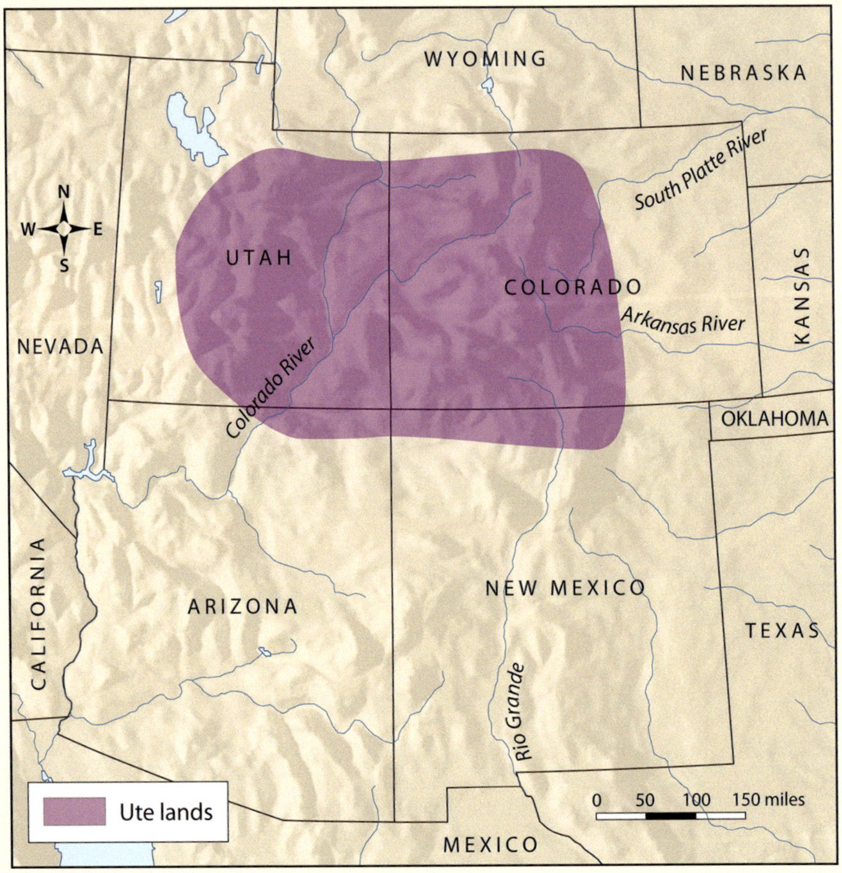

Where the Utes lived

Focus Your Reading

- What life zones did the Utes visit during the year?
- What kinds of plants and animals did they eat?
- How did getting horses change the Utes' diet?

THE SEARCH FOR FOOD

Colorado must have looked better to the Utes than the desert they had left. Even in a drought, they found enough food in the plateaus and mountains to survive. They did not have to eat ants and lizards. Still, finding enough food was a struggle.

The Utes moved with the seasons. They traveled in small groups, harvesting the plants as they ripened. In the spring, they gathered green plants in the lower foothills. In early summer, they gathered roots and grass seeds in the mountain forests. They reached the subalpine forests in late summer. Chokecherries, serviceberries, and elderberries that grew in the mountain meadows were ripe by that time. The Utes went back to the foothills in the fall to harvest piñon nuts, juniper seeds, and ricegrass seeds. At the first snowfall, they set up winter camps in the lowlands. Food was scarce during the winter. The Utes tried to gather enough food during the summer to last until the next spring.

While You Read

Make a list in your notebook of the animals and plants the Utes could eat as they traveled through different life zones.

Food Gathering

At first, the Utes lived mainly by gathering plant food. They did not eat much meat. Killing big game was difficult for small groups of hunters who were on foot. Now and then, Ute hunters came upon a small herd of bison in the mountain parks. These animals usually escaped. Hunters sometimes killed pronghorn antelopes by driving herds over cliffs. Deer were easier to kill. Rabbits were the easiest of all. The Utes drove rabbits into nets and killed them with clubs.

Seeds, dried meat, wild plants, berries, and roots made nourishing meals. To prepare ricegrass and sunflower seeds, Ute women first roasted them over hot coals. The heat caused the hard shells to pop off. Then they boiled the tender seed grains to make mush or shaped them into patties to be cooked. Ute women also made tasty meat stews. They stirred wild onions, carrots, and berries into meat as it boiled. Wild potatoes and baked yampa roots added starch to their diet.

Elderberries

Yampa Roots

The roots of yampa plants were a favorite Ute food. Women cooked them in pits lined with rocks, which they had heated in a fire pit. They placed layers of damp grass over the rocks to protect the roots. When the pit was filled with roots, the Utes covered it with another layer of heated rocks. Roots that had steamed overnight tasted like cooked carrots.

While You Read

In your notebook, draw a Venn diagram and add words and phrases that compare and contrast the Utes' life "before horses" and "after horses."

Bison Hunting

The Utes' diet changed after the 1640s, when they got horses. Horses arrived with the Spanish farmers and ranchers who settled in New Mexico. In 1637 the Spanish captured eighty Ute men and made them work as slaves. Three years later some of the men escaped, taking horses with them. The Utes got still more horses by raiding Spanish settlements. Mounted Utes could travel farther to search for food. Horses also made it easier for the Utes to hunt bison.

Bison provided the Utes with protein-rich food and many useful items. They found a use for almost every part of the animal. They used thick bison hides to make winter coats, robes, and tepee covers. Bison sinew made strong thread. Ute women made cups, ladles, and spoons from bison horns. The flat shoulder bones made good scrapers. Utes also traded bison meat for **Navajo** cotton cloth and pottery and for Spanish knives and axes.

A bison

Skills and Tools for Learning

Inquiry Learning

Real learning is inquiry learning. That is, it comes from asking questions. Geographers ask questions about people and places. Economists ask questions about choices people face. Historians ask questions about the past. The best way to learn about Colorado history is by asking questions.

Each chapter in this book begins with a question about a topic. For this chapter the question is "How did horses change the Utes' way of life?" Keep coming back to this question as you read the chapter. Each topic includes information to help answer it. For example, let's use the information about shelter. As you will see, the Utes relied on wickiups before they had horses. After getting horses, they began using tepees. Did getting horses lead them to change the kind of shelter they used?

Begin your inquiry by reading the description of wickiups (pages 108–109). Then read the information about tepees (page 109). Now, can you think of reasons wickiups worked better for people without horses and tepees were better for people with horses? If so, write a paragraph explaining why getting horses changed the kind of shelter Utes preferred.

Ute wickiups

Ute tepees

Focus Your Reading

- How did Ute clothing change over time?
- What kind of shelters did Utes build before they had horses?
- How did their shelters change after they had horses?

CLOTHING AND SHELTER

Hunting supplied the Utes with clothing as well as food. Most of their clothes were made of deer hides. Ute women were widely known for their skill in preparing deerskins. The finished skins, which they bleached almost white, were soft to the touch. Ute deerskins were in great demand. The Spanish settlers in New Mexico traded corn, knives, iron pots, and woven cloth for deerskins.

Deerskin Clothing

To make their best dresses, Ute women used doeskin. Doeskin, the hide of a female deer, was softer than buckskin. The women used buckskin from a male deer to make men's clothing and moccasins. In warm weather, Ute men only wore breechcloths. In winter, they added buckskin shirts and leggings. Both men and women wore moccasins.

In summertime, children under age six wore nothing at all. In winter, they wore small versions of the adults' dresses and shirts. Ute mothers wrapped their infants in buckskin blankets and laced them into cradleboards. The boards kept them safe while their mothers worked.

Ute dress made of deerskin

Pair of Ute men's moccasins made of buckskin and decorated with beads

Learning from Primary Sources

Ute Food Gathering

The following are descriptions of Ute food gathering. The author of the first source was a fur trapper in the 1830s, who kept a journal of his travels in Ute country. The second source is by a Ute elder whose mother taught her how to harvest chokecherries.

Gathering Food

"Women and children are employed in gathering grass-hoppers, crickets, ants, and various other insects, which are carefully preserved for food, together with roots, and grass seed. From the mountains, they bring the nuts, which are found in the cones of the pine, acorns from dwarf oaks, different kinds of berries, and the inner bark of the pine, which has a sweet acid taste, not unlike lemon syrup."

Warren Angus Ferris, *Life in the Rocky Mountains*

Chokecherries

"If you've seen a chokecherry tree, it's all filled with berries . . . The upper part is for the birds. The middle part is ours, the human's, the rest, the bottom part is for the animals that cannot climb. That's why we were taught that we don't pick the whole thing. We leave some, because God gave us this wonderful food, not just for the human beings but for all of us. So we have to share with the little birds and little wild animals at the bottom."

Isabel Kent, quoted in Jan Pettit, *Utes: The Mountain People*

- **What food did the Utes gather from the mountains?**
- **Why did Utes not pick all the chokecherries?**

Chokecherries

Oak acorns

Pinecones

Ute man in camp

Cotton and Wool Cloth

Ute clothing changed over time. By trading with the Navajo and the Spanish, the Utes acquired cotton and wool cloth. The Navajos wove fine cotton cloth, which Ute women used to make dresses. Sheep the Spanish brought with them to New Mexico provided wool. The Spanish settlers traded wool to the Utes in exchange for deerskins.

UTE SHELTER

The Utes lived in wickiups. These were huts made of willow sticks or poles covered with brush. Brush huts were adequate for summer

Ute Wickiups

Utes built different kinds of wickiups. They made small, dome-shaped shelters by laying brush over a willow frame. Tall wickiups were made by leaning poles against a tree. They covered the poles with brush. If the poles were placed close enough together, a brush cover was not needed.

Before the Utes had tepees, they lived in wickiups like these.

shelter. In winter, the Utes covered the brush wickiups with animal skins. These shelters were warm enough, but they were not portable. The Utes had to build completely new shelters each time they moved.

Getting horses helped the Utes solve that problem. With bison now easier to kill, the Utes built tepees covered with bison hides. Tepees were easy to move. The Utes fastened the tepee poles to a horse's neck to make a travois. A **travois** was a platform mounted on poles behind the horse. When they moved camp, the Utes loaded the tepee covers, household goods, and even small children onto the travois. A horse could pull several times more weight than it could carry on its back.

Ute tepee

FAMILIES, COMMUNITY LIFE, AND GOVERNMENT

In early times, Utes lived in family groups most of the year. Their **extended families** were larger than most families are today. A Ute family often included grandparents and a married daughter and her husband, as well as parents and children.

Large families were very useful. Groups of adults hunted and gathered food. Everyone helped raise the children. Grandparents took care of young children when their mothers were busy. They helped teach them how to behave. Aunts and uncles, as well as the parents, taught the children the skills they would need as adults.

Focus Your Reading

- Why did Utes have extended families?
- What was camp life like for Ute children?
- Why did all the Ute bands come together each spring?

Ute mother and child. The baby is in a cradleboard.

Ute children

Ute Children

Ute children had a good life. Their parents did not believe in spanking them. Instead, they let children learn from their mistakes, pointing out what they did wrong. Young people did not go off to school in the morning. They watched and listened to adults to learn what they needed to know. Fathers and uncles taught boys to hunt. Girls learned to sew and cook from their mothers and aunts. Children also helped adults with daily chores. Ute children were taught to be quiet when adults talked. They had to listen to learn new things. Children had pets, usually a dog but sometimes a hawk or a young deer.

Ute Camps

At first, the Ute camps were small. The Utes could find enough food in one place to feed only a few families. After the Utes got horses, their camps became much larger. Bison hunters could bring back enough meat to feed dozens of families. Two hundred or more people lived in some of these camps.

The camps were lively places. Children played beside the long rows of tepees. During their free time, men raced their best horses, held footraces, and gambled. Women scraped bison and deer hides while sharing camp news and gossip. Dogs were everywhere. A visitor to a Ute camp said he could not walk around without dogs yelping at him.

Ute camp

Ute Bands

Spring was a special time for the Utes. At that time, the Ute families met together in their **bands**. The Ute tribe in Colorado was made up of six bands. Bands were large groups of families that had remained friends over the years. Three bands had their winter camps in southern Colorado and northern New Mexico (the Mouache, Capote, and Weeminuche bands). The other three spent winters farther north (the Tabeguache, Grand River, and Yampa bands). Six other Ute bands lived in Utah. The family groups in each band met together in the spring for a Bear Dance celebration.

While You Read

Use sticky notes in the margin whenever you make a connection. Label the notes **TT** (text to text), **TS** (text to self), or **TW** (text to world). Choose the strongest connection you make and write about it in your notebook.

Bear Dance

Origin of the Bear Dance

According to Ute legend, a Ute hunter once came upon a bear. The bear had not awakened from its long winter sleep, even though it was spring. The hunter woke the bear to keep it from starving to death. To repay him for his kindness, the bear taught his hunter friend the Bear Dance. Thereafter, the Utes held a Bear Dance each year to celebrate the waking of the bears.

The Bear Dance

The spring Bear Dance was a religious event that lasted for several days. The bands came together to thank the Great Spirit for helping them survive the winter. For the Bear Dance, men and women formed two lines inside a dance circle. The lines moved back and forth. The dancers sang and kept in step to the beat of drums and the rubbing of notched sticks. The noise represented spring thunder and bears growling. The dance celebrated the waking of the bears and the renewal of life.

The Bear Dance was also a social event. It brought old friends together again. Young men and women used the Bear Dance to meet, court, and get married. When the dance ended, the family groups once again went their own ways.

Bands Governed Themselves

Each Ute band governed itself. A band had one or more leaders. The chief was an older man whose judgment everyone trusted. He decided important matters, such as when the Bear Dance should be held. For advice, he relied on a council or group of elders. They would meet in the chief's tepee to discuss the question. Then the chief would announce his decision.

The chief's power was not unlimited. If individuals in a chief's village disagreed with him, they could move away and form a new village. The band could select a braver man who was a better fighter to lead them into war. When members of two Ute bands came together to visit or hunt, they chose the most respected band leader to be the head man. The most successful hunter became the leader of a hunt or rabbit drive.

The chief had to be a wise man. He had no police power and could not force people to do anything. He gained people's trust by making good decisions. It also helped that Utes respected the elderly and valued obedience. Children were taught to obey their parents and others in authority.

THE UTES TODAY

Most of the Ute Indians in Colorado today live on two **reservations**. They are the Southern Ute Reservation and the Ute Mountain Reservation. Both are located in the southwestern part of the state. Descendants of the Utes also live in towns and cities throughout the West. The small

Modern Utes dancing a Bear Dance

Focus Your Reading

- Where do most Colorado Utes live today?
- How do Utes make a living?
- How have Utes kept their culture alive?

reservations are all that is left of the thousands of square miles of land that was once the Utes' hunting and camping grounds. (How the Utes lost their land is explained in chapters 9 and 10.)

What is Ute life like today? The Southern Utes live much like people in other rural places. Most live on small farms near the town of Ignacio or in the town itself. The Ute Mountain Utes support themselves mainly by herding sheep and cattle. A few live in the town of Towaoc (*toy-yahk*), which is on the reservation. The Ute Mountain Utes refused to divide their land into small farms. It is owned jointly by the people.

While You Read

Study the photo of modern Utes on the previous page. How is life different for the Utes today compared with the way their ancestors lived? Talk about your conclusions with a partner.

Many Utes are poor. Jobs are hard to find in that part of Colorado. Some Utes work in the tribal offices. Both reservations operate casinos, which provide a few jobs. The Ute Mountain Utes also hire people to work in their pottery factory.

The Utes still dance the Bear Dance. Both reservations hold dances each year in May or June that last three or four days. The dances give Utes who live off the reservation a chance to spend time with family and friends. The Utes also invite guests from other tribes.

After You Read

1. Think about the chapter you've just read. In your notebook, write just **two** words that best describe your thinking, feeling, or understanding after reading about the Utes. Then, write why you chose these two words, quoting a sentence or two from the text that support your thinking.
2. On the left side of a page in your notebook, quote a few sentences from this chapter to which you feel a strong response (positive or negative). On the right side of the page, write your reaction to the quote, and be prepared to talk about it with your small group.

Asking Historical Questions
Your Response

This chapter began with this question:

How did horses change the Utes' way of life?

1. **Review**
   Review the information in your notes and in this chapter about how horses changed the Utes' way of life.
2. **Reflect**
   With a partner or in a small group, discuss how horses changed the Utes' way of life.
3. **Respond**
   In your notebook, explain how horses changed the Utes' way of life.

CHAPTER 6

The Plains Indians

FOCUS QUESTION

How did the Plains Indians create a way of life based on hunting bison on horses?

Before You Read

Brainstorm everything you know about the Plains Indians of Colorado and everything you **wonder** about these tribes. Afterward, make a "What I Wonder" list in your notebook. As you read the chapter, put a check beside the questions for which you find answers.

KEY WORDS

- **raid**
- **villages**
- **scout**
- **rawhide**
- **reservation**
- **tribal government**
- **powwow**

After the year 1400, new groups of people arrived in Colorado. They were the ancestors of modern-day Indians. Like many hunters before them, they followed herds of bison. They were different from one another in many ways. But they all had one thing in common: they made a living hunting on Colorado's Eastern Plains. They are known as the Plains Indians.

THE PLAINS TRIBES

The Apaches were the first Plains Indian tribe to reach Colorado. They arrived from Alaska and Canada around the year 1400. Many of the Apaches kept moving and finally settled in what is now Arizona. Those that we know as the Plains Apaches stayed in Colorado to hunt bison. Their only enemies were the Utes. The Utes lived in the mountains but hunted on the plains.

Focus Your Reading

- What tribes lived on the Colorado plains?
- When did they arrive?
- Why did some tribes leave Colorado?

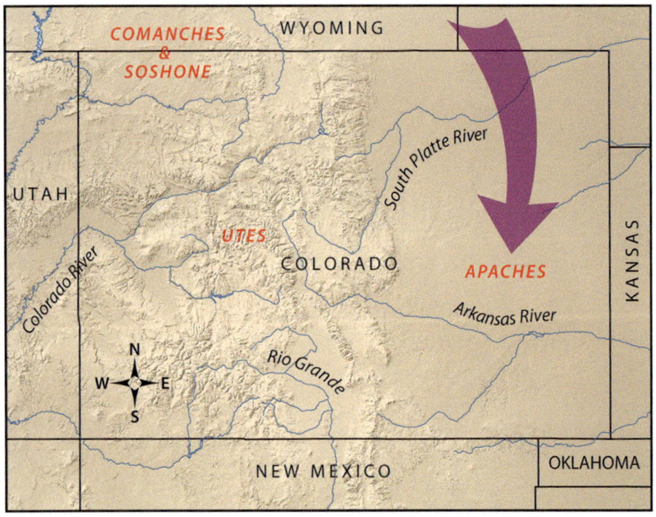

AD 1400

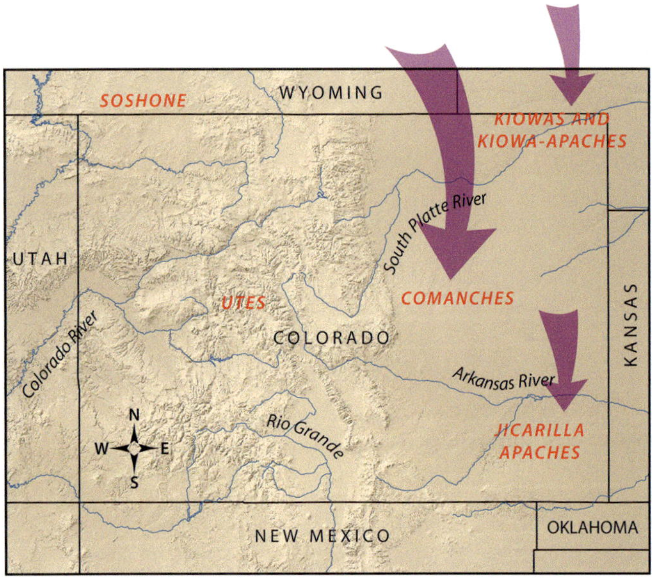

AD 1700

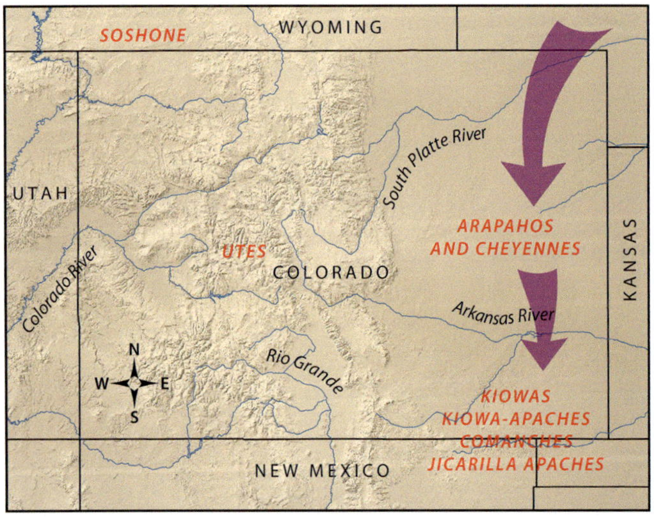

AD 1800

Locations and movements of the Plains Indians in Colorado, AD 1400, AD 1700, and AD 1800

The Comanches

The Comanches were the next to arrive. They came from central Wyoming and were cousins of the Utes. The Comanches arrived about the year 1700 to hunt bison and to **raid** the Apache **villages**. With help from the Utes, the Comanches drove the Apaches south into New Mexico. Then they fought the Utes. The word *Comanche* comes from the Ute word *Komantcia*. It means "anyone who wants to fight me all the time."

Comanche man

Newcomers Arrive

In the 1750s, the Comanches faced a new enemy: the Kiowas and Kiowa-Apaches. The Kiowas came from the Black Hills of South Dakota. With them were the Kiowa-Apaches, a group of Apaches from Canada. Following bison herds south, the Kiowas and Kiowa-Apaches ran into the Comanches on the Colorado plains.

The newcomers pushed the Comanches south to the Arkansas River. The Kiowas and Kiowa-Apaches mainly hunted north of the Arkansas River. When they and the Comanches were not hunting, they raided each other's villages. The three tribes made peace in the 1790s because they all faced new enemies—the Arapahos and Cheyennes.

While You Read

Why did tribes come to the Colorado plains? Why did they leave? Talk about this as you read with a partner. What are your conclusions?

Arapahos and Cheyennes

The Arapahos arrived in Colorado in the late 1700s. Their good friends, the Cheyennes, came shortly thereafter. Both tribes had once lived as farmers near the Mississippi River.

Arapaho woman named Freckled Face

Arapaho man named Runs Medicine

Jicarilla girl, 1907

Jicarilla boy, 2009

The Jicarilla Apaches

In 1541, Francisco Vásquez de Coronado found bands of buffalo-hunting Querechos (ker-ay-chos) on the plains. Later Spanish settlers called them the Apache de la Xicarilla, or "People of the Baskets." The Apache women made fine baskets. Their descendants, the Jicarilla band of Apaches, now live in northern New Mexico.

They were pushed west by other tribes. By the time they reached the plains, the Cheyennes and Arapahos had given up farming. They decided that hunting bison was an easier way of life.

In the early 1800s the Arapahos and Cheyennes fought the Kiowas and the Kiowa-Apaches for control of the Colorado plains. The Comanches joined the fight against the Arapahos and Cheyennes. But the three tribes combined were no match for the newcomers. Like the Comanches, the Kiowas and the Kiowa-Apaches were pushed south of the Arkansas River.

Hunters skinning a bison

Plains Indians Make Peace

In 1840, these Plains Indians finally made peace. Thereafter, the Cheyennes and Arapahos hunted north of the Arkansas River. The other tribes hunted south of that river.

Skills and Tools for Learning

Weighing Costs and Benefits

In the 1770s the Cheyenne tribe made a decision. Their villages and farms along the Missouri River were under attack by enemy tribes. Many Cheyennes were killed. Others had died from smallpox brought up the river by white fur traders. They decided to leave their homes, give up farming, and move west to become bison hunters.

In making their decision, the Cheyenne had to weigh what economists call benefits and costs. The benefits included:

- Moving a safe distance from their enemies
- Avoiding the traders who brought diseases
- Having a ready supply of bison meat

Moving west also involved costs, mainly:

- Needing to learn a new way of life
- Becoming more dependent on trade for corn and vegetables
- Making new enemies on the plains

They decided that the benefits outweighed the costs.

We all make decisions that involve costs and benefits. Should we spend money on new clothes or on entertainment? Think of a decision you made lately. What were the costs? What were the benefits?

The Cheyennes' decision to move turned out to be a wise choice. They became owners of large herds of horses, skillful bison hunters, and successful traders.

Focus Your Reading

- How did bison hunting change over time?
- What work did men and women do during and after a hunt?
- What other work did men and women do around the camp?

BISON HUNTERS

The Plains Indians were hunters and gatherers. They hunted bison, elk, antelope, and rabbits and other small animals. Bison supplied most of their meat. Meat was the main item in their diet. The Plains Indians also ate vegetables, roots, and fruit that grew wild on the plains. They dug up turnips and carrots, gathered greens, and picked berries.

When they first arrived, the Apaches hunted bison on foot. They drove bison herds over cliffs, much as the Paleo-Indians had done. Hunters dressed in coyote skins also killed bison by creeping up on the herds. In the winter, they chased bison into snowdrifts. Stuck in the snow, the big animals made easy targets.

Plains Indians Get Horses

After the Spanish settled in New Mexico, the Apaches got horses. The Spanish had brought these animals with them from Europe. The Apaches raided Spanish ranches for horses. They also got them by trading women and children from other tribes who had been captured in battle. The Spanish used Indian slaves to work in their fields and homes.

Hunting bison on horseback

Plains Indians drying meat

Bison Hunts

Bison hunts were well-planned events. First, a **scout** located a bison herd and brought the news back to the village. The hunters then rode out quietly in a group. One man dashing ahead might spook the herd. Then, mounted on their fastest horses, the hunters charged into the herd. Horses and bison raced neck-and-neck across the plains. The hunters let fly one arrow after another. A man mounted on a fast horse could kill two or three bison in half an hour. That was enough meat to feed a village for several weeks.

After the hunt, both men and women had work to do. The hunters skinned the bison where they lay. They could tell which animals they had killed from marks on their arrows. The hunter kept the hide, tongue, and other choice parts. He cut up the rest of the animal and brought it back to the village. The meat was shared with the entire village. Some of it was roasted over a fire and eaten immediately. The women cut up the rest and hung the strips of meat in the sun to dry. This kept the meat from spoiling.

While You Read

Make two columns in your notebook. Write "Men's Work" at the top of the first column and "Women's Work" at the top of the second column. As you read, list the kinds of work Plains Indian men and women were responsible for.

Spoon made from an animal bone

Camp Work

Men, women, and children shared the work of the camp. Men protected the camp against enemy raids. To do this, they had to keep their weapons in good repair. Young men went on raids to steal horses and to prove that they were brave. Women and girls did most of the work around the camp. They gathered wood, cooked, scraped and prepared hides, made clothing, took care of the young children, and gathered roots and other food. Women also put up the tepees and took them down again each time a village moved. Very young children watched older people work. They had to learn the skills they would need as adults.

Focus Your Reading

- How did Indian women make their families' clothing?
- How did getting horses change the kind of shelters the Indians lived in?
- In what other ways did horses change their way of life?

CLOTHING AND SHELTER

The Plains Indians wore clothes made from animal skins. When skinning an animal, a hunter took care not to damage the hide. It was almost as valuable as the meat. Women prepared the hides the men brought home. First they staked the hide down to let it dry. Then they scraped off any flesh that remained. If they wanted leather that was smooth on both sides, they also scraped off the hair. Then they tanned the hide by rubbing a liquid into it. This liquid, made partly from animal brains, turned the stiff **rawhide** into soft leather.

Plains Fruits and Vegetables

For the Indians, the Great Plains were like a fruit and vegetable market. Depending on the season, the region produced eight to ten different roots, a dozen to fifteen vegetable stalks, and sixteen varieties of fruit. Among the Indians' favorites were red turnips, chokecherries, and thistle stalks. The stalks tasted like bananas.

Chokecherries

Deerskin Clothing

Plains Indian women made clothing from different kinds of skins. Doeskin, the hide of a female deer, made the best dresses. They used buckskin from a male deer to make men's shirts, moccasins, belts, and bags. A man's shirt or a girl's dress required one skin. A woman's long dress needed two skins. Women made bed covers, warm robes, and tepee covers with bison or elk hides.

The Plains Indians' first shelters were small and simple. The Apaches lived in low, rounded huts made of sticks covered with a bison hide or two. Their shelters were small because the Apaches had to move often to keep up with the bison herds. They had to carry everything in bundles on their backs or in packs carried by dogs.

While You Read

Add to your list of the work men and women were responsible for. Which group do you think worked harder? Talk about this with a partner.

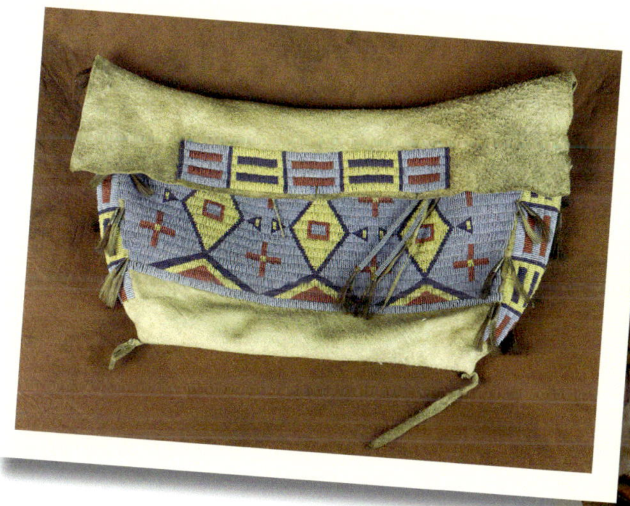

Items made from bison

With Horses Come Tepees

Once they had horses, the Plains Indians built larger shelters. A horse could pull thirty-foot tepee poles from one camp to another. Cheyenne tepees were large enough for five or so people to live in comfort. The family sat and slept on bison robes placed around the tepee walls. A small fire in the center kept the tepee warm in winter. The smoke escaped through a hole in the roof, which could be closed when it rained.

A Tepee-Making Feast

Making a new tepee was a social event. Women held a sewing bee to cut up the hides and stitch them together. When they finished, the village held a feast. The man known as the bravest warrior had to count coup and approve of the tepee by touching it with his coup stick before anyone could enter it. Then the leading men of the village entered and praised the women for their good work.

Cheyenne tepee

Modern-day tepee

Plains Indian women attached tepee poles to a horse to make a travois. They laid a platform across the poles. The platform could hold tepee covers and household goods. Horses and travois allowed Plains Indians to acquire more goods. The early plains hunters had very few household or personal items. They could own no more than they could carry. Indians with horses could carry more blankets and iron tools and kettles.

Horse pulling a travois

Raiding Other Tribes

Raiding also became more important to the Plains Indians' way of life after they had horses. The quickest way to get new horses was to raid a Spanish village or an enemy tribe's camp. Raiding also gave young men a chance to prove how brave they were.

FAMILIES AND COMMUNITY LIFE

The family was the center of Plains Indian life. Some families included only the father, mother, and a child or two. Other families were extended; that is, they included grandparents or an uncle or an aunt. Large families were very useful. Grandparents helped take care of the young children when mothers and fathers were busy. Uncles and aunts helped with the hunting and cooking.

Focus Your Reading

- How did Plains Indian families treat their children?
- Why did Plains Indians spend most of their time living in scattered villages?
- Why did they hold a tribal meeting each spring?

Arapaho family

While You Read

Make two columns on a page in your notebook. Write "Family," "Village," and "Tribe" down the left-hand column. As you read, fill in the right-hand column with information about these topics.

Plains Indian Children

Plains Indian children were well treated. Parents seldom punished or yelled at their children. They thought it best to correct bad behavior with kind words. Adults also tried to set good examples for the children to follow. Children were not allowed to cry. A crying child might give away the location of the village to an enemy raiding party. Indian mothers kept babies from crying by promptly taking care of their needs. They stopped a crying baby by pinching its nostrils.

Plains Indian children did not go to school. Boys learned the skills they needed as adults from their fathers or uncles. Mothers taught their daughters to cook and sew. Children also learned by playing with one another. Boys made their own toy bows and arrows. They went on make-believe raids and pretend bison hunts. Girls made dolls of soft cedar bark, built small tepees, and "played house." Children listened to stories told around campfires at night to learn the history and legends of their people. They had to listen carefully. Sometimes a storyteller called on them to repeat a story they had heard the night before.

A busy Plains Indian camp

Learning from Primary Sources

Arapaho Children

Carl Sweezy, who grew up on a reservation, remembered how Arapaho infants were cared for and how children were educated.

"Nearly every Arapaho mother had a carrier, or what white people call a cradle board, for her baby . . . It kept the baby safe from falls or accidents, and comfortable when he traveled. Strapped in his cradle, he learned to look at and listen to everything that went on around him, and he grew straight and strong.

"Fathers and mothers made fine toys for their children. For their little girls, Arapaho mothers made dolls dressed in perfect buckskin costumes, beaded and fringed just as our own costumes were. The tiny moccasins these dolls wore were made as carefully as moccasins for people.

"Fathers made bows and arrows for their sons, and made them so true that little boys could bring down squirrels or birds with them. Sometimes the boys dressed the squirrel they had shot, and cooked and ate it, and then sat around their fire telling their 'buffalo story,' as if they were old hunters."

Althea Bass, *The Arapaho Way: A Memoir of an Indian Boyhood (as told by Carl Sweezy)*

- **What toys did Arapaho children play with?**
- **What were they made of?**

Doll made from corn husks

Village Life

Next to the family, the village was the Plains Indians' most important group. Villages were made up of several families, usually of 50 to 100 people. Families could live in whichever village they wished.

Plains Indian villages were busy places. People did most of their work outside. Women cooked meals over open fires in front of the family's tepee. Men sat on bison robes getting bows and arrows ready for the next hunt. Children played games, went to fetch water, or helped their parents in other ways. Older boys stood watch over the horse herd in a nearby pasture. One of their jobs was to watch out for enemies trying to steal the village's horses.

Dogs were everywhere. Dozens of barking dogs might greet a stranger who visited a village for the first time. Dogs were seldom fed, but they ran loose in the camp, eating whatever bones and food scraps they could find. Dogs helped keep the campsite clean.

The largest group to which a Plains Indian belonged was the tribe. The people of a tribe spoke the same language and shared many of the same beliefs. The most important Plains Indian tribes in Colorado were the Apache, Comanche, Kiowa, Arapaho, and Cheyenne.

A drawing of a Comanche camp

Indian Sign Language

The first sign an Indian child learned was the name of his or her tribe. If he or she were an Arapaho, the child would first make the sign for "Indian," and then the sign for "mother." The word *Arapaho* means "the mother of all tribes." The word *Cheyenne* means "finger chopper." You can practice sign language by making the signs for "hungry," "cold," and "hot."

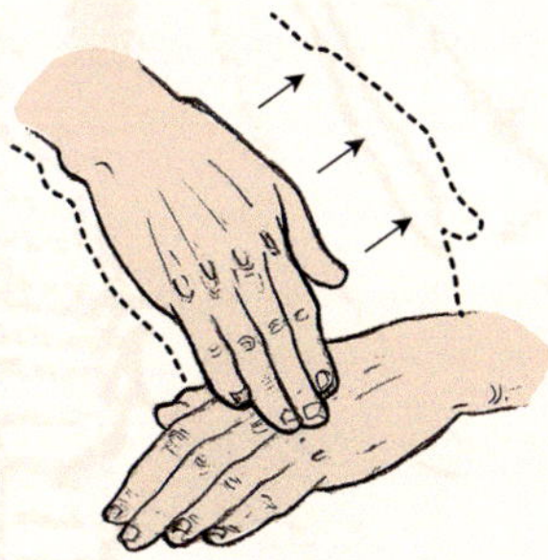

Indian

Mother

I am

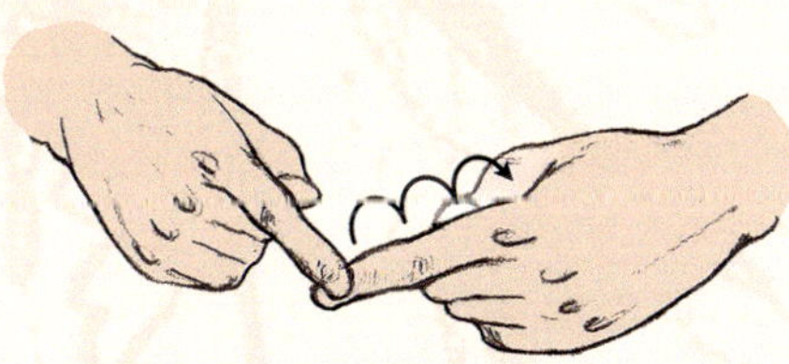

Cheyenne (finger chopper)

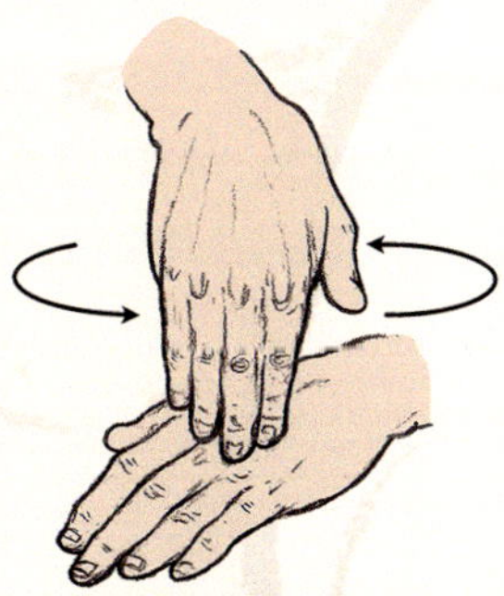

Color

Red

Hungry

Hot

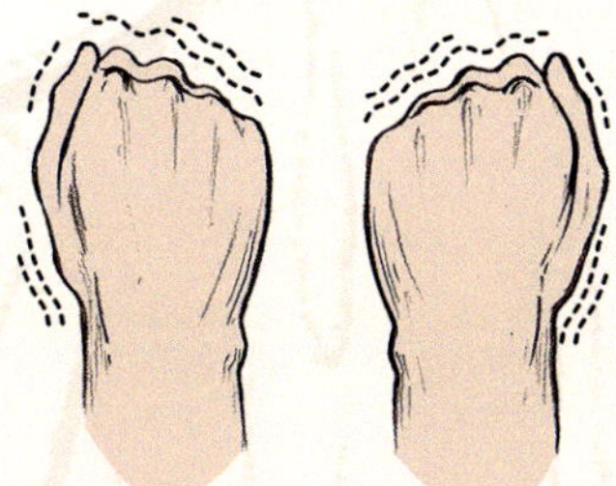

Cold

Plains Tribes

Each spring or early summer, the Plains Indians met together as a tribe. It was a time to visit and renew old friendships. It was a time for dancing and religious ceremonies. These gatherings also gave young men and women time to meet, court, and get married. The spring meetings ended with a tribal hunt. Early summer was a good time for a big hunt. At this time of year, large herds of bison grazed on the lush, green grass of the plains. The hunt ended with a great feast. People stuffed themselves with bison meat.

Bands and Villages

Each plains tribe was made up of smaller groups called bands. The Cheyenne lived in ten separate bands. The members of each band lived in villages close enough that they could visit one another and get together to hunt or go on raids.

After the tribe gathered in the summer, the bands left to hunt on their own. They tried to end up in the fall with enough dried bison meat to last through the winter. They spent the winter scattered in small villages. That was the only

Horses grazing in winter

way each village would have enough grass for its horses. A big herd could eat up all the grass before winter was over.

Focus Your Reading

- What was the Council of Chiefs?
- What matters did the Council of Chiefs decide upon?
- What were the soldier societies?

TRIBAL AND BAND GOVERNMENTS

The Plains Indians had tribal and band governments. When the Cheyenne came together for their summer hunt, a Council of Chiefs decided important matters. It could decide to go to war, where to hunt, or when to move camp. The council did not make laws. The basic rules or laws that people lived by were customs the Cheyenne had long followed. When the tribe broke up to spend the winter in smaller villages, the band chiefs became the village leaders.

Council of Chiefs

The council was made up of forty-four chiefs. It included four chiefs from each of the tribe's ten bands and four head chiefs respected for their wisdom and leadership. The council listened carefully to the head chiefs' advice and usually followed their lead. Chiefs served for a ten-year period, at which time the council chose new chiefs to replace them.

The Council of Chiefs was also the tribe's only court. If it got word of a serious disagreement in the camp, it ordered the individuals involved to appear before it. After hearing both sides, it would make a decision. Usually, it required the person it decided against to pay something to the other person. Less important disputes were often settled by the individuals' families.

While You Read

With a partner, make a brief list of items on which Cheyennes might disagree. Consider possible conflicts that might arise during a hunt or over who owns what. How might conflicts between men and women be different?

Wolf Robe, a Cheyenne chief

Soldier Societies

The council's decisions were carried out by the Cheyenne soldier societies. These were groups of young warriors

Military Societies

Plains Indian men belonged to military societies. The members of these warrior clubs went on raids and fought together. They also served as tribal police, keeping order during tribal ceremonies or communal hunts. The Cheyenne Dog Soldiers were a famous military society.

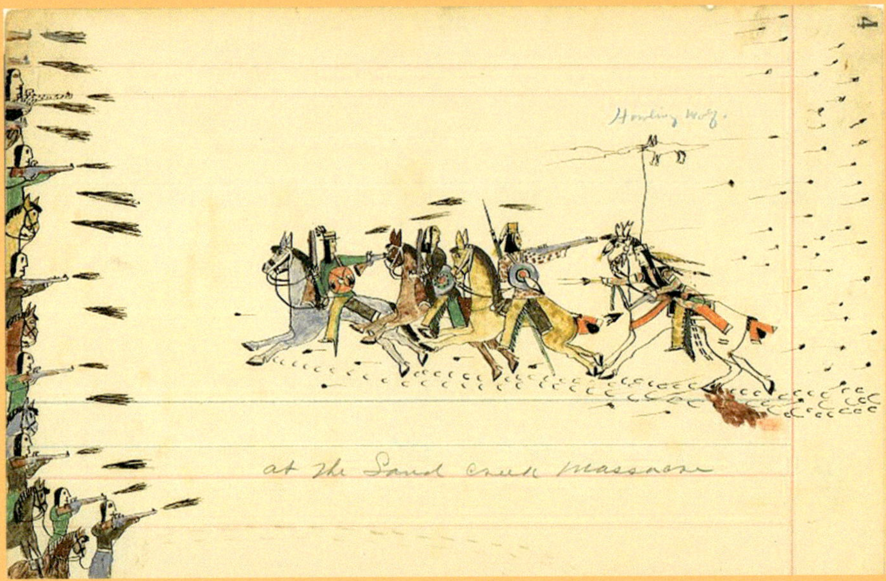

Drawing of the Sand Creek Massacre by Cheyenne warrior Howling Wolf

who belonged to their own bands. They served as the tribe's police and were its most skillful fighters. They enforced the rules or customs governing a bison hunt. They took charge of moving the camp and led the march to the new campground.

THE PLAINS INDIANS TODAY

Focus Your Reading

- Where do Plains Indians live today?
- What kinds of work do they do?
- How do Plains Indians keep their traditions alive?

Today, the Plains Indians live in many western states. Most of the Plains Apaches ended up in New Mexico. The Comanches, for the most part, live in Oklahoma. The Arapaho and Cheyenne are divided into northern and southern tribes. The Northern Arapaho have a reservation in Wyoming. A **reservation** is an area set aside for an Indian tribe, although not all members of the tribe live there. The Northern Cheyenne have a reservation in Montana. Many Southern Arapaho and Southern Cheyenne live in western Oklahoma. Few Plains Indians still live in Colorado.

The Northern Arapaho Wind River Reservation

New Ways of Life

The Plains Indians today live very differently than their ancestors did. They no longer hunt for a living. Some Northern Cheyenne own cattle ranches in Montana. Others fight wildfires during the summer. The Comanches in Oklahoma are farmers, teachers, and oil-field workers. Many Plains Indians, especially Kiowas, live in Los Angeles, Dallas, and other big cities. They work at many different kinds of jobs. Most of the Indians who live on reservations are very poor. It is hard to find work on a reservation.

While You Read

Use a map of the western United States to locate the states and cities in which the descendants of the Plains Indians live today. Make a list of these locations in your notebook.

Keeping Traditions Alive

Plains Indians have kept many of their traditional ways alive. Indians who live on reservations have a **tribal government** and elect tribal leaders. Most tribes bring people together each summer for a big gathering called a

powwow. They do not have community hunts, but they do have dances and religious ceremonies. The Kiowas meet in Oklahoma in July for a Sun Dance celebration. The Northern Cheyenne hold a ceremony each year to renew the sacred Medicine Arrows. The tribes have also tried to keep their native languages alive. The Northern Arapaho hold language classes to make sure their children learn to speak Arapaho.

After You Read

1. Return to your "What I Wonder" list in your notebook. Do you still need answers for any of these questions? Talk with a partner about resources you have that might help you find answers to your questions.
2. With a small group, create a poster about the everyday life of Plains Indian men and women.

Colorful regalia at a summer powwow

Asking Historical Questions
Your Response

This chapter began with this question:

How did the Plains Indians create a way of life based on hunting bison on horses?

1. **Review**

   Review the information in your notes and in this chapter about how bison hunting shaped the Plains Indians' way of life.

2. **Reflect**

   With a partner or in a small group, discuss how bison hunting shaped their way of life.

3. **Respond**

   In your notebook, explain how their way of life was shaped by bison hunting.

UNIT FOUR

More People Scout Out the Land

1694 de Vargas visits San Luis Valley

1706 de Ulibarri enters eastern Colorado

1739 The Mallets cross the Platte and Arkansas Rivers

1650 — 1700 — 17

People

In the early 1800s, newcomers arrived in Colorado. The first newcomers explored the land. Then others came to trap beaver and trade with the Indians. Hispanic people from New Mexico came looking for land to farm.

Places

The new people scouted out different places in Colorado. Most of the explorers traveled through eastern Colorado. Fur trappers went directly to the mountains. Hispanic farmers had their eyes on southern Colorado.

Times

It was a time of adventure for the newcomers. They explored a land new to them. They found new opportunities and ways to make money. These pathfinders opened the way to Colorado for others.

1765 de Rivera explores Colorado's San Juan Mountains

1776 Escalante and Domínguez explore western Colorado

1800

1803 Louisiana Purchase

1806–1807 Pike spends the winter in Colorado

1820 Long explores eastern Colorado

1835 Bent's Fort built

1849 First Hispanic farmers arrive in San Luis Valley

1850

CHAPTER 7

The Pathfinders

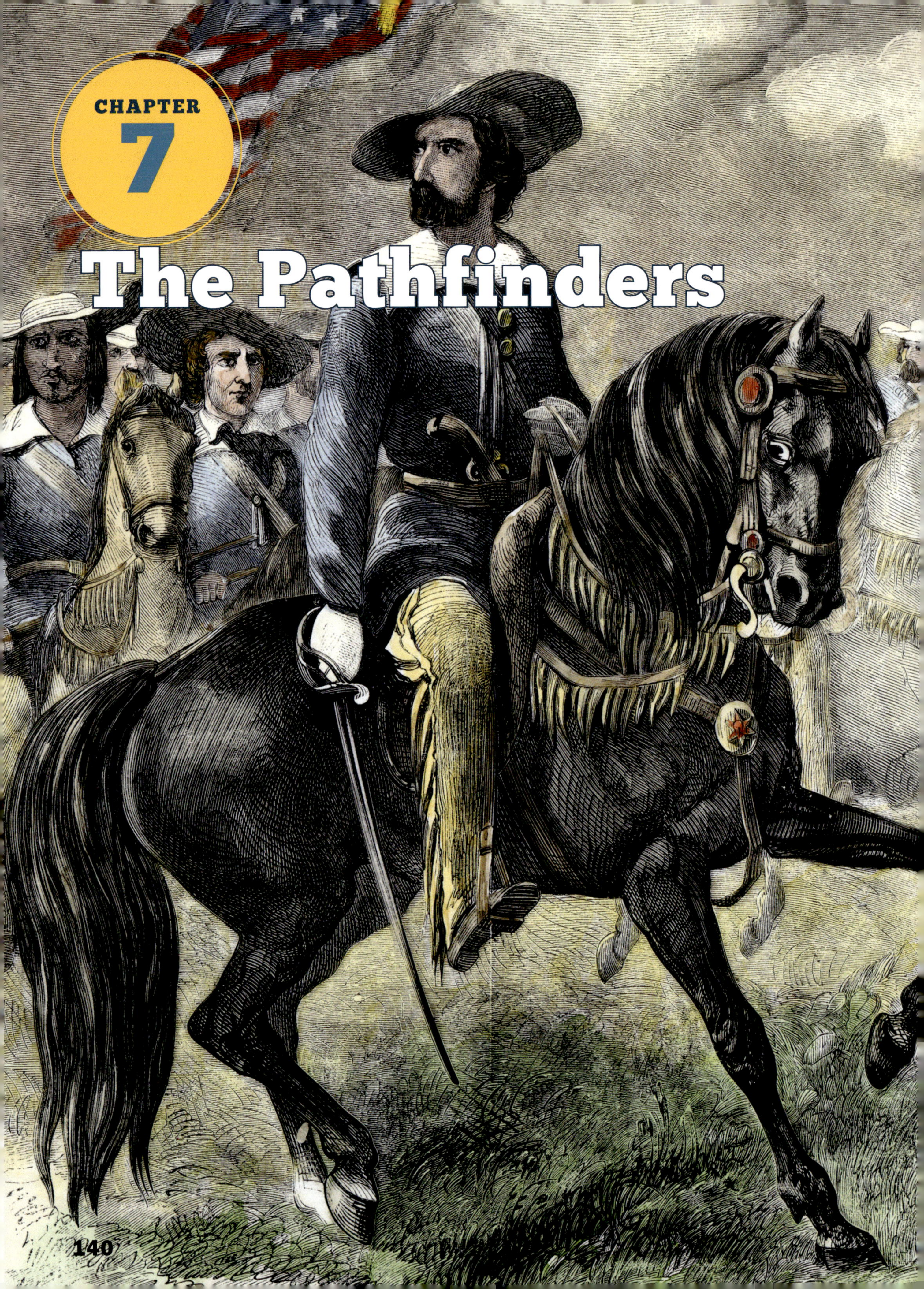

FOCUS QUESTION

For what reasons did explorers, trappers, and traders come to Colorado, and how were they different?

Before You Read

Make a three-column pathfinder chart in your notebook. Label the columns "European Explorers," "American Explorers," and "Fur Trappers." As you read this chapter, fill in the chart with words or phrases that answer the "While You Read" questions below.

KEY-WORDS

- **European**
- **trappers**
- **pathfinders**
- **precious metals**
- **expeditions**
- **rendezvous**
- **trading posts**
- **adobe**

In 1540, Francisco Vásquez de Coronado set out from Mexico. With him were 200 Spanish soldiers and 1,000 friendly Indians. They marched north to look for the Seven Cities of Gold. The Indians had told Coronado that such cities existed. For the next two years, Coronado explored New Mexico, Texas, and the Great Plains. He found endless grasslands. He met Apache Indians. He saw great herds of bison. But he found no cities of gold.

Coronado was the first **European** to explore the West. He claimed the land for Spain, then returned to Mexico. Later, priests, fur traders, and **trappers** passed through. They were **pathfinders** for those who came later.

Spanish explorers

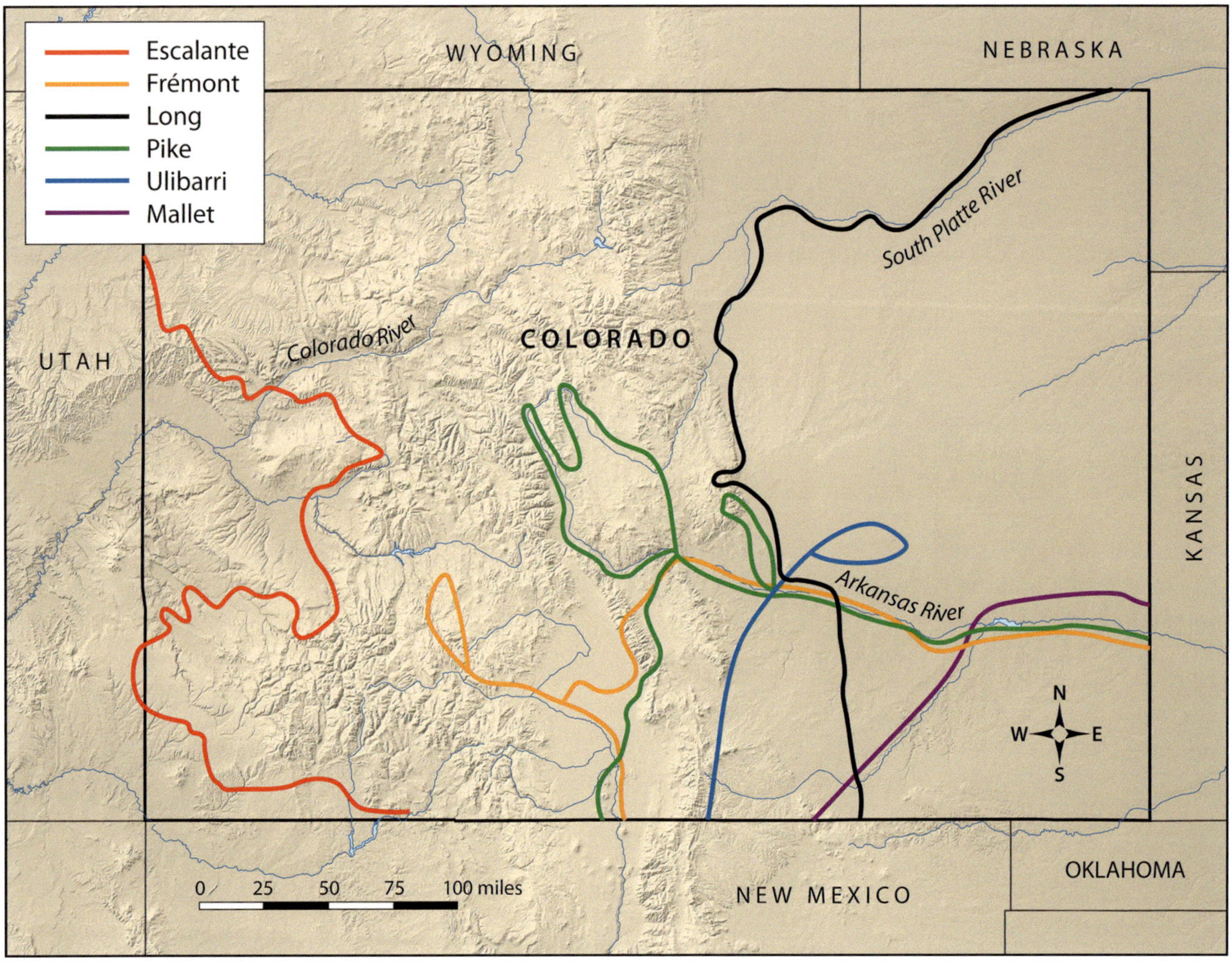

Routes of six early explorers in Colorado

Focus Your Reading

- Which Europeans explored Colorado?
- What did they hope to find?
- What did they discover?

EUROPEAN EXPLORERS

In 1694, Diego de Vargas visited the San Luis Valley. He was the first European to set foot in Colorado. Vargas, the governor of New Mexico, went to open trade with the Utes. He also asked for their help in fighting the Comanches, who had attacked the Spanish towns in New Mexico.

Explorers of Eastern Colorado

In 1706, Juan de Ulibarri and forty soldiers marched north from New Mexico. They headed for the plains to find some Pueblo Indians who had run away from New Mexico to live with the Apaches. They wanted to come home but were afraid to cross the Comanches' hunting ground. Ulibarri brought the runaways back to New Mexico. He also claimed eastern Colorado for Spain.

The next Europeans to reach Colorado were French traders. In 1739, Peter and Paul Mallet set out from Canada. They wanted to open trade with the Spanish. On their way to Santa Fe, they crossed the Platte and Arkansas Rivers. Their plans came to nothing, as the Spanish turned them away. The Frenchmen did give the Platte River its name. *Platte* means "flat" in French.

Exploring Western Colorado

In 1765, Juan María de Rivera explored Colorado's San Juan Mountains. He and his men were looking for gold and silver. They failed to find **precious metals**. They did give Spanish names to several rivers in Colorado.

In July 1776, two Spanish priests set out from Santa Fe. Silvestre Escalante and Francisco Domínguez were looking for an easy way to California. They explored the western part of Colorado. Then they headed west into central Utah. Stopped by winter storms, Escalante and Domínguez returned to Santa Fe. Their journal contained the first good description of the Western Slope of Colorado. They also made the first maps of that area.

While You Read

Answer these questions on your three-column chart:

1. What are the names of the European explorers included in this chapter?
2. Where in Colorado did they explore? (See the map on page 142)
3. When did they arrive?
4. Why did they explore Colorado?

Escalante Pueblo is named after Silvestre Escalante.

Skills and Tools for Learning

Primary Sources and Secondary Accounts

Historians use firsthand, or eyewitness, accounts to write historical narratives about what happened in the past. Firsthand accounts are called "primary sources." The narratives based on them are called "secondary accounts."

A Primary Source

The following are passages from the journal Silvestre Escalante kept during the 1776 Domínguez-Escalante expedition.

> "August 9: It [the La Plata River] rises in the same west end of the Sierra de la Plata and flows through the canyon in which they say there are veins and outcroppings of metal . . . Accounts of various Indians and of some citizens of this kingdom that they were silver mines, caused the mountain to be called Sierra de la Plata . . . The land is very moist, for, because of the nearness of the sierra it rains very frequently. For this reason, in the forests, which consist of very tall straight pines, small oaks and several kinds of wild fruits, as well as in its valleys, there are the finest of pastures."

Fray Angelico Chavez (translator), *Diary and Itinerary by Silvestre Vélez de Escalante*

A Secondary Account

Historian Hubert Howe Bancroft used Escalante's journal to describe the expedition's journey through southern Colorado in his history of Nevada, Colorado, and Wyoming.

> "Escalante's descriptions of the country passed over avoid dwelling upon the exceeding roughness of this region, dwelling rather upon the beauty and fertility of the small valleys, the grandeur of the forests of pine which grew upon the high benches and mountain sides, and the abundance of water, even that which fell from the clouds, of which he complained a little. At the Rio Mancos, or San Lizaro, he again heard reports of mines."

Hubert Howe Bancroft, *The Works of Hubert Howe Bancroft*, volume 25: *History of Nevada, Colorado, and Wyoming, 1540–1888*

Silvestre Escalante and Francisco Domínguez

- **How are primary sources and secondary sources different?**
- **What is one benefit of a primary source?**
- **What is one advantage of a secondary source?**

Location of the Louisiana Purchase and Spanish territory

AMERICAN EXPLORERS

In 1803, the United States bought Louisiana from France. The purchase nearly doubled the size of the United States. It included part of what is now Colorado. To explore this region, the United States sent out two **expeditions**. In 1804, Meriwether Lewis and William Clark led one expedition. They crossed the Rockies and traveled to the Pacific coast. Two years later, the US Army sent Lieutenant Zebulon Montgomery Pike with twenty-two men to explore the Arkansas Valley.

Pike and his men set out in July 1806. In November, they reached the future site of the city of Pueblo. To the north, they saw a tall peak. It looked like a "small blue cloud." Pike, with three of his men, hiked to the base of the peak. The snow was too deep for them to climb to the top. Pike called this mountain "Grand Peak." A later explorer, John C. Frémont, named it Pikes Peak.

Focus Your Reading

- Which Americans explored Colorado?
- Why were the plains called the "Great American Desert"?
- Which Front Range mountain peaks are named for explorers?

While You Read

Answer these questions on your three-column chart:

1. Which American explorers led expeditions to Colorado?
2. Where did they explore? (See the map on page 142)
3. When did they arrive?
4. Why did they come?

Pike's Expedition

Pike and his men spent the winter in Colorado. They hiked through deep snow in the mountains. Many of the soldiers froze their feet. They set up camp in the San Luis Valley, which was Spanish territory. Spanish soldiers captured them. In July 1807 the Spanish finally set them free.

Pike wrote a book about his journey. It was the first report about the West published in English. It helped Americans learn about what is now Colorado.

Long Explores the Plains

In 1820 the United States sent Major Stephen H. Long to explore the plains. Long led his group of nineteen men up the Platte Valley. As they approached the mountains, they saw a high peak. Long did not give it a name, as he thought it was Pike's "Grand Peak." In fact, Pikes Peak was 100 miles to the south. The high peak to the north is now named for Major Long. Long returned home by way of the Arkansas River.

Long took careful notes about the plains. The grass in July was dry and brown. In some places, the wind had formed sand dunes. Nothing was growing. On his maps, Long labeled the plains the "Great American Desert." That led many people to think the plains were unfit for farming. For years, few farmers settled there. In fact, the plains now are one of the world's best wheat-growing areas.

John C. Frémont explored the West

Frémont's Trips to Colorado

Lieutenant John C. Frémont led five expeditions into the American West. He explored parts of Colorado on each trip. He mapped its rivers and mountain passes. On his fourth trip, in 1848, Frémont and his party were trapped in the mountains by snow. Ten of his thirty-three men and 120 of their pack mules froze to death. Some explorers paid a high price to find paths to the West.

Learning from Primary Sources

The Great American Desert

These accounts by Zebulon M. Pike and Edwin James, a member of Stephen H. Long's expedition, describe the plains of eastern Colorado.

The Arkansas Valley

"In that vast country of which we speak, we find the soil generally dry and sandy, with gravel . . . But here a barren soil, parched and dried up for eight months in the year, presents neither moisture nor nutrition necessary to nourish the timber. These vast plains of the western hemisphere may become in time as celebrated as the sandy deserts of Africa."

Zebulon M. Pike, *Account of Expeditions to the Sources of the Mississippi and through the Western Parts of Louisiana*

The Base of the Rockies

"In regard to this extensive section of the country, I do not hesitate in giving the opinion, that it is almost wholly unfit for cultivation, and of course uninhabitable by a people depending upon agriculture . . . The scarcity of wood and water, almost uniformly prevalent, will prove an insuperable obstacle in the way of settling the country . . . This region, however, may . . . serve as a barrier to prevent too great an extension of our population westward."

Edwin James, *Account of an Expedition from Pittsburgh to the Rocky Mountains*

- **To what other region did Pike compare the western plains?**
- **What did Pike and James's accounts have in common?**

Zebulon Montgomery Pike

Stephen H. Long

Focus Your Reading

- Why did fur trapping appeal to young men?
- How did mountain men spend each season of the year?
- Why did beaver trapping come to an end?

FUR TRAPPERS

In the 1820s, new pathfinders arrived. They were fur trappers. At that time, beaver pelts, or skins with the fur on them, were in great demand. Hat makers used them to make men's felt hats. The mountain men, as the trappers were called, also explored the West. They found the trails and passes used by Indian hunters. They knew more about the region than anyone except the Indians.

The trappers had two "hunts" each year. The spring hunt was more important. The beaver still had their thick winter pelts, which brought the most money. Pelts taken in the fall were not worth as much.

To protect themselves from Indians, the trappers worked in groups of ten or so. Each group had a base camp in the mountains. From there, they went out in pairs to set traps.

The Rendezvous

Each summer, the trappers gathered at an agreed-upon place for a **rendezvous**. There they met the fur company

While You Read

Answer these questions on your three-column chart:

1. Which fur trappers are included in this chapter?
2. Where in Colorado did they trap?
3. When were they most successful?
4. Why did they stop trapping?

Fur trappers, or mountain men

agents who had come to buy their pelts. The agents sold the trappers new traps, gunpowder, and other supplies for the coming year. After doing business, the rendezvous became a monthlong social event. A visitor said he watched trappers at a rendezvous "running, jumping, wrestling, shooting with the rifle, and running horses . . . They drank together, they sang, they laughed, they whooped; they tried to out-brag and out-lie each other in stories of their adventures and achievements." The trappers finally left to prepare for the fall hunt. By then, they had spent most of their money gambling and having a good time.

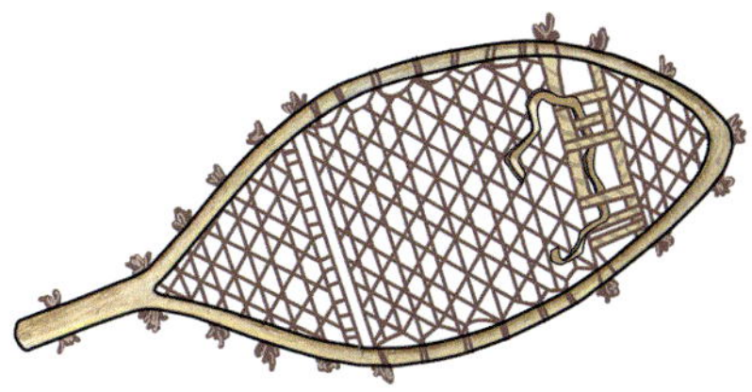

Snowshoes

Possibles Bag

Fur trappers used special equipment when they traveled to where the beaver lived. Here are two items.

A Dangerous Life

Fur trapping was a dangerous life. Trappers were mauled by grizzly bears and bitten by rattlesnakes. They suffered frostbite in winter blizzards. The Blackfeet, Crow, and Comanche Indians were a constant threat. They killed

A rendezvous

trappers for their horses and guns and to drive the trappers out of the Indians' hunting grounds.

The trappers' life attracted young men like Kit Carson. Carson grew up in a small town in Missouri. At age sixteen he left home to work on a wagon train headed for Santa Fe. In New Mexico, Carson became a fur trapper. He saw it as a quick way to make money. Beaver pelts were worth six to eight

Fur trapper with a packhorse

Hat made from beaver pelts

Tanned beaver pelt

dollars each. That was nearly a week's wages for a hired man at that time. Carson trapped beaver for the next twenty years.

The End of an Era

The era of the mountain men did not last long. By 1840 the trappers had killed most of the beaver. Hat styles had also changed. Men quit wearing beaver felt hats. Tall silk hats became the fashion. The price of beaver skins dropped to one dollar a pelt.

The mountain men went their separate ways. Some settled as farmers in Colorado's river valleys. Others, like Kit Carson, used their knowledge of the West to become hired guides. Carson guided Lieutenant John C. Frémont on his first three expeditions. Still others went to work at **trading posts**.

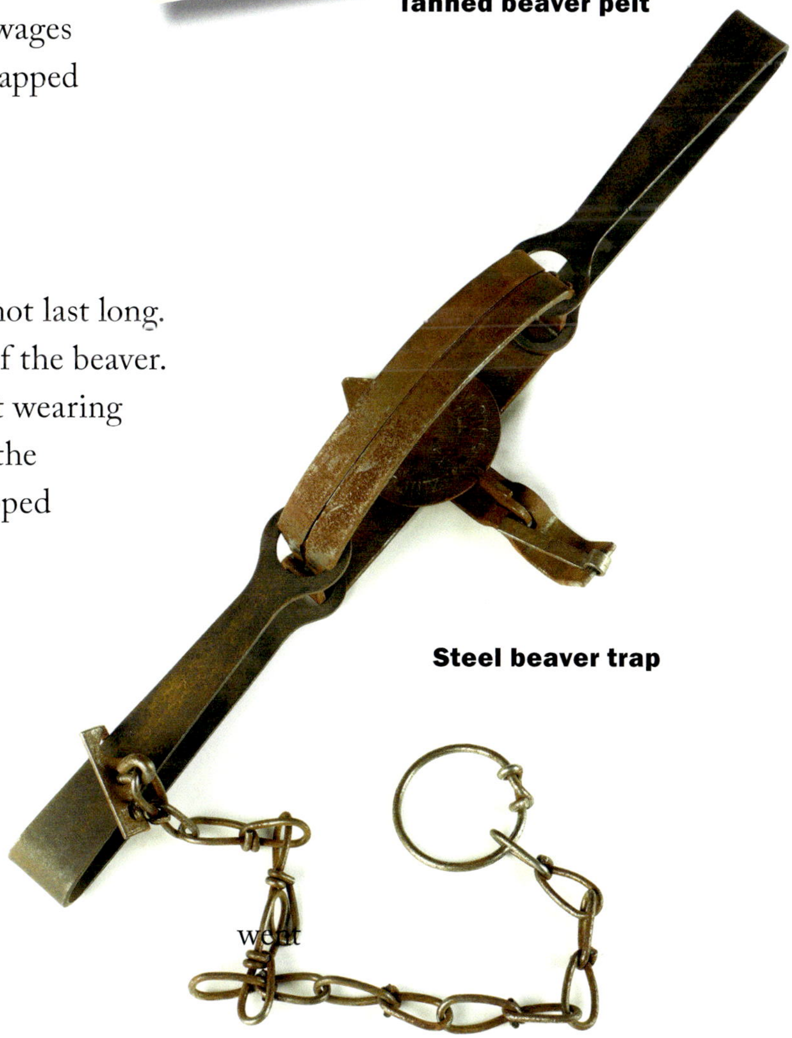

Steel beaver trap

Kit Carson's Near Escape

In March 1834, two grizzly bears attacked Kit Carson. He had just shot an elk and did not have time to reload his rifle. "There were some trees at a short distance. I made for them, the bears after me. As I got to one of the trees, I had to drop my gun—the bears rushing for me, I had to make all haste to ascend the tree." One grizzly tried to uproot the tree, but it was too big. "He finally concluded to leave, of which I was heartily pleased, never having been so scared in my life."

Kit Carson, *Memoirs, 1809–1856*

Kit Carson as an older man

Focus Your Reading

- What was Bent's Fort?
- What did traders exchange for bison hides?
- What other trading posts did Colorado have?
- What effect did the hide trade have on the Plains Indians?

THE INDIAN TRADE

By the 1830s, trade in bison hides was more important than fur trapping. Traders could buy a bison hide from the Indians for three dollars' worth of trade goods. They sold them in the East for two or three times that amount. Thick bison hides made good winter lap robes. Every American family wanted one.

Trading Forts

The center of the hide trade in Colorado was Bent's Fort. Two American brothers, Charles and William Bent, had built this trading post on the Arkansas River in 1835. With the help of a partner, Ceran St. Vrain, they bought hides and pelts from the Plains Indians. Bent's Fort was well named. The building was like a fort. It had fifteen-foot-high **adobe** walls and towers at two corners.

Bent's Fort was a popular place. It was a rest stop on the Santa Fe Trail. Wagon trains stopped there on their way to

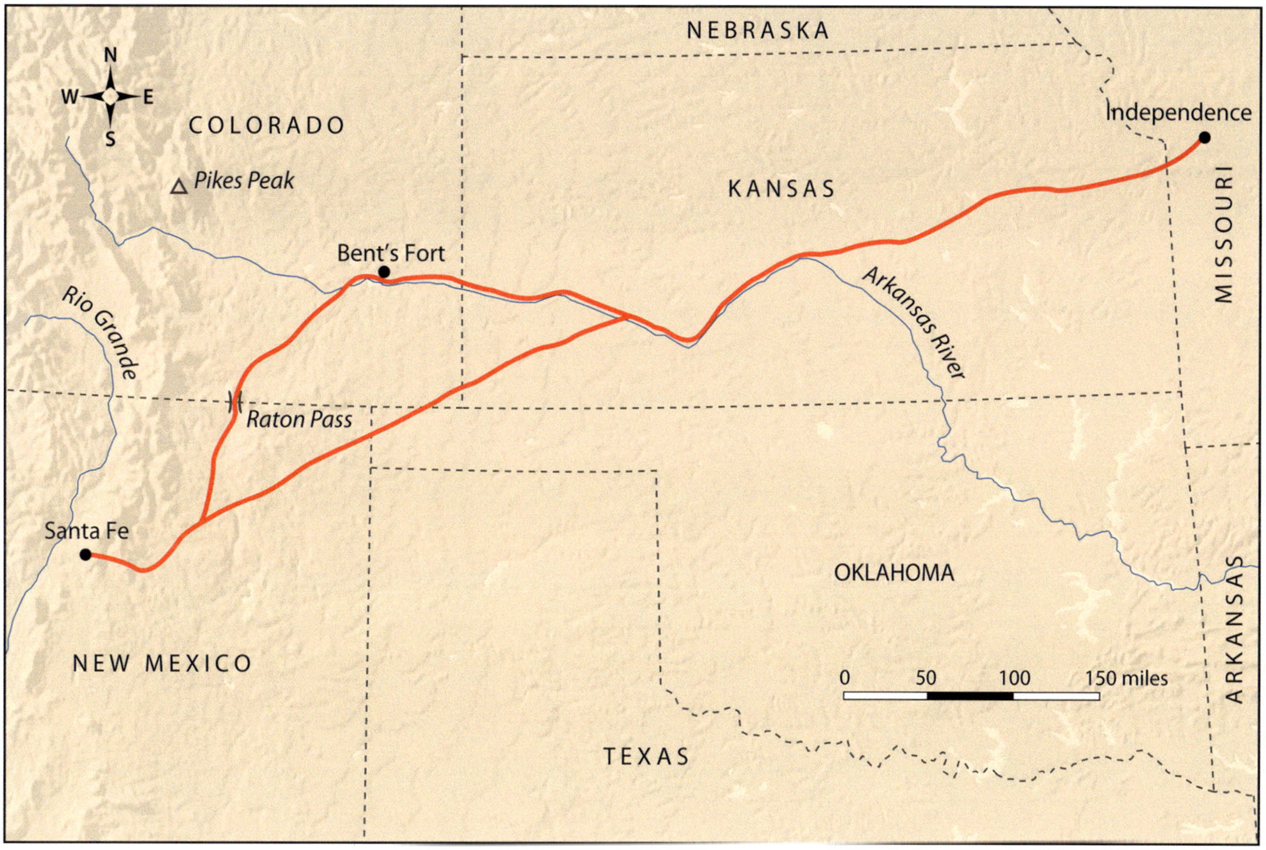

Route of the Santa Fe Trail

New Mexico. Retired mountain men hung out at the fort. Kit Carson worked there for several months. He hunted bison to provide the fort with meat. Cheyenne and Arapaho Indians came there to trade. So did their enemies, the Comanche and Kiowa. William Bent finally convinced these tribes to stop fighting each other.

While You Read

What were the good and bad aspects of the bison trade from the Indians' point of view? If you could change any part of it for the Indians' benefit, what would you do? Talk about this with your partner or in a small group.

Trade Goods

Retired trappers also built trading forts in Colorado. Louis Vasquez and Andrew Sublette built Fort Vasquez on the South Platte River. Lancaster P. Lupton built a second fort on the Platte River. He named it Fort Lupton. Other mountain men built Fort Jackson farther north. In time, the Bent brothers built their own trading post on the Platte River. They named it Fort St. Vrain in honor of their partner, Ceran St. Vrain.

Bent's Fort

Bent's Fort was like a walled town. It contained a store or trading room, a storage room, apartments with fireplaces, a dining hall, kitchens, an office, a carpenter's shop, a blacksmith's shop, a tailor's shop, a billiard room, a press for packing buffalo hides, and a large corral for horses. The fort had room enough for 200 people and 300 to 400 animals.

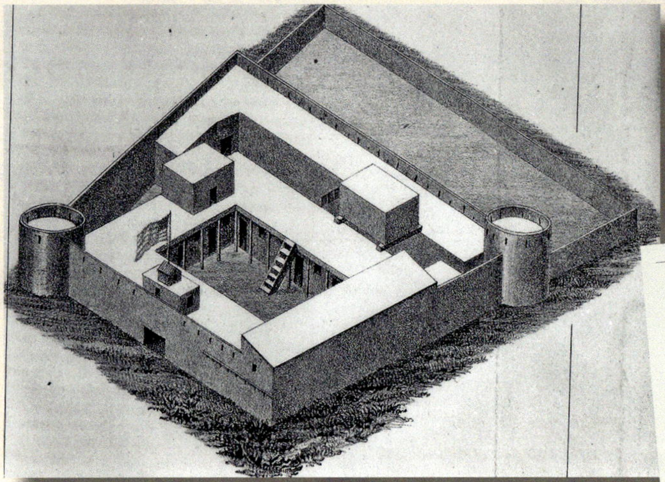

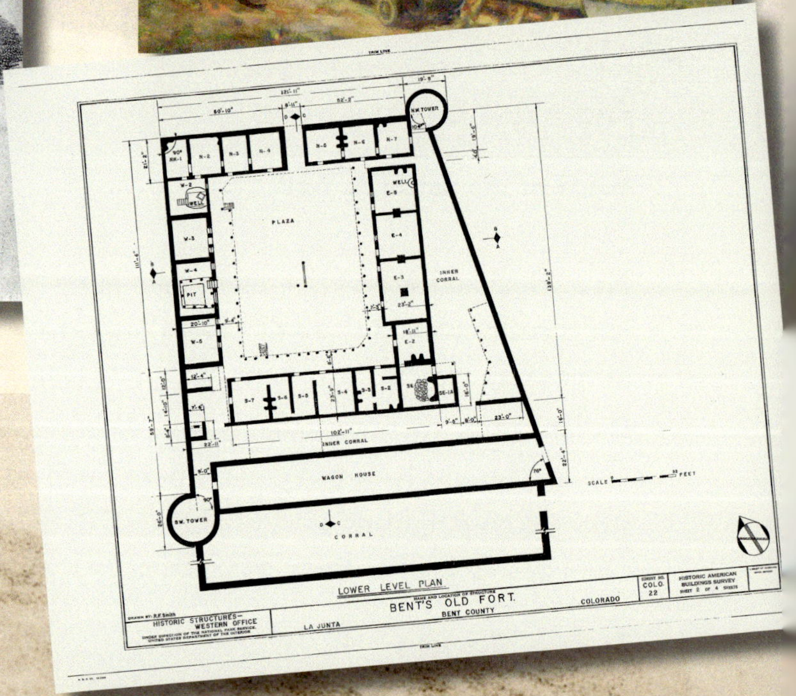

Drawings and layout of Bent's Fort

Fort Vasquez today

Traders from Bent's Fort also went to Indian villages to trade. They took packhorses loaded with trade goods. These items included glass beads, knives, whiskey, and Navajo blankets. The traders spread out their goods in the chief's tepee. The trading session might last for hours or days. Indian customers took their time deciding what to buy. They often gave ten bison hides for a brightly colored Navajo blanket.

The hide trade both helped and hurt the Plains Indians. The iron pots, guns, and knives made their lives easier. The whiskey was harmful. Many Indians became addicted to alcohol. The hide trade also changed the way Indians used the bison. They had once killed them mainly for meat, but they put every part of the bison to good use. The hide trade led them to kill the animals mainly for their hides. They killed many more bison than they needed for their own use.

Coat made from bison hide

While You Read

In your notebook, name the pathfinder you would like to know more about. What resources would be helpful in your research? Make a list of them.

THE PATHFINDERS TODAY

The pathfinders of the early 1800s are gone but not forgotten. The people of Colorado remember them in various ways. Zebulon M. Pike and Stephen H. Long have mountain peaks named for them. Fort Carson near Colorado Springs is named for Kit Carson. People today check out biographies of the pathfinders from public libraries. People get together to reenact what life was like at that time. Coloradans can also visit historic sites linked to the pathfinders.

Pike's Stockade

Pike and his men erected a log stockade in the San Luis Valley in February 1807. In 1952 the Colorado Historical Society built a replica of this little fort to honor the explorer. Pike's Stockade is located on the Conejos River about forty-five miles southwest of Fort Garland. It is open only during the summer. There is no charge to visitors.

Many Coloradans take part in fur-trapper reenactments. They get together to act out a fur trappers' rendezvous. They dress in pre-1840s clothes and try to live like trappers for a few days.

Replica of Pike's Stockade, or camp, in the San Luis Valley

Two views of
Bent's Fort today

Bent's Fort and Fort Vasquez

People in Colorado can learn about the trappers and traders at two reconstructed forts. The larger of the two is Bent's Old Fort National Historic Site. The National Park Service built this replica, or copy, of Bent's first trading post in 1976. It includes shops and rooms equipped as they were in the 1830s. The fort is east of La Junta and is open year-round. Fort Vasquez, near Platteville, is a smaller fort. This fort and museum are also open all year.

After You Read

1. Which pathfinders do you think were the most successful in accomplishing their goals? Write a paragraph to explain why you think so. Use quotes from the chapter to support your opinion.
2. Suppose you had been a pathfinder in Colorado. What advice would you have for those who wanted to follow in your footsteps? Make a list of suggestions in your notebook.

Thinking about Colorado Water

Do you know . . . why eastern Colorado has a dry climate?

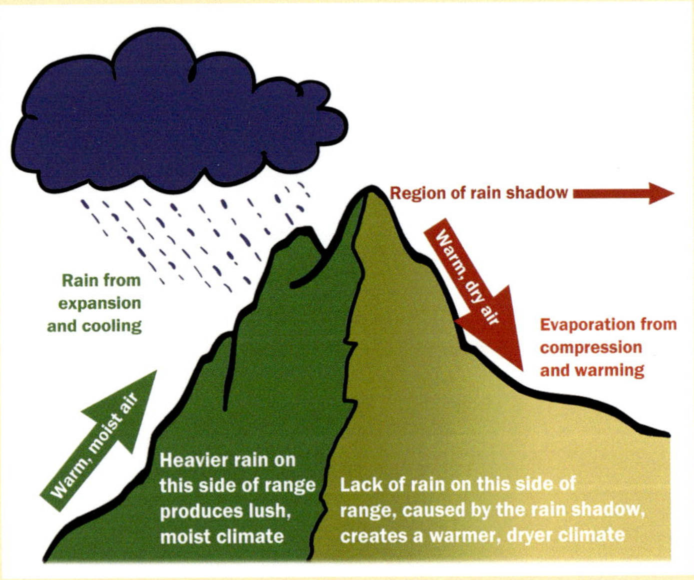

Early explorers called eastern Colorado a desert. The eastern plains do have a very dry climate. Few trees grow there because of the lack of moisture. The explorers visited during hot summers, when streams dried up and the grass turned brown. It looked more like a desert than like the farmland to the east.

Have you ever wondered why eastern Colorado gets so little rain and snow?

Geographers call this the rain shadow effect. It is created by currents of warm air and moisture that flow into Colorado from the west. This warm, moist air rises when it reaches the mountains. Air cools when it is pushed upward and releases much of its moisture. (Cool air holds less moisture than warm air.) This moisture falls on the west-facing slopes and the higher peaks as rain or snow. After the air currents cross the mountains, little moisture is left. That leaves the region to the east in a precipitation or moisture shadow.

How is a rain shadow like a light shadow?

- Make a long triangle by folding a sheet of paper into thirds.
- Hold one of the three sides up to a light.
- Imagine that the light is moisture falling as rain or snow.
- The opposite side is in the rain shadow.

Asking Historical Questions
Your Response

This chapter began with this question:

For what reasons did explorers, trappers, and traders come to Colorado, and how were they different?

1. **Review**
   Review the information in your notes and in this chapter about the reasons explorers, trappers, and traders came to Colorado.
2. **Reflect**
   With a partner or in a small group, discuss the reasons explorers, trappers, and traders came to Colorado.
3. **Respond**
   In your notebook, explain the different reasons explorers, trappers, and traders came to Colorado.

CHAPTER 8

Hispanic Settlers

FOCUS QUESTION

In what ways and why did Hispanic settlers in the San Luis Valley have to depend on themselves?

Before You Read

Skim this chapter. On sticky notes, write two **big** questions and two **little** questions you have about the chapter. **Big** questions are about big ideas. **Little** questions are about details or words. Place the notes in your notebook. Try to answer the questions as you read the chapter.

KEY-WORDS

- **Hispanic**
- **oxen**
- **mules**
- **patron saint**
- **plaza**
- **irrigate**

On May 6, 1859, Juan Bautista Silva and his family set out for the San Luis Valley. With them were thirteen other **Hispanic**, or Spanish-speaking, families from New Mexico. They left to find better farm country in Colorado. The farmers had suffered from a long drought. Corn and bean plants wilted in the fields. The Silvas hoped the San Luis Valley's creeks would provide water for crops.

The trip north was difficult. The **oxen** and **mules** struggled to pull the settlers' heavy carts. They lost an entire day repairing a broken wheel. The Ute Indians were a constant threat. Once before, the Utes had forced them to turn back. To guard against the Utes, they put their carts in a circle at night.

Tired and dirty, the families arrived in the San Luis Valley on June 6, 1859. They dropped to their knees and thanked Saint Joseph for getting them there safely. Saint Joseph was their **patron saint**. This was a holy person who lived long ago and to whom the townspeople prayed to keep

Focus Your Reading

- Why did the Utes claim the San Luis Valley?
- How were the settlers different from other people who had come to the valley?
- How did they build their first settlements?

them safe. They made camp on a hill. That summer, they laid out the village of La Loma de San José. It means "the Hill of Saint Joseph." Then they planted their fields.

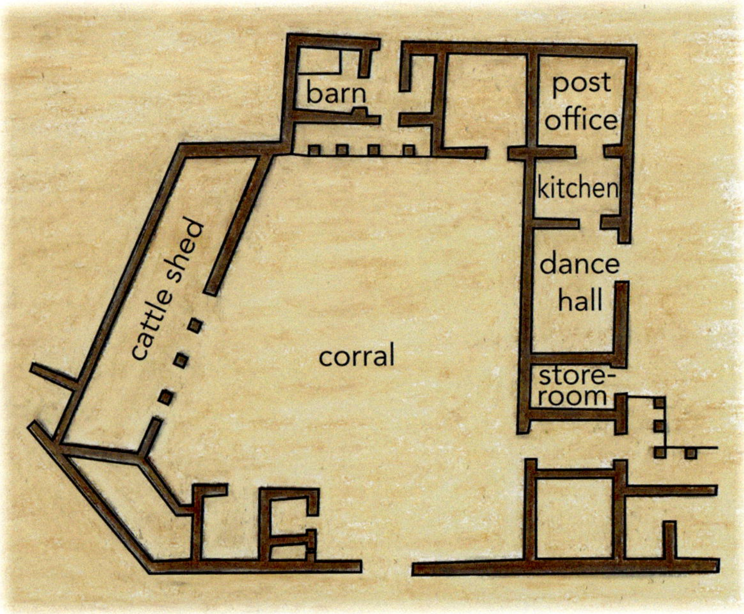

Layout of a plaza-style Hispanic settlement

EARLY SETTLEMENT

The Silvas were not the first outsiders to arrive in the San Luis Valley. Fur trappers from Taos and Santa Fe had trapped beaver there. In 1807, Zebulon Montgomery Pike explored the valley. Even as settlers, the Silvas were late arrivals. In 1849, farmers from New Mexico established the first settlement in the valley. This settlement, which they called Plaza de los Manzanares, is now the town of Garcia. The first Hispanic farmers built **plaza**-style settlements. A plaza was an open square enclosed by rooms. A heavy gate closed the single opening. Women worked and prepared food in the plaza during the daytime. At night, the settlers kept their cattle there to protect them from Ute raids.

The San Luis Valley

Settlers and Utes

The new settlements led to conflict between farmers and Utes. The valley had long been the Utes' winter camp and hunting ground. What settlers saw as a new opportunity, the Utes viewed as a threat to their old way of life. These different people had very different perspectives.

The Utes attacked the settlers in 1851, killing three Hispanic farmers. To protect the settlers, the United States sent army troops to the valley. The soldiers attacked a Ute camp, killing forty people and wounding many more. In 1858, the United States built Fort Garland, which is now a museum in the town of Fort Garland. Outnumbered by settlers and soldiers, the Utes were driven out of the valley.

Fort Garland

After the Utes left, the settlers built ribbon-type settlements. They built houses in a row along the main road. The fields extended back from the road in narrow strip.

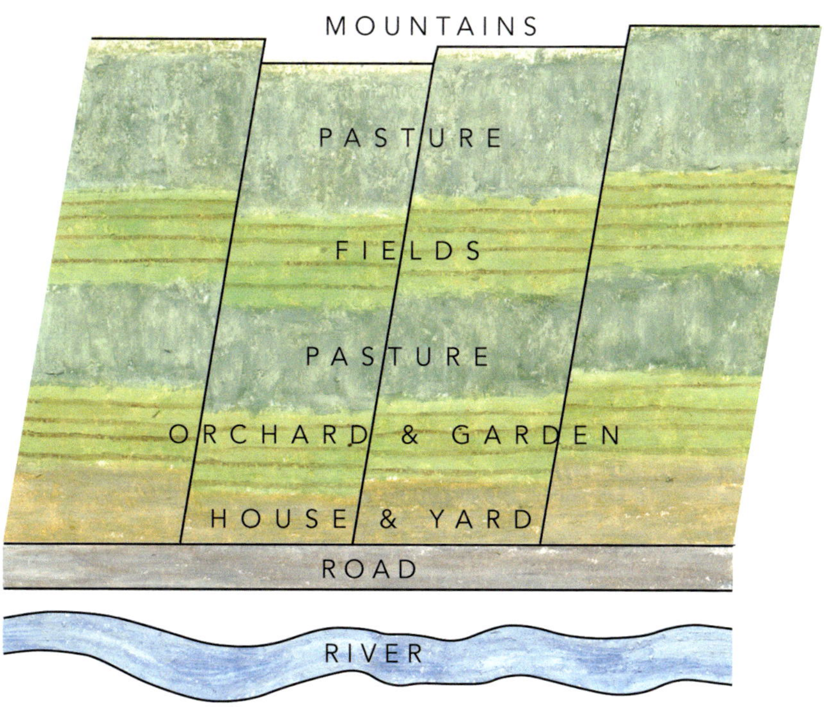

Ribbon-type Hispanic settlement

While You Read

In your notebook, quickly sketch a bird's-eye view of two kinds of Hispanic settlements. Why did the settlers design them this way? Write about this in your notebook.

Skills and Tools for Learning

Farm workers in the San Luis Valley

Analyzing Perspectives

People see things from different perspectives, or points of view. American explorers saw the plains of eastern Colorado as a desert. It was such a dry, treeless region that they doubted that farmers would ever settle there. The San Luis Valley was also a semiarid grassland, much like the Eastern Plains. Yet the Hispanic farmers who moved there never thought of it as a desert. They risked their lives from Ute attacks to make new settlements there.

Historical thinkers try to account for different perspectives. It helps explain why things happened differently in different places. It also helps explain why people disagree. Why did explorers and Hispanic settlers have such different perspectives about semiarid places?

American explorers came from a humid woodland region. Unlike Colorado's Eastern Plains, the climate was well suited for farming. They could depend on enough rain to raise crops and for trees to grow. The Hispanic farmers came from a dry climate. They were used to raising crops by irrigating their fields with ditches dug from nearby streams. They were used to living in a semiarid place.

Think of an example of when you disagreed with someone. How were your two perspectives different? Do you and your parents ever have different perspectives? Why?

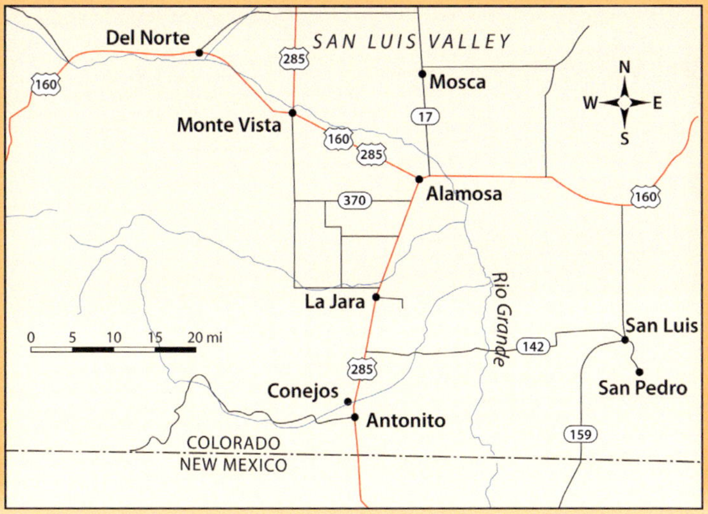

Hispanic Town Names

The people chose different kinds of names for their settlements. They named some after saints (San Luis, San Pedro). Others were named for plants that grew nearby (Alamosa, or "cottonwood grove"; La Jara, or "thickets of wild roses"). Still other towns had the names of animals (Conejos, or "rabbits"; Mosca, or "fly").

FOOD, CLOTHING, AND SHELTER

Having moved so far away from their homes, the settlers had to depend on themselves. They raised their own food. They made most of the things they needed by hand. Most of them were too poor to afford store-bought goods. They grew their own food, including wheat to make flour, as well as corn, beans, peas, and chili peppers. Some planted fruit trees that provided them with peaches, apricots, and plums. They raised chickens and cows for eggs, milk, and meat and sheep for wool.

Focus Your Reading

- What kinds of food did the settlers eat?
- What kind of clothing did they wear?
- How did they furnish their houses?

An outdoor oven used to bake bread

While You Read

Make a three-column chart in your notebook. Label the columns "Food," "Clothing," and "Shelter." Write words or phrases in each column that describe what the early settlers ate, wore, and used to build and furnish their houses.

Homemade Clothing

The women made most of their families' clothes. They spun and wove wool into yarn. From the yarn, they made dresses, men's trousers, and blankets. They tanned deerskin to make moccasins. In winter, people also wore overshoes made of sheepskin. The wool was turned inside to keep their feet warm. In cold weather, men wore wool blankets over their shoulders with an opening for the head. These are called serapes. Women wore heavy wool shawls.

Rich families wore some store-bought clothes. Women wore imported silk scarves called *rebozos*. They covered their heads with mantillas, or veils made of lace.

Houses Made of Earth

The settlers built their first houses jacale-style. Jacales are wooden posts stood upright. The builders filled in the cracks between posts with mud that dried in the sun. These houses were easy and cheap to build.

When the settlers had time to build better houses, they used adobe bricks. These were large, sun-dried bricks. On top of the adobe walls, the builders laid poles to support the roof. They made the roof of smaller sticks covered over with dirt.

Building an adobe house

Inside the House

The early houses were simply furnished. The main items were a bed for the husband and wife, a table, and homemade chairs. Few chairs were needed, as the walls in most rooms were lined with adobe benches. They were covered during the day with long, wool cushions that were placed on the floor as mattresses at night. Children and guests slept on the floor. The floors were made of earth.

The settlers knew how to live in houses made of earth. Tamping the floors and sprinkling them with water made the earth almost as hard as tiles. Some families used rugs made of rags or cowhides with the hair left on. Wool sheets fastened to the ceiling caught the dirt that sifted down from the roof. Wealthy families covered the lower half of the inside walls with calico cloth. This kept clothes from getting dirty when people brushed against the adobe walls.

Focus Your Reading

- What things did the settlers make for themselves?
- What work did men do on a farm?
- What work did women do?

WORK

The early farmers of the San Luis Valley were very poor. They raised or made everything they needed with few tools. The men plowed the fields with homemade plows made of tree limbs sharpened at the end. Oxen pulled the

Farmer plowing with oxen

Irrigation ditches in the San Luis Valley

plows. At harvesttime, the men cut hay and wheat by hand with curved blades called scythes. They walked oxen back and forth over the stems to thresh the grain. To grow crops, the farmers had to **irrigate** their fields. They brought water to the fields by digging ditches to the nearest river or creek.

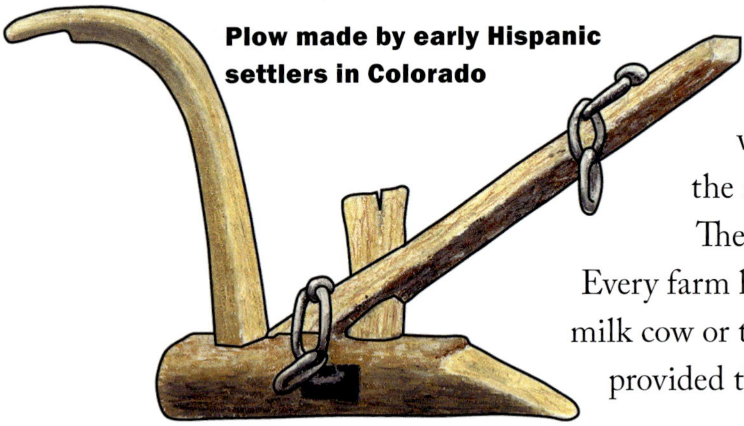

Plow made by early Hispanic settlers in Colorado

The men also took care of the farm animals. Every farm had a team of oxen, sheep and goats, a milk cow or two, chickens, and a few pigs. The sheep provided the wool used to make clothing.

Making Cloth

Making clothing took much of the women's time. First, they had to wash and card the wool. Carding with a wire-tooth brush straightened the fibers for spinning. Then the wool was dyed. To make natural dyes, women collected and boiled flower petals, roots, and leaves. After dyeing the wool, they spun it into yarn. Coarse yarn made good rugs, blankets, and serapes. Sheets, shirts, skirts, and curtains required finer yarn. The women then wove the yarn into cloth. Finally, they cut up the cloth and made the clothing.

While You Read

In your notebook, write three sentences that summarize the differences between men's and women's work on a Hispanic farm.

Learning from Primary Sources

The San Luis Valley

An Adobe House

In July 1864, Nathaniel P. Hill, a scientist visiting Colorado, traveled through the San Luis Valley. He left this description of the adobe house of a wealthy landowner he visited.

Nathaniel P. Hill

"After a days travel over an arid plain, destitute alike of water and vegetation, we have arrived at the . . . town known as Culebra . . . It contains only adobe houses, extending along for half a mile on either side of the road and all joined together. The adobe is made of a fine alluvial soil ground with water into a stiff paste. It is then moulded into forms about three times the size of an ordinary brick. These are baked in the sun for a few days, and then used for building . . .

"We are staying at the house of Amidor Sanchez, one of the old and rich men of the place . . . The house is quite splendid in its way. The walls are covered with calico. Instead of carpets, they use cowhides, dressed with the hair on. The floor is entirely covered with them. A cushioned seat extends entirely around each room, and the walls are well covered with small paintings, most of which represent the crucifixion or some event in the life of Christ. The house contains eight rooms, each about 12 × 20 ft. . . .

"All the people in the place are Catholics. A cross is stuck up in the room of almost every mud house."

Nathaniel P. Hill, "Nathaniel P. Hill Inspects Colorado: Letters Written in 1864"

- **How were the adobe bricks made?**
- **How were the rooms in the Sanchez house decorated?**

Modern-day adobe bricks

Grinding Corn

Women also did all the cooking, cleaning, and caring for children. In the early days, women in the San Luis Valley had to grind corn to make tortillas and *atole*, or cornmeal mush. They spent hours hunched over a metate, or grinding stone. Nobody was happier than they were to see the village build its first gristmill. The mill used water-powered grindstones to grind wheat and corn into meal and flour. Women also made soap and molded candles.

A gristmill

FAMILY AND COMMUNITY LIFE

The family and the community played important roles in the lives of Hispanic settlers. Most families were related to other families in the town. The next-door neighbors might be one's grandparents, aunts and uncles, or cousins. The community was like an extended family.

The family was the center of life. Family members worked together on their farms. Children were taught what they needed to know at home. Boys watched their fathers to learn how to grow corn and beans, shear sheep, and raise cattle. Girls learned homemaking skills from their mothers. The few schools that did exist were Catholic schools that mainly taught religion.

Indian Slaves

Indian slaves helped many early San Luis Valley families with cooking and farmwork. Most were Utes who had been captured and sold by other Indian tribes. In 1865, a government worker identified more than 150 Indian slaves. They were freed after the Civil War, when the Thirteenth Amendment to the US Constitution abolished slavery throughout the nation.

Focus Your Reading

- What did people do with leisure time?
- What role did religion play in community life?
- What special days did people celebrate?

Social Events

Most social events took place during the winter. Farmers had fewer chores to do then. The men gathered to talk and listen to stories. They also held cockfights, in which their prized roosters fought one another. Young men enjoyed horse races, footraces, and wrestling. Men also played pelota, a game like field hockey, and gambling games. Women's social life centered on their work. They often got together to help each other bake, weave cloth, and make clothing.

Religion was also important. In most towns, the first public building was an adobe Catholic Church. At first, few communities had a priest to lead the services. People gathered on their own to pray or sing hymns. Those who had a priest attended church for Sunday mass and for weddings and baptisms.

While You Read

Divide a page in your notebook into thirds. As you read this section, quickly sketch scenes that represent the settlers' leisure-time activities, religious practices, and village celebrations. Talk about your sketches with a partner.

Religious Holidays

Many of the holidays were special religious days. Each village had a day set aside for its patron saint. The saint's day began with a mass or church service. Then the people paraded through the village. In the afternoon, the men might hold a *corrida de gallo*, or cock race. Mounted on horses, they would see who could pick up a rooster that was buried in the ground up to its neck. That night the village held a dance. Townspeople with guitars or violins provided the music.

Colorado's first Catholic church, built in Conejos, 1858

Statue of a saint

Christmas was the biggest event of the year. The celebration began on Christmas Eve. In many towns, the people put on a play called *Los Pastores*. It was a play about the birth of Christ. Christmas Eve was also the time the *abuelo* (grandparent) came to visit young children. The abuelo came to see if the children had been good and had said their prayers every night. If not, the abuelo cracked a whip until prayers were said. The night ended with a midnight mass at the church. Christmas Day was a day for family dinners and dancing.

New Year's Day was the day of the Manueles. On New Year's morning, a group of men went to each house in which a man or boy named Manuel lived. Manuel is a special name. It is short for Emmanuel, which refers to Christ. The group would honor the Manuel who lived at that house with guitar music and singing.

THE SAN LUIS VALLEY TODAY

What is the San Luis Valley like today? In many respects, it is like the rest of Colorado. Cars and pickup trucks are parked in driveways. The city of Alamosa has a shopping center with a Wal-Mart store and a movie theater. People come to the annual Crestone music festival from miles around to listen to country-western, blues, and rock bands. Fast-food restaurants and gas stations line the highways. People watch the same TV programs that everyone in Colorado watches. Schools are much like those everywhere, with sports teams that compete in regional competitions.

Focus Your Reading

- What is the San Luis Valley like today?
- What changes have taken place since the early years of settlement?

Former US senator Ken Salazar. His ancestors were early settlers of the San Luis Valley.

Present-day Hispanic Catholic Church in the town of San Luis

The
Great Sand Dunes

The San Luis Valley is known for its sand dunes. Sand and dust blown by strong winds pile up against the foothills along the eastern edge of the valley. The tallest sand dunes are more than 700 feet high. People from all over the world visit the Great Sand Dunes National Park and Preserve.

A Changing Way of Life

The San Luis Valley is similar to other places in Colorado because many changes have taken place. They began during the lifetimes of the first settlers. Beginning in the 1870s, miners, railroad builders, and English-speaking farmers, ranchers, and merchants arrived. Many were Anglo-Americans from eastern Colorado. They spoke English rather than Spanish. Most of them were Protestants rather than Catholics. They ate steak and potatoes instead of tortillas and beans. They wore store-bought clothes and lived in wood-frame houses. They celebrated July 4 instead of saints' days. These cultural changes made the San Luis Valley more like the rest of Colorado.

While You Read

Look for the answers to the "Focus Your Reading" questions as you read. How did the authors organize the paragraphs to help you with this? Talk about your thinking with a partner when you finish reading.

Traces of the Past

The past is still present in the San Luis Valley. The area still has a Hispanic character. Many people still speak Spanish and have Hispanic names. San Luis, Garcia, and other early settlements have survived, along with their adobe houses and churches. The people who live there enjoy the good things of modern life. Yet by present-day standards, many people in the San Luis Valley are still poor. Much has changed in the San Luis Valley, but much remains the same.

After You Read

1. Share and compare your **big** and **little** questions and answers with a partner, a small group, or the whole class. Star the answers you found "right there" in the text. Put a check beside the answers that were inferred or found in other resources.
2. Imagine that you are a girl or boy living in the San Luis Valley in the 1850s. Draw a scene in your notebook that depicts your village, your home, the work you do, and your family and community life.

Thinking about Colorado Water

Do you know . . .

why Hispanic farmers made irrigation a community effort?

San Luis People's Ditch

In the dry San Luis Valley, Hispanic farmers needed irrigation to produce the food they and their animals needed. They grew wheat, corn, and beans, as well as hay for their animals. Unlike farmers in Colorado today, they did not sell water rights to individuals.

Hispanic farmers worked together to dig the ditches, to keep them repaired, and to divide up the water. During dry periods, they shared water so that everyone benefited. When there was not enough water for each farmer, they shared the fields that did have water.

The oldest community-owned ditch in Colorado is the San Luis People's Ditch. Begun in 1852, it is still in use today.

Have you ever wondered why Hispanic farmers made irrigation a community effort?

Sharing resources was a custom that Hispanic settlers brought with them from New Mexico and before that from Spain. Sharing was often necessary in poor communities. Most families in the San Luis Valley could not afford to have their own irrigation system.

Can you think of ways that people share resources today?

- How are they similar to a community-owned irrigation ditch?
- Would sharing irrigation water work in Colorado today?

Asking Historical Questions
Your Response

This chapter began with this question:

In what ways and why did Hispanic settlers in the San Luis Valley have to depend on themselves?

1. **Review**
   Review the information in your notes and in this chapter about how and why settlers in the San Luis Valley became self-sufficient farmers.
2. **Reflect**
   With a partner or in a small group, discuss how and why settlers in the San Luis Valley became self-sufficient farmers.
3. **Respond**
   In your notebook, explain how and why settlers in the San Luis Valley became self-sufficient farmers.

UNIT FIVE
New Settlers Come to Colorado

- **1855**
- **1858** Discovery of gold at Cherry Creek
- **1859** Gold rush begins
- **1860**
- **1861** Colorado becomes a territory
- **1862** Homestead Act
- **1862** Pacific Railway Act
- **1864** Sand Creek Massacre
- **1864–1867** Warfare on the plains
- **1865**
- **1867** Plains Indians agree to leave Colorado
- **1868** Utes give up territory in eastern Colorado
- **1870**
- **1870** Denver Pacific Railr and Kansas & Paci Railroad complet

People

The discovery of gold in 1858 brought thousands of new settlers to Colorado. Many came to work in the mines. Others became farmers, store owners, or hotel keepers. Many of these new settlers came to stay.

Places

The newcomers settled throughout Colorado. The miners found gold and silver in the mountains. Farmers settled in the river valleys. Others raised cattle on the Eastern Plains and in mountain parks.

Times

This was a time of change in Colorado. The new settlers built railroads, plowed up the plains, and killed bison to sell their hides. It was a bad time for the Indians, who were driven off their land.

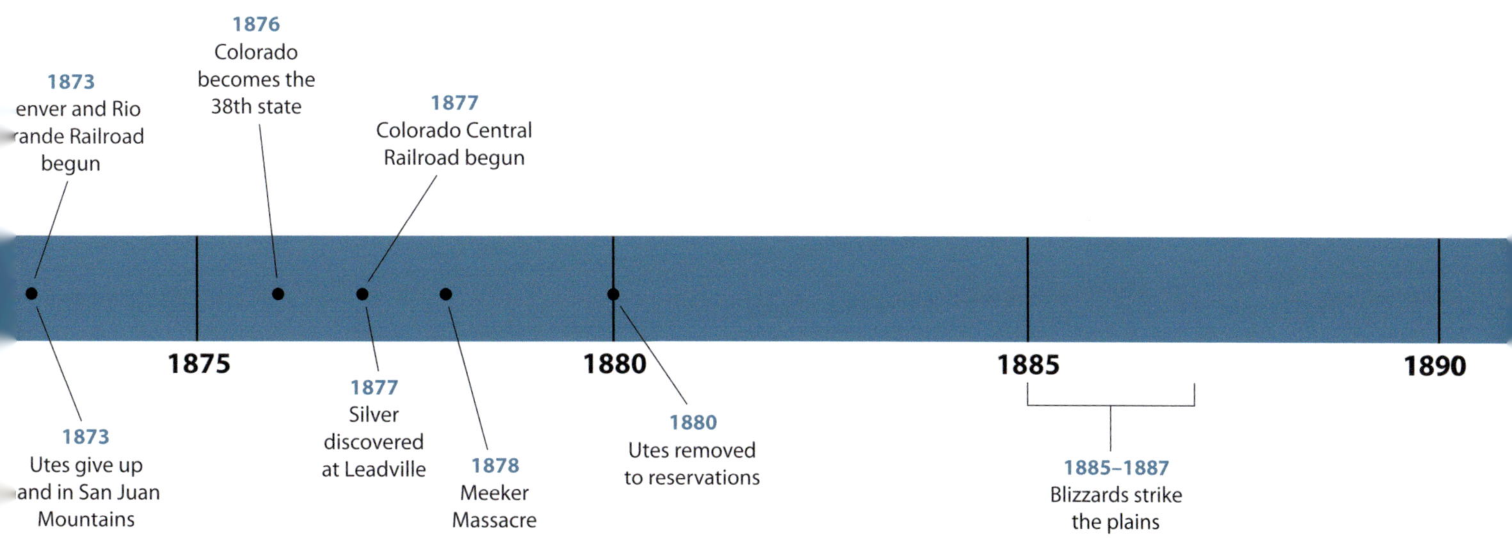

Economics

Before You Read

Scan this chapter. Look at the section headings, photos, captions, and the bold printed words. Then make a list in your notebook of these big ideas of economics: scarcity, opportunity cost, incentives, and economic risks. Leave space under each term so you have room later to explain what the term means.

KEY-WORDS

- **economics**
- **scarcity**
- **opportunity cost**
- **economic incentives**
- **economic risk**
- **natural resources**
- **human resources**
- **capital resources**

WHAT IS ECONOMICS?

Economics is the study of how people make choices. Usually, these are choices about how goods and services are produced and consumed. Goods are material things like clothes, houses, and automobiles. Services are things people get paid to do, such as delivering the mail, teaching, or painting a house. Economics is also about how people make and spend money. We have to make choices about how we spend money because our material wants are greater than our means to get what we want. This is what economists—people who are trained in economics—call **scarcity**.

Focus Your Reading

- What is economics?
- Why do economic thinkers determine costs and benefits?
- What is involved in making good economic choices?

WHAT IS AN ECONOMY?

An economy is the way people and societies organize themselves to deal with the problem of scarcity. In some societies, such as North Korea, the central government makes nearly all of the decisions about how goods and services are produced and consumed. Economists call this

Children's parka

Family car

House

Goods

Services

Worker painting a building

Mailman

Teacher with student

While You Read

In your own words, explain what the term *scarcity* means under the word you wrote in your notebook. Then give an example of scarcity in your own life.

a command economy. In other societies, such as the United States, most of the choices are made by individuals and privately owned businesses. That is called a market economy. Many societies have a mixed economy, in which both government and ordinary people make decisions. Even in the United States, state and national governments play a role in the economy. They have some say about the quality of goods made and sold, what workers are paid, and conditions of the workplace.

THE PROBLEM OF SCARCITY

Scarcity is the central problem of economics. To illustrate the problem, let's assume that you have twenty-five dollars that you can spend on anything you want. Perhaps it is a birthday gift from a favorite aunt or uncle. Make a list on a sheet of paper of the things you want that cost about that amount. The list may include a ticket to an event, an item of clothing, recreational equipment, or anything else. On the top half of a sheet of paper, list as many of these wants as you can think of.

On the bottom half of the page, answer these questions: Which want did you choose from your list? How and why did you decide to choose this one? We will look next at how economic decisions are usually made.

COSTS AND BENEFITS

In making economic decisions, most people weigh the costs and benefits of the choices they make. Deciding that the cost of an item outweighs the benefits they will gain by having it helps people decide what not to buy. Deciding that the benefits are worth the cost involved sends a "buy" signal. In making your decision, did you weigh the cost and benefits of possible choices? Did some items seem to be of greater benefit to you than others?

OPPORTUNITY COST

Making an economic choice involves another kind of cost that goes beyond the price you pay. We have to give up the next best thing we could have chosen but did not. This is what economists call the **opportunity cost** of making a choice. In other words, making choices involves tradeoffs. In a world of scarcity, we have to give up things to get things.

> **While You Read**
>
> In your own words, explain what the term *opportunity cost* means under the words you wrote in your notebook. Then give an example of opportunity cost in your own life.

POSITIVE AND NEGATIVE INCENTIVES

Individuals and societies also make choices based on **economic incentives**. An incentive is something that makes one choice more or less attractive than other choices. Incentives may be positive or negative. A positive incentive means there is more

Positive incentive
Sale sign in store window

Negative incentives

Do Not Bicycle sign

No Dogs Allowed sign

Do Not Enter sign

to be gained by making a particular choice. Having more to lose by choosing it is a negative incentive.

Businesses that sell products often rely on incentives in their television and radio ads. Think of an ad you have seen or heard recently that uses positive incentives to promote a product. How does the ad claim you will be better off by buying this product? Can you remember ads that use negative incentives? How will you be worse off if you do not buy it or you buy a competitor's product?

While You Read

In your own words, explain what the term *incentives* means under the word you wrote in your notebook. Then give an example of incentives in your own life.

ECONOMIC RISKS

Making economic choices also involves risk. *Risk* means the possibility of injury or loss. Buying a product involves the risk that it will not be all that you expected. Loaning money to a friend involves the risk of it not being paid back.

Even spending money on a good choice may be risky. What if a better choice comes along tomorrow? Did the choice you made for spending the twenty-five dollars involve any **economic risk**?

While You Read

In your own words, explain what the term *economic risk* means under the words you wrote in your notebook. Then give an example of economic risk in your own life.

Man shopping for shoes

MAKING GOOD CHOICES

The goal in making choices is to get the best possible outcome. We want to get the most from our choices. To choose wisely, we need to consider both the facts at hand and our own likes and dislikes.

The facts may include the price of an item. Is it on sale, selling at a fair price, or overpriced? Is it of good quality? Can we find a similar item of better quality at the same or a lower price? Shopping around for information about price and quality helps us know more about what we are buying. Good choices are usually well-informed decisions. Paying little attention to price and quality is likely to lead to a bad decision and a poor choice.

Facts are not the only consideration in making a good choice. Economic decisions should also be based on our own preferences. Buying an item of good quality at a fair price may not be a good choice if it does not suit your tastes. Why buy a pair of shoes at a good price if you cannot see yourself wearing them? Making good economic decisions involves both facts and our likes and dislikes.

ECONOMIC RESOURCES

The kinds of goods and services an economy produces depend on the resources available to it. Resources come in various kinds. There are **natural resources**, which include underground minerals, the quality of the soil, and the climate. **Human resources** are people who have valuable skills and knowledge. A third kind of resource includes the tools, machines, and buildings needed to produce goods and services. These are called **capital resources**.

Natural Resources

Colorado has always had an abundance of natural resources. Its mineral resources, especially gold and silver, attracted the first wave of settlers from the East. As gold and silver production fell, coal mining brought new immigrants

Natural resource: coal being mined

Human resource: mechanic repairing robot

to the state. Over the years, Colorado's scenic beauty and healthful climate have attracted thousands of tourists and health seekers. Many of the people attracted to Colorado settled here as miners, farmers, store clerks, and business owners. They brought valuable skills with them and learned new ways to develop the state's natural resources.

Human Resources

At each stage of Colorado's development, hardworking people provided the human resources needed for success. Skilled miners blasted gold and silver ore out of the mountains. Farmers made the soil productive by knowing or learning how to irrigate their fields. Laborers built a railroad system to ship ore to smelters and crops to market. Later, skilled workers turned iron ore into steel rails, pipe, and wire. Over the years, businessmen and -women have opened new banks, law offices, restaurants, and resort hotels to provide the services Colorado's residents needed.

Capital resource: a building under construction

Capital Resources

The growth of Colorado's capital resources has helped make all this possible. At first, prospectors spent money on burros, picks, and gold pans. Later, mining companies built stamp mills and smelters. Farmers invested in horses, plows, and irrigation ditches. Railroad companies bought locomotives, ore cars, and cattle cars to provide needed transportation. More recent generations have invested in factories, office buildings, research centers, airports, and ski resorts. Capital resources help Colorado's hardworking people put its natural resources to good use.

After You Read

Go back to the list of terms and definitions you included in your notebook. Under each, give an example of how that term can be applied to your personal experience. For example, give an example of your own experience with scarcity.

CHAPTER 9

Gold and Silver Miners

FOCUS QUESTION

How did the discovery of gold and silver affect Colorado's environment and people's lives?

Before You Read

Make a four-column chart in your notebook. Label the columns "What I Know," "What I Wonder," "What I Learned," and "What I Still Wonder." In the first column, write everything you know about gold and silver mining in Colorado. Then look at the photos and read the captions in this chapter. In the "What I Wonder" column, write all the questions you now have about Colorado mining.

KEY WORDS

- **veins**
- **placer miner**
- **ore**
- **hard-rock mining**
- **immigrants**
- **territory**
- **statehood**
- **mine tailings**

"Our fortune is made," William Green Russell yelled to his friends. On that day in May 1858, Russell and twelve other men were panning for gold in Colorado. In the bottom of his pan, he saw flakes of gold.

Russell was not the first person to find gold in Colorado. In 1850 John Ralston, a Cherokee Indian, found gold flakes in a creek near the South Platte River. A Delaware Indian named Fall Leaf had also found a gold nugget along the South Platte. These were small finds. They did not attract much attention.

Russell's discovery was different. During the next two weeks, he and his friends from Georgia found more gold-bearing sand. At Dry Creek, which flowed into the South Platte, they each panned out four to ten dollars of gold per day. That was enough to persuade others that they could get rich in Colorado.

Pikes Peak Fever

"Those two little words [Pikes Peak] are everywhere," wrote a St. Louis newspaper reporter in August 1859. "Every clothing store is a depot [storehouse] for outfits for Pikes Peak. There are Pikes Peak hats, and Pikes Peak gloves, Pikes Peak boots, Pikes Peak shoes and goodness-knows-what all."

Prospectors' camp

Focus Your Reading

- How did people find out about the gold discovery?
- Why were many people disappointed when they arrived?
- Where did George A. Jackson find gold?

THE PIKES PEAK GOLD RUSH

The news of the gold strike spread quickly. Hide traders who visited the miners took flakes of gold east with them. They talked to newspaper reporters. Soon the gold discovery was front-page news. The headlines of a Kansas City newspaper read:

> "The New Eldorado!!! Gold in Kansas Territory!!! The Pikes Peak Mines! First Arrival of Gold Dust at Kansas City!!!"

As the news spread, "gold fever" swept through the United States. In hotels and stores and on street corners, gold became the main topic of conversation. People called it the Pikes Peak gold region, as that peak was the only Colorado landmark most of them knew.

While You Read

If you were trying to persuade the people of Kansas City to travel to the Pikes Peak gold region, what would you want them to know? In your notebook, sketch a small poster with convincing phrases on it.

Pikes Peak Gold Rush

The result was the Pikes Peak Gold Rush of 1859. Thousands of men spent their savings getting ready for the trip. They bought shovels, picks, gold pans, tents, and other supplies. A few left for Colorado that fall. Most set out across the plains in the spring. They drove covered wagons, some with "Pikes Peak or Bust" painted on the sides. They used trails made by Indians, trappers, and traders.

Skills and Tools for Learning

Note Taking and Note Making

Good readers take notes while they read. They write short comments in the margin, such as "Important point" or "What does this mean?" If it's a textbook or a library book, they write on sticky notes instead of on the page itself. They also stop from time to time to take longer notes in a journal or a learning log. It helps them remember what they have read and makes information available for later use.

Notes look different than the sentences or paragraphs written for an assignment to be turned in. They do not have to be complete sentences or start with capital letters. Notes can be messy, so long as they are readable. Notes put the author's language into his or her own words. Notes are not quotes.

Successful learners also *make* notes. Note making includes your thoughts about why information is important or what it means to you. The best way to do this is by creating two-column notes.

Divide a note page into two columns. Read one of the sections in this chapter, *taking* notes in the left-hand column. Use the right-hand column for *making* notes about what you have just learned. Does this change your ideas about the topic? Does it help answer the Focus Question asked at the beginning of this chapter?

A gold nugget

The first "Pikes Peakers" to arrive that spring expected to find gold nuggets in every streambed. Instead, they found two small log-cabin towns and men standing around. The towns of Auraria and Denver City were laid out by the gold seekers who had spent the winter there. These men had also taken out most of the gold from the South Platte River. The men still looking for gold earned only a few cents for a hard day's work. Hundreds of newcomers decided they had been "humbugged," or misled. They left for home.

Early in May, George A. Jackson walked into Denver City with $1,900 in Colorado gold dust. He had spent time in the California mines. He knew that the gold found in rivers came from **veins** in the mountains. Instead of looking for gold along the South Platte, he headed for the high country. That winter, he found a gold nugget in a creek. He told only a few close friends about his find. In April, they went out to stake claims near present-day Idaho Springs. There they found a very rich pocket of gold. They had mined the gold Jackson brought to town in just seven days.

Prospector ready to pan for gold

Staking a Claim

Placer miners staked out claims on a "first-come, first-served" basis. A placer miner could stake only one claim along a river or creek. It could be no longer than 100 feet. An exception was granted to the person who made the first discovery. He was allowed two claims. Miners had to work the claim to hold it. The rules were set by mining custom and were enforced by the miners themselves.

Miner using a rocker

PLACER MINING

George A. Jackson saved the day for Pikes Peak gold seekers. They rushed to the mountains to search for gold. They looked for placers, or deposits of gold in streams. These were flakes of gold that had settled into the sand at the bottom. Lucky prospectors might find a nugget, or a larger piece of gold. To pan for gold, they shoveled gravel into a metal pan. Then they dipped the pan in water and swirled the contents around. This washed out the lighter gravel and sand. Gold was heavier than sand. It settled to the bottom. They picked out the flakes of gold with tweezers.

Focus Your Reading

- How did prospectors use pans to hunt for gold?
- Why did they use rockers and sluices to mine gold?
- How did mining companies remove the gold that was left?

Placer Miners' Tools

Miners who found a paying placer used other tools. They could work faster with a rocker than with a pan. It was a box mounted on rockers, often used by two miners. First they

shoveled dirt into the box. There one man rocked it back and forth while his partner poured in water. The rocking washed out the lighter sand and dirt. Gold flakes settled behind slats nailed to the bottom of the box.

Larger groups of miners used a sluice, or Long Tom. This was a long trough connected to a water source. Miners shoveled dirt into the sluice, letting the flow of water carry away the lighter gravel. The miners stopped the flow of water once a day to collect the gold that had settled to the bottom of the sluice.

Can you identify the tools these placer miners are using?

While You Read

In your notebook, make a list of all the supplies a **placer miner** would need.

Other Placer Methods

After mining the rich deposits, miners often sold their claims. The low-grade **ore** left behind required more work than it was worth. Tons of it might produce only a few ounces of gold. They sold their claims to big mining companies. These companies used a method called ground sluicing. At the upper end of a valley, they built a dam across a stream. At the lower end, they built a giant sluice. When they opened the dam, a wall of water rushed down the valley. It carried tons of dirt into the sluice at the lower end. Mining companies also mined low-grade ore by hydraulic mining. This method used high-pressure hoses to wash sand

and gravel from the side of a gulch. Both methods polluted streams and ruined the banks of rivers.

Miners using a sluice

Most of the gold found in Colorado from 1859 to 1867 was placer gold. Placer miners found rich deposits near Breckenridge, Gunnison, and Steamboat Springs and at California Gulch near Leadville. However, few of them "struck it rich." Most were lucky to make a living.

HARD-ROCK MINING

In June 1859, John Gregory "struck pay dirt." He found the first quartz gold in Colorado. A longtime miner, Gregory knew that gold flakes in streams came from veins in the mountains. Most veins of gold were locked inside quartz rock. It became free, or placer, gold when the rock weathered into sand and gravel.

Focus Your Reading

- What did John Gregory look for in the mountains?
- Why did most quartz miners sell their claims?
- Where did prospectors find silver?

Inside a gold mine

Quartz Rock Gold

Gregory set out to find the quartz rock that had produced the placer gold. Panning in Clear Creek, he kept finding bits of "color" in his pan. He followed the color up a narrow gulch to its source: a ledge of quartz rock. The first pan of gravel he chipped out contained $4 worth of gold.

The news of his find brought another rush of miners into the mountains. This time they came with picks and hammers. To get at quartz gold, miners first had to hammer the rock into bits. Then they hauled the gravel down to a creek, where they panned out the gold. Few places produced enough gold to make it worth the effort. "Gregory's Diggings" (pre–Central City) was one that did. The first miners there made $50 to $100 per day. When John Gregory got tired of hammering rock, he sold his two claims for $21,000. That was as close as most miners ever came to "striking it rich."

Removing large amounts of gold from quartz rock required stamp mills and smelters. Stamp mills used heavy weights to crush the quartz into powder. The powder was then sent to a smelter. There it was mixed with chemicals and

While You Read

Make a quick sketch of the way John Gregory dug for quartz gold. Why do you suppose very few hard-rock miners got rich?

Hard-Rock Mining

To mine quartz gold, miners drilled holes into the rock using a steel drill and a hammer. A single miner held the drill in one hand and a four-pound hammer in the other. When two men worked together, one held the drill and the other hit it with a two-hand, eight-pound hammer. After drilling eight to ten holes, they placed sticks of dynamite in the holes and lit the fuses. They hauled the rock brought down by the explosion to a stamp mill.

roasted over high heat. Few quartz miners could afford to build a mill and smelter. Most sold their claims, then went to work at the mill or smelter.

Smelter at Black Hawk, Colorado

Silver Ore

Early miners like Sam Conger failed to see fortunes that were at their feet. In 1860 he was elk hunting near the town of Nederland. He found an outcropping of mineral but had no idea what it was. Nine years later, he saw a railroad car in Wyoming filled with the same kind of mineral. An armed man guarding it told him it was silver ore. Conger returned to Nederland and opened the Caribou Mine. It produced $8 million worth of silver.

Over the years, miners in Colorado found more silver than gold. The biggest discovery took place in 1877 at Leadville. Miners there had long complained about the gray sand that clogged up their sluices. The "sand" turned out to be silver mixed with lead. Mines there soon produced $10 million in silver each year. Miners also found rich veins of silver ore near Georgetown, Aspen, Gunnison, and in the San Juan Mountains.

Learning from Primary Sources

Mining and the Environment

Central City is a good place to investigate mining's impact on the environment. In the summer of 1859, miners rushed there by the thousands. In the primary sources below written at two different times, the authors mention the area's natural environment. What can you learn about mining's impact from these accounts?

Central City, 1859

"This narrow valley is densely wooded, mainly with the inevitable yellow pine, which sheltered from the fierce winds which sweep the mountaintops, here grows to a height of sixty or eighty feet . . . Of these pines, log cabins are constructed . . . and probably one hundred are now being built."

Horace Greeley, *An Overland Journey*

Central City, 1866

"The gulch miner has been here in all his pristine strength and glory. Gravel, sand, bowlders [boulders], rocks—not one where Nature put it . . . Trees and vegetation have long since disappeared. Holes, shafts, and excavations almost obliterate the original surface."

James F. Meline, *Two Thousand Miles on Horseback*

Central City, 1866

"The timber has been wholly cut away . . . The great, awkwardly rounded mountains are cut up and down by the lines of paying 'lodes,' and pitted all over by the holes and heaps of rocks made either by prospectors or to secure claims. My experience in California taught me that gold-mining utterly ruins the appearance of a country, and therefore I am not surprised at what I see here."

Bayard Taylor, *Colorado: A Summer Trip*

- **How did mining modify the landscape?**
- **How did it alter the natural vegetation?**

Central City, 1864. The bare hillside was once covered with trees. The miners used the trees for lumber to build the town.

MINING CAMPS AND TOWNS

With each new gold or silver discovery, miners rushed in to stake out claims. Tent cities grew up almost overnight. Miners lived in tents. Stores set up in tents sold food, tools, and clothing. Most camps were short-lived. It took only a few weeks to mine out the best deposits. Then the miners moved on to the next camp.

Tent lunchroom in a mining town

From Camp to Mining Town

Camps near rich ore deposits grew into towns. Jackson's Diggings became Idaho Springs. Central City and Black Hawk grew up in Gregory's Gulch. There, tents and shacks gave way to log cabins and frame or brick storefronts. By 1866, Central City had a drugstore, a bookstore, a bank, a hardware store, and many saloons.

Saloons were popular places. They were social centers as well as places to buy beer, wine, or whiskey. Miners went there to relax and learn the news. Saloons also served as banks. The owners kept the miners' gold dust locked in their safes.

Focus Your Reading

- Why were most mining camps short-lived?
- What services did mining towns provide?
- What purpose did supply towns serve?

Miner's cabin

Inside a miner's cabin

Clara Brown, a freed slave, washed clothes for miners in Central City. She used her income to bring twenty-six relatives and orphans to Colorado.

Mining Town People

Mining towns attracted people of different ethnic groups and races. At first, most of the miners were born in the United States. In time, skilled miners arrived from England. The mills and smelters hired many Irish **immigrants**. Newcomers from Europe opened banks, saloons, and hardware stores. While most miners were white, African Americans also worked in Colorado's mining towns. By 1890, 1,447 Chinese were living in Colorado. Many of them were miners.

At first, most of the people there were men. Most married men had left their wives and children at home. As mining towns grew, more women and children arrived. Married men who found a rich placer or a good job sent for their families. Some wives opened boardinghouses or cooked for the single men. Other women taught in the mining town school.

Classroom in the mining town of Silver Plume

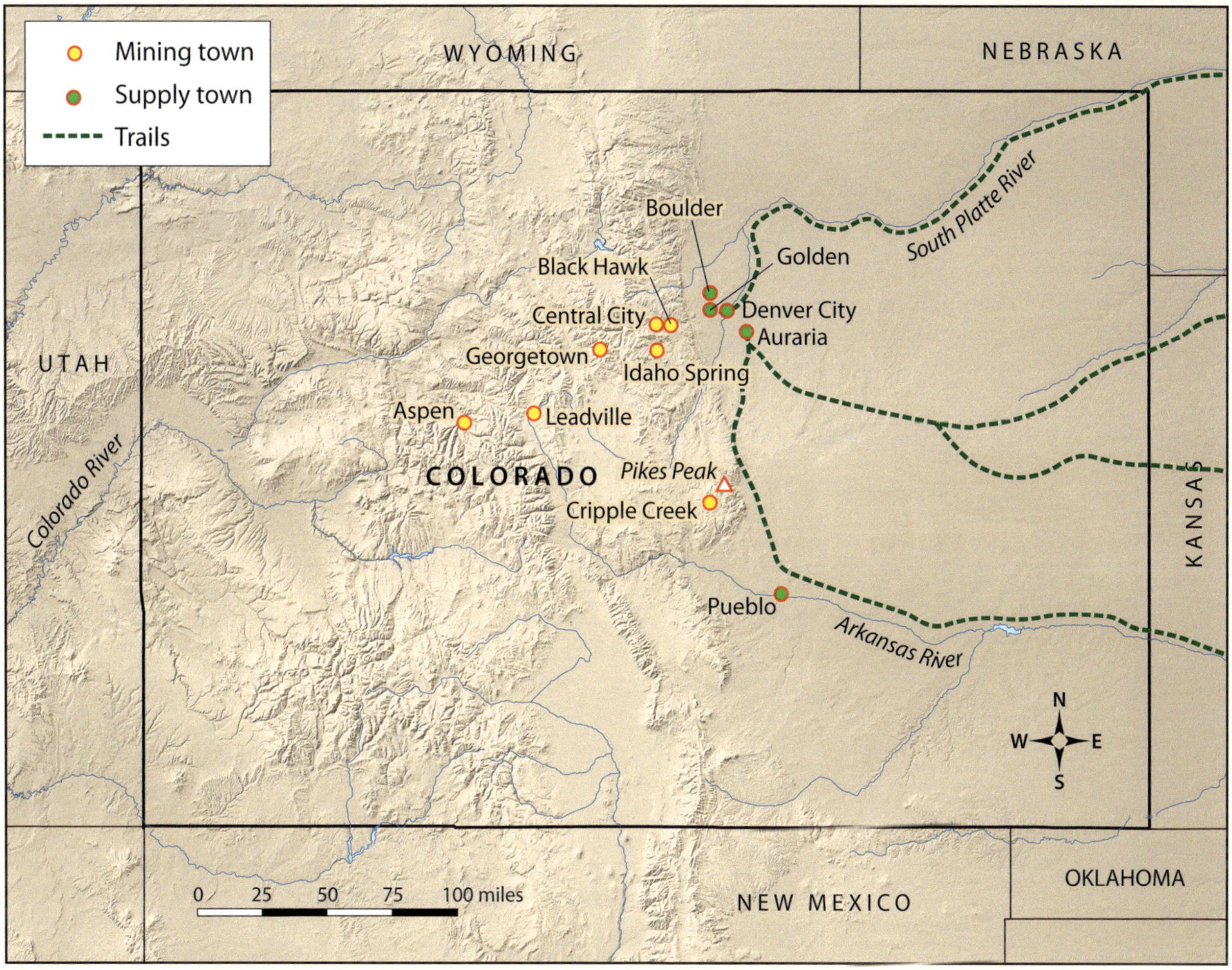

Early mining and supply towns in Colorado and the main trails leading to the towns

Supply Towns

The mining towns were linked to supply towns down on the plains. The merchants of Denver and Pueblo, the largest supply towns, shipped food, clothing, and hardware to the mining towns' storekeepers. The Denver and Pueblo merchants received these goods from eastern cities from freight wagons pulled by oxen. It took several weeks for the wagons to cross the plains. Horse-drawn wagons and pack trains of mules spent additional days hauling the goods up the steep mountain roads to the mining towns. Slow transportation presented a problem. The money spent feeding animals and paying wagon drivers for weeks at a time kept transportation costs high. Building and repairing

While You Read

In your notebook, make a word web with the topic "Mining Camps and Towns" at the center. As you read, write words and phrases in the web boxes about the things camps and towns provided for miners and their families.

Freight wagons that hauled supplies across the plains to Denver

Mule train, Nellie Mine

steep and dangerous mountain roads added other expenses. These costs, in turn, drove up the price miners had to pay the storekeepers in the mining town for food and tools.

Railroads Solve a Problem

The US Congress helped solve the transportation problem in 1862 when it passed the Pacific Railway Act. This law provided government aid for building railroads across the West. Railroad companies needed government help to lay tracks across the Great Plains and the western deserts. Not enough people lived there to make a railroad profitable. Too few goods were shipped to pay the cost of construction. The government aided the railroads by giving them public land, which they sold to land buyers. They used that money to build the railroad and equip it with locomotives and railroad cars.

Two railroads linked Denver to the east in 1870. The Denver Pacific connected Denver to the Union Pacific Railroad at Cheyenne, Wyoming. The Kansas Pacific connected Denver to Kansas City and other eastern cities. These railroads reduced the cost of hauling goods from the east. Their steam locomotives could haul more goods faster and cheaper than ox-drawn wagons. This allowed merchants

1873 Denver and Rio Grande Railway map

and storekeepers to lower prices and sell more groceries and other items.

Mountain Railroads

Other railroads soon connected the supply towns to the mining towns. The first was the Denver and Rio Grande Railroad, begun in 1873. It extended south to Pueblo and west into the mountains. It was a narrow-gauge railroad, which means its tracks were narrower than those of most railroads. It also had smaller locomotives and cars. This made it easier for its trains to wind through narrow canyons and climb steep mountains. By 1877, a second narrow-gauge railroad, the Colorado Central Railroad, connected Denver to Blackhawk, Central City, and other gold mining towns. These mountain railroads lowered the cost of getting food and tools to the miners and shipping gold and silver ore to smelters. Lower costs made mining in Colorado more profitable.

Denver and Rio Grande narrow-gauge train

Auraria and Denver City, 1859

Focus Your Reading

- What problems did miners create for the Plains Indians?
- What happened to the Plains Indians?
- How much land did the Utes lose?

MINERS, SETTLERS, AND INDIANS

The miners who arrived in 1859 found Plains Indians living nearby. At first, they were on friendly terms. Indians came to Denver to trade. The miners bought bison hides from them. But the peace did not last.

Early in 1864, fighting between Indians and soldiers broke out on the plains. Men were killed on both sides. In June of that year, four Arapaho Indians attacked a ranch east of Denver. They killed the rancher, his wife, and two children. In July, Indians attacked stagecoach stations and wagon trains on the plains. Fearing an Indian attack, the people of Denver panicked.

They demanded help from John Evans, the governor of the **territory**. In 1861 the US Congress had declared

Leadville Ice Palace

In 1896, Leadville held a winter fair. To house the fair, the city built a castle made of ice. It covered an entire city block. Inside were a skating rink, a ballroom for dancing, a restaurant, and concession booths. The Ice Palace, as it was called, opened on January 1 and closed on June 1, when the ice began to melt.

Colorado a territory, which was the first step toward **statehood**. Evans ordered all peaceful Indians to gather at Fort Lyon in eastern Colorado. Any Indian who remained on the plains would be considered hostile. To calm the people of Denver, he sent soldiers to hunt down hostile Indians. Colonel John M. Chivington was placed in command.

While You Read

In your opinion, what caused problems between the Indians and the newcomers? Why were Indians moved to reservations? Write your opinions in your notebook, and be prepared to defend them using information from this section for support.

Sand Creek Massacre

Instead of looking for hostile Indians, Colonel Chivington led the soldiers to Fort Lyon. At daybreak on November 29, 1864, they attacked an Indian village camped at nearby Sand Creek. The soldiers killed nearly 100 Cheyennes and Arapahos. Most of those killed were women and children. This attack is known as the Sand Creek Massacre.

The result was an Indian war. To get even for Sand Creek, the Plains Indians attacked white towns and farms. They burned down the town of Julesburg. For three years, Indians and soldiers fought each other. In October 1867 the Plains Indians agreed to leave Colorado. They moved to reservations in Kansas and Oklahoma.

John M. Chivington

The Sand Creek Massacre

Sand Creek Massacre

Chief Black Kettle

The Sand Creek site

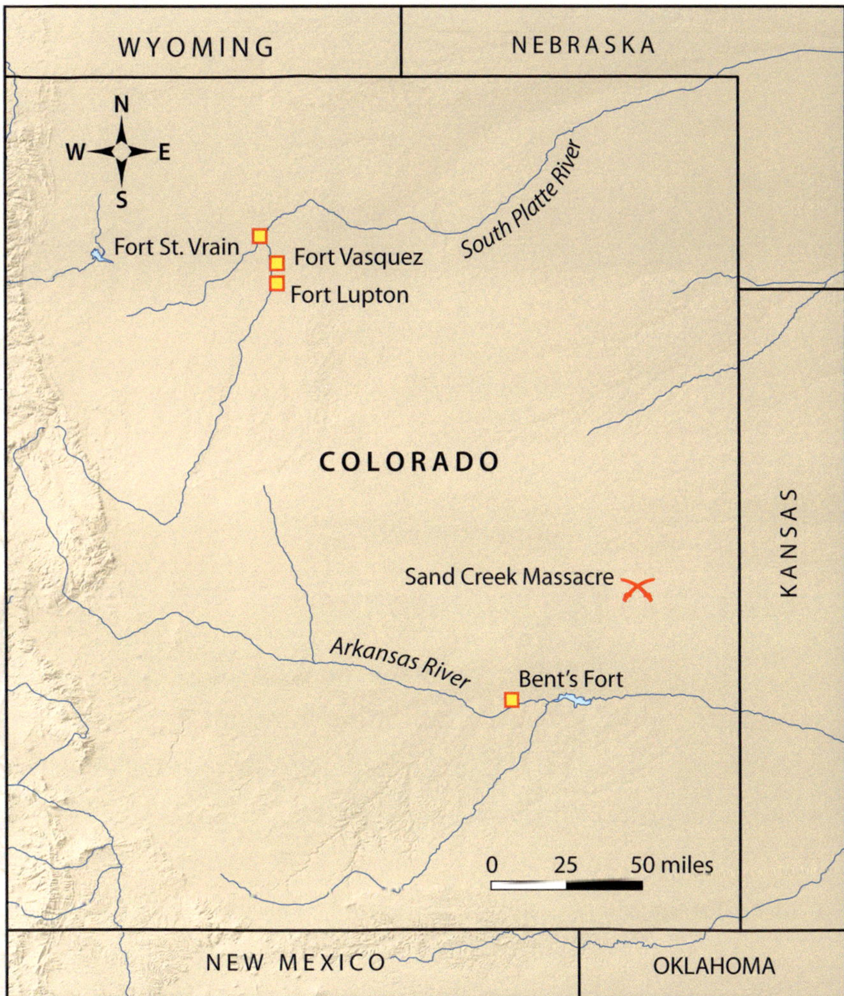

Cheyenne warrior Howling Wolf was fifteen years old at the time of the Sand Creek Massacre.

Location of the Sand Creek Massacre in relation to Bent's Fort, Fort Vasquez, Fort Lupton, and Fort St. Vrain

George Bent and his first wife, Magpie

George Bent on Sand Creek

George Bent, the son of William Bent and his Cheyenne wife, Mis-stan-stur (Owl Woman), was in one of the lodges at Sand Creek when the soldiers attacked. He survived and later described the scene: "The Indians all began running, but they did not seem to know what to do or where to turn. The women and children were screaming and wailing, the men running to the lodges for their arms and shouting advice and directions to one another."

George E. Hyde, *Life of George Bent*

This sketch of the final battle in Colorado between Plains Indians and US soldiers was drawn by a Cheyenne who was there that day.

Utes Leave the Mountains

Miners also had their eyes on the Utes' land. They wanted the Utes out of the rich mineral region in the Rocky Mountains. In 1868 the Utes signed a treaty that created a Ute reservation on the Western Slope. They gave up their claim to the Rocky Mountains and to northwestern Colorado. In return, the government agreed to pay them $60,000. Three years later, miners found placer gold in the San Juan Mountains. Again, the Utes had to give up land. In 1873 they agreed to leave the San Juans in return for a $25,000 payment each year.

Focus Your Reading

- How is gold mined in Colorado today?
- What evidence of past mining activity still exists?
- What activities take place in mining towns today?

MINING TODAY

Gold is still mined in Colorado today. The Cripple Creek and Victor Gold Mining Company mines most of it. Since 1994, its Cresson Mine near Cripple Creek has produced more than 2 million ounces of gold.

Gold mining is not what it used to be. The Cresson Mine is an open pit. Huge earthmovers dig the ore out of the ground. Giant dump trucks haul it to a crusher. The digging goes on twenty-four hours a day.

People still pan for gold in Colorado. Placer mining is a popular hobby. Hobby shops and other stores sell gold pans, picks, and shovels. Few of the gold seekers hope to make

Trucks hauling ore at the Cresson Mine near Cripple Creek

much money. But a few still do. In 1990, Shane Dodge found an eight-ounce nugget in Park County. It is on display at the Denver Museum of Nature and Science.

Mining from Colorado's past is still visible. Dozens of mountainsides are stained by yellow and brown **mine tailings**. They mark the places where miners dumped waste rock as they dug into the mountain. Old mining towns are cluttered with ruins of stamp mills and miners' cabins. Many people enjoy hiking into these "ghost towns."

Many of Colorado's mining towns are still busy places. Tour buses take people to Central City, Black Hawk, and Cripple Creek to play slot machines. Aspen, Breckenridge, and Telluride are popular ski resorts. During the summer, thousands of tourists stop at Georgetown, Leadville, and Silverton. These towns' historic sites and museums help teach people about Colorado's mining past.

While You Read

With a map of Colorado, locate mining towns that are still active communities today.

This turtle-shaped nugget was found in 1990 near the town of Alma, Colorado. It weighs 8.6 ounces.

After You Read

1. Return to your four-column chart in your notebook. Write five important things you have learned in the "What I Learned" column. Then write questions you still have in the "What I Still Wonder" column.
2. In a small group or as a whole class, defend your opinions about the problems between the Indians and the newcomers.

Thinking about Colorado Water

Do you know . . . that water is used to make and do things?

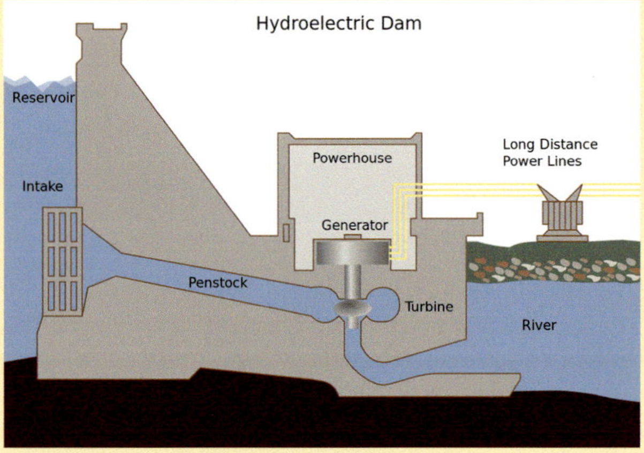

Diagram of a hydroelectric dam

Hydraulic mining

We usually think of water as something that we drink and cook with or that farmers use to grow crops. But water is also used to make and do things.

Water was a placer miner's most important tool. Prospectors swirled water in their pans to separate gold dust from sand and gravel. Placer miners used water to flush dirt out of their sluices, leaving flakes of gold behind. Hydraulic miners used powerful blasts of water to wash away entire stream banks.

Have you ever wondered why Colorado's placer miners found so many uses for water?

By swirling, flushing, and washing away, placer miners turned water into waterpower. Waterpower made mining easier and saved time. The miners did not have to spend time picking the tiny specks of gold out of the the sand and gravel by hand.

Can you think of ways that we use waterpower today to make and do things?

- How do electric companies use water-power to make electricity?
- How do oil drillers use water to fracture oil-bearing layers of rock?
- How do all of us use water to make things cleaner?

Asking Historical Questions
Your Response

This chapter began with this question:

How did the discovery of gold and silver affect Colorado's environment and people's lives?

1. **Review**
   Review the information in your notes and in this chapter about how the discovery of gold and silver affected the environment and people's lives.
2. **Reflect**
   With a partner or in a small group, discuss the information you have found.
3. **Respond**
   In your notebook, describe the effects of these discoveries.

CHAPTER 10

Farmers and Ranchers

FOCUS QUESTION

How and why was farming in eastern Colorado different from farming in the San Luis Valley?

Before You Read

Scan this chapter. Look carefully at the section headings, photos, captions, and the bold printed words. If you were the author, what title would you have given this chapter?

KEY WORDS

- **open range**
- **brand**
- **sod house**
- **sorghum**
- **rural**
- **livestock**
- **blacksmith**
- **constitution**
- **treaty**

In the spring of 1859, David K. Wall set out for Colorado in a team and wagon. Wall was an Indiana farmer. Packed in his wagon were a plow, bags of potatoes and flour, and garden seeds. That summer he planted a two-acre field along Clear Creek. Wall made $2,000 selling fresh vegetables to miners. He also sold the potatoes and flour he had hauled across the plains.

The miner John Gregory was one of Wall's customers. Gregory had just found a vein of quartz gold. But he had to quit digging, as he had run out of money. Wall grubstaked Gregory. That means he gave Gregory tools and other supplies in return for a share in his mine. During the next year, he made $1,000 from Gregory's quartz mine. Finding gold was not the only way to strike it rich in Colorado.

Focus Your Reading

- What cash crops did Colorado's farms produce?
- Why did farmers irrigate their fields?
- In what ways did miners depend on farmers?

RIVER VALLEY FARMING

William N. Byers, Denver's first newspaper editor, urged gold seekers to take up farming. To prove that it would pay off, he laid out a farm along the South Platte River. Byers

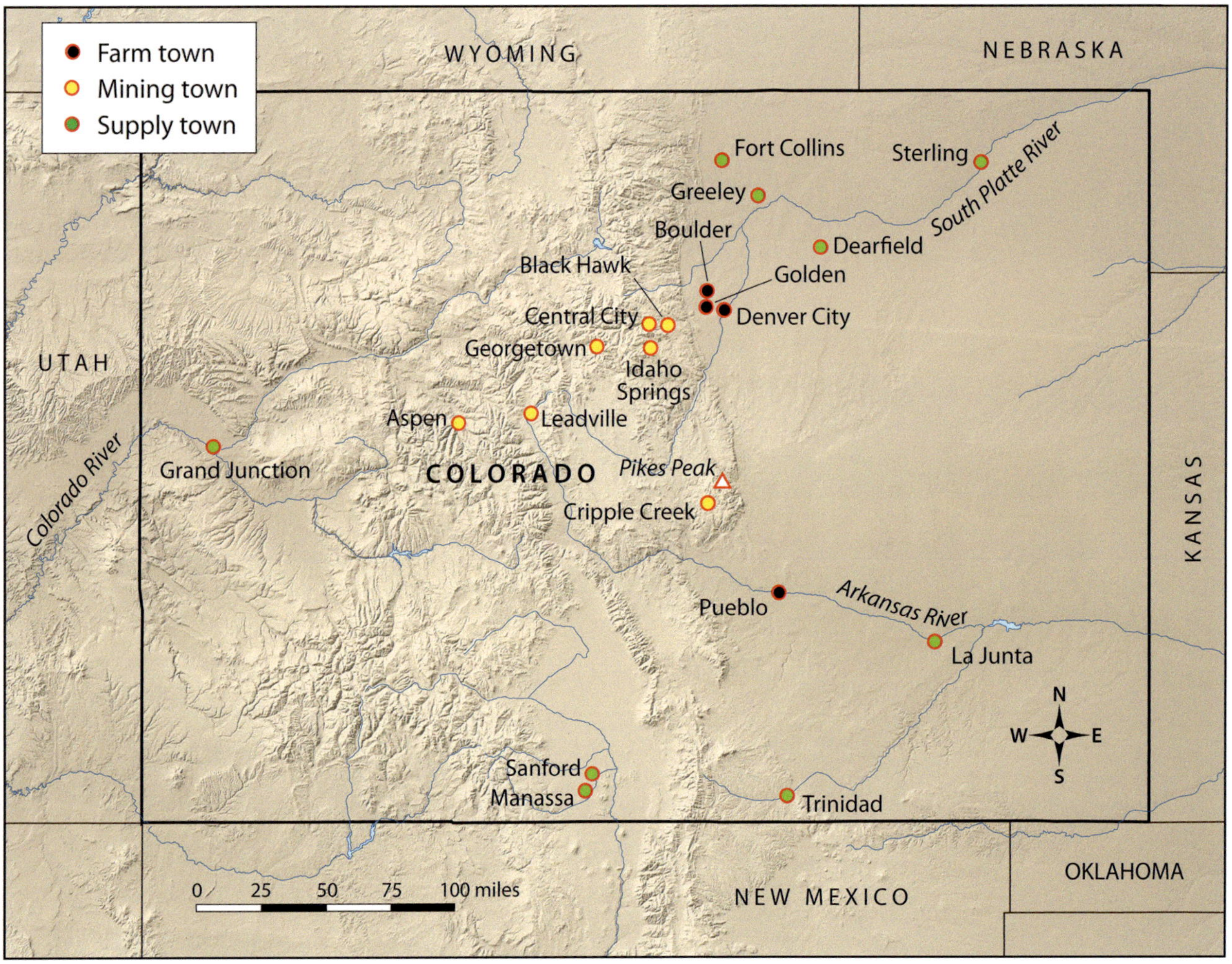

Early farming, mining, and supply towns in Colorado

While You Read

Find the river valleys of eastern Colorado on a map. In your notebook, list the names of major cities located on these rivers. Explain how you think rivers and cities are connected.

planted potatoes, tomatoes, cabbages, onions, eggplants, beets, peas, and beans. The farm provided Byers with all the food he needed. The crops he sold paid him about $3,000 a year. Many miners took his advice.

Farmers grew some crops to sell for cash. They included food crops, wheat, corn, and fruit. John McBroom planted fruit trees and sold apples and plums to miners. Farmers in the Arkansas River Valley planted melons. Hay was a major cash crop. Miners needed hay to feed their horses. Farmers cut and

Farmers who settled on the plains in the 1870s used plows made of steel.

baled the wild grass that grew along the South Platte River. They sold the hay for $100 a wagonload in the mining towns.

Farmers Irrigate Their Fields

The first farms along the Front Range were close to a river or stream. Farmers had to irrigate their crops, as less than fifteen inches of rain and snow fell per year. Most crops require at least twenty inches a year. Farmers dug ditches to bring water from the nearest stream to their fields.

Large canals soon replaced these small ditches. In 1870 farmers at Greeley dug a canal big enough to serve dozens of farms. In other places, businesspeople dug canals and sold farmers water for a profit. Most of the rainfall and snowmelt came during the spring. To store water for the summer, farmers dug lakes and ponds.

Irrigation ditch on the plains

Skills and Tools for Learning

Time Lines

Time lines are useful tools. They help us see events in the order in which they happened. Time lines do this by using dates. The following time line has a beginning date (1855) and an ending date (1875). The space between each date equals five years.

Settlement in Colorado

1855 1860 1865 1870 1875

When Events Happened

We can place events either above or below the dates on the time line with a connecting line to show when they happened. Placing events close together or far apart shows how little or how much time passed between them.

Make Your Own Time Line

To make your own Settlement in Colorado time line, copy the 1855–1875 time line in your notebook. Select the five or six events from chapters 9 and 10 that you think were the most important events of this time. Include one or two that took place elsewhere in the United States.

Other Kinds of Time Lines

You can make other kinds of time lines. To create an illustrated time line, draw a picture for each event that you included. Making a time line on the classroom floor will allow you to "walk through time." By standing in front of the classroom, students representing historical events can make a human time line.

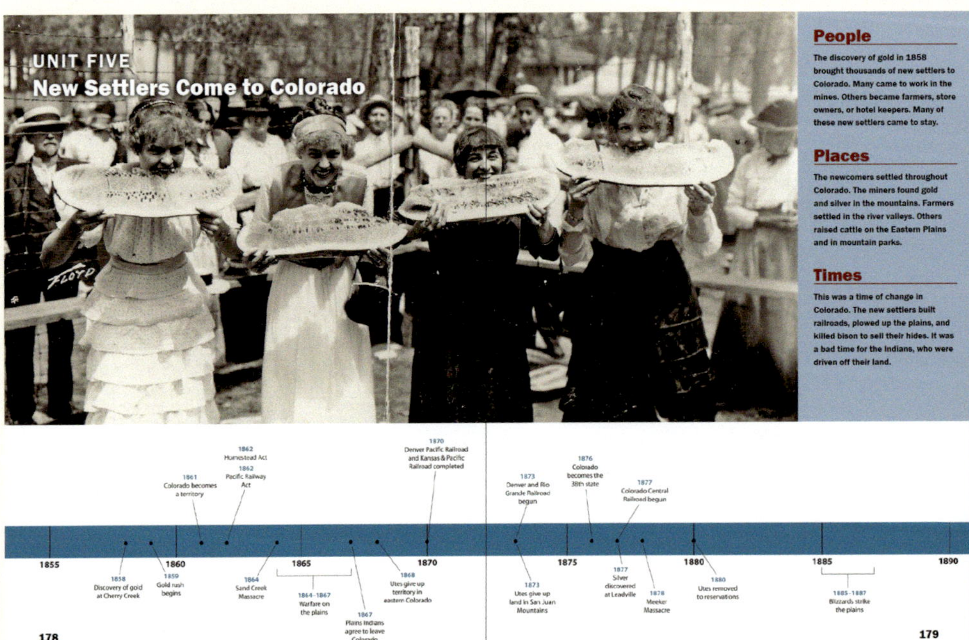

UNIT FIVE
New Settlers Come to Colorado

People

The discovery of gold in 1858 brought thousands of new settlers to Colorado. Many came to work in the mines. Others became farmers, store owners, or hotel keepers. Many of these new settlers came to stay.

Places

The newcomers settled throughout Colorado. The miners found gold and silver in the mountains. Farmers settled in the river valleys. Others raised cattle on the Eastern Plains and in mountain parks.

Times

This was a time of change in Colorado. The new settlers built railroads, plowed up the plains, and killed bison to sell their hides. It was a bad time for the Indians, who were driven off their land.

1855 1860 1865 1870 1875 1880 1885 1890

1858 Discovery of gold at Cherry Creek
1859 Gold rush begins
1861 Colorado becomes a territory
1862 Homestead Act
1862 Pacific Railway Act
1864 Sand Creek Massacre
1864–1867 Warfare on the plains
1867 Plains Indians agree to leave Colorado
1868 Utes give up territory in eastern Colorado
1870 Denver Pacific Railroad and Kansas & Pacific Railroad completed
1873 Denver and Rio Grande Railroad begun
1873 Utes give up land in San Juan Mountains
1876 Colorado becomes the 38th state
1877 Silver discovered at Leadville
1877 Colorado Central Railroad begun
1878 Meeker Massacre
1880 Utes removed to reservations
1885–1887 Blizzards strike the plains

178

179

An example of a time line

Crop Days

Colorado farmers took pride in the crops that were their specialty. As Richard T. Ely, a visitor to the state, reported in *Harper's Monthly Magazine* in 1902, "It is customary in various parts of Colorado to have an annual celebration . . . connected in each case with the harvesting of the crop which, in the particular section, plays the chief role. At Rocky Ford we have a melon day; in Boulder, the strawberry day; in Grand Junction the peach day; and in Greeley, the potato day."

Farmers along the Arkansas River grew melons. The town of Rocky Ford celebrated Melon Day.

CATTLE RAISING

The first cattle along the Front Range were oxen used to pull freight wagons across the plains. Many of the "bull whackers," as the drivers were called, stayed to look for gold. They turned the oxen loose on the plains to survive as best they could. The next spring the bull whackers found that their animals had not only survived, they had put on weight. The plains grass was like hay. Dried in the summer heat, it kept its nutrients. The plains were a natural, year-round cattle pasture.

Some settlers began raising cattle. At first, the market for beef was small. The stock raisers sold their cattle to meat markets in Denver and in the mining camps. That changed after

A cowboy

Focus Your Reading

- Why were the plains a good place to raise cattle?
- Where did the cattle come from?
- How did cattlemen tell which cattle belonged to them?
- Why did cattlemen begin fencing the open range?

While You Read

As you read about "open-range" cattle raising, choose one word or phrase each to describe its advantages and disadvantages. Write these words in your notebook, along with quotes from the text that support your choices.

1870, when the first railroad reached Colorado. The railroads hauled carloads of cattle to eastern markets.

Most of the cattle in Colorado came from Texas. Each spring, Texas cowboys rounded up wild longhorn cattle and drove them north. In Colorado, cattlemen bought the herds and turned the cattle out to graze on the plains.

Cattle on the Open Range

John W. Iliff usually kept 10,000 to 15,000 cattle on his range. He paid about eleven dollars a head for them. He could sell them within two years for thirty dollars a head. The Prairie Cattle Company had as many as 54,000 cattle on its range south of the Arkansas River. Raising cattle on the **open range** was a good business. Cowboys worked for low wages, and the grass was free.

Thousands of cattle grazed on the unfenced plains. To keep track of who owned which cattle, each owner marked his cattle with a distinctive **brand**. Cowboys from the different ranches rounded up their cattle twice each year. The spring roundup was held to brand new calves. The fall roundup separated out the steers to be sold.

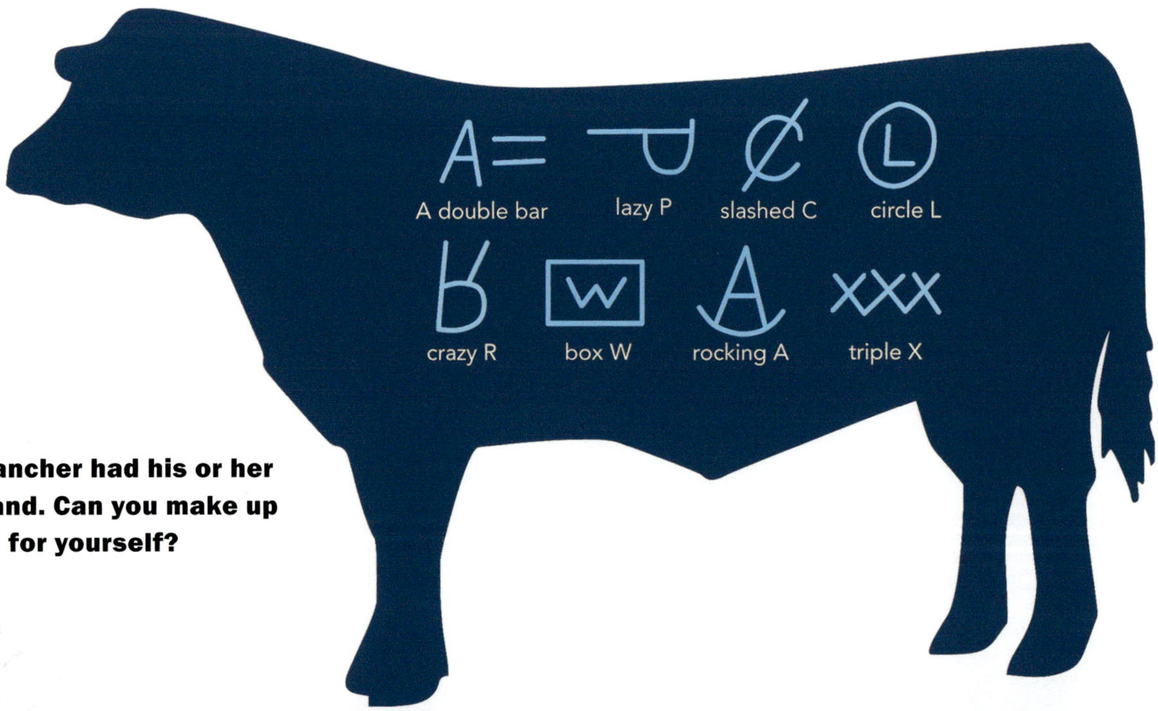

Every rancher had his or her own brand. Can you make up a brand for yourself?

Texas longhorn cow

Texas Longhorn Cattle

By the 1870s, most of the cattle on the Colorado plains were longhorn cattle. Spanish settlers had brought this breed of cattle to Mexico in the 1500s. Three hundred years later, thousands of wild longhorns grazed on the Texas plains. Cowboys rounded them up and drove them north to buyers in Kansas, Colorado, and other states.

The open-range cattle business was short-lived. By the mid-1880s, the open range was overstocked. The cattle barely had enough grass to survive. Then came two harsh winters. Blizzards in 1885 wiped out thousands of starving cattle. A blizzard the next winter killed even more. That brought an end to the open-range cattle business. After that, the cattle were fenced in. The cattlemen fed their herds hay during the winter.

Cattle in corral

A Sod House

"No more pleasant or delightful house can be built than those old sod houses of the Platte valley," wrote Clara H. Erlich, who lived in one when she was a child. "The great thickness of the walls and their perfect joining with the earth itself provided a shelter so cozy and proof against the extremes of either heat or cold that no housewife who had once lived in one cared to abandon it completely" (Clara Hilderman Ehrlich, "My Childhood on the Prairie"). People who built larger frame houses often kept the sod house as a kitchen.

Sod house on the Colorado plains

Focus Your Reading

- Why did settlers try to raise crops on the plains?
- How did they build houses on the plains?
- What are dryland farming methods?

PLAINS FARMING

In the 1880s, hundreds of farm families settled on the plains of eastern Colorado. They arrived in covered wagons and low-fare railroad cars. The railroads provided cheap transportation, as they had land to sell. They advertised the plains as the nation's new "rain belt," even though it was an arid region. The settlers had no reason to doubt it. "It was in the early summer and everything was green and thriving," wrote Thomas Sisk, who brought his family to eastern Colorado in 1889. The ads did not say that the mid-1880s had been a period of wet years.

Sod Houses

As soon as the settlers arrived, they built houses. These were **sod houses**, as few trees grew on the plains. To build a sod house, the settlers plowed up strips of sod. They built the walls by laying one strip on top of another. They placed poles across the walls to support a roof, also made of sod. Sod houses, they discovered, had real benefits. The thick walls kept the houses cool in summer and warm in winter. The only problem was the roof, which tended to leak mud during a hard rain.

As long as the wet years continued, the settlers did well. They planted corn, wheat, and other crops that grew well in a moist climate. They had good harvests. But in 1889 the rain stopped.

End of the Wet Years

For the next ten years, most summers were hot and dry. Crops wilted and died in the fields. Farmers could not irrigate because the plains' shallow streams also dried up.

Most of the settlers returned to the Midwest. Some could not leave, as they had gone into debt to buy their farms. The banks wanted their money back. "A great many people have left the country, in fact nearly all that could get

While You Read

Copy these sentences into your notebook and then complete them:

- The farmers who stayed learned how to farm in an ____________ region.
- They began to use ____________ methods.
- These methods included ________________.
- Farmers also learned to ________________.

Farmworkers cutting wheat with horse-pulled machines

Farmers brought bundles of wheat from the fields in wagons. They pitched the bundles into a separator or threshing machine. It separated the grain from the stems. The grain was collected in bags. The stems were blown into piles of straw.

away, for there are so many mortgages that compel people to stay," a girl in Burlington, Colorado, wrote in 1894. "A few families left in the night." The Thomas Sisk family left. They lost most of the $10,000 they had invested in their farm.

Dryland Farming

The farmers who stayed learned how to farm in an arid region. They began to use "dryland farming" methods. These methods included plowing the earth to a greater depth. Deep plowing brought more moisture to the surface. Farmers also learned to plow the fields after a rain to keep the moisture from evaporating. They also planted crops such as winter wheat and **sorghum**, which did better in an arid climate.

Focus Your Reading

- What work did different family members do?
- Why did neighbors get together?
- What purposes did towns serve?
- How were colony towns different?

FAMILIES, NEIGHBORHOODS, AND COMMUNITIES

Cheap land attracted settlers to Colorado. To help settle the West, the US Congress passed the Homestead Act in 1862. This law allowed any adult to claim 160 acres of government land at virtually no cost. The land belonged to the "home-steader" after he or she paid a small fee, built a house, and lived in it for five years. Many settlers claimed land under this act of Congress. Settlers could also buy land from some of the railroads. Those that received public land from the government sold it to settlers as fast as they could. They needed farmers to raise crops they could ship to markets in the East.

While You Read

Take turns reading each paragraph in this section out loud with a partner. Each time you finish your reading, explain in your own words what the paragraph says.

Family Life

Most settlers in **rural** Colorado had families. The husband often came out first to buy land and build a house. His wife and children soon followed. The few single men who lived there were cowboys or hired farmhands. Every member of the family had work to do. Men worked in the fields, took care of **livestock**, and herded cattle. Women took care of the garden, raised chickens, and milked the cows. They also cooked, cleaned house, and cared for the children. The children had chores to do. They helped feed farm animals, weeded the garden, and helped their parents.

The early settlers were good neighbors. They helped one another build their houses, harvest crops, and care for the sick. They invited neighbors over for dances, religious services, and holidays such as the Fourth of July.

The Gully Homestead in Aurora, Colorado, was founded in 1871.

One-Room Schools

Starting a school also brought neighbors together. A one-room schoolhouse was often their first public building. On the plains, it was most likely made of sod. The teacher might be the teenage daughter of one of the families. She mainly taught reading, writing, and arithmetic. School was also a social occasion for the children. At lunchtime they played tag, hide-and-seek, and pom-pom-pull-away. Boys also played games with marbles. Older children went to school only during the winter. They had to work on the farm from spring until fall. Summer school was only for young children.

Farm Towns

Each rural area had at least one small town. It usually had a general store, a **blacksmith** shop, a flour mill, and a post office. The post office was frequently part of the general store. Towns were like service stations that supplied farmers with things they needed. On Saturdays, farm families came to town to sell butter and eggs, buy supplies, pick up their mail, and chat with friends.

Greeley was named for Horace Greeley.

Some farm communities in Colorado were "colony" towns. That is, they were settled by groups of people who came to Colorado together. People from New York City founded the town of Greeley. After sending an agent to buy land, the people arrived and laid out the town. Most of the new settlers built houses in town. They walked out to their fields each day. A group from Chicago started a colony at Longmont. The towns of Colfax, Evans, Fort Collins, and Sterling began as colonies. The Mormon Church founded colonies in the San Luis Valley at Ephraim, Manassa, Richfield, and Sanford.

Learning from Primary Sources

One-Room Schools

One-room schools were common on the plains of eastern Colorado. They also served as community centers. What do these primary sources tell you about the advantages and disadvantages of the rural schools?

Benches

"There were about twelve pupils. We sat in high straight benches that a carpenter had made. They were much too high and our feet seldom touched the floor. At class time we recited from a big long bench up near the teacher's desk."

Mrs. Jennie Lucas, "Pioneer Education"

Plenty of Activity

"I still have a soft spot in my heart for the one-room school. It is true, perhaps, that you cannot have as many activities—of some kinds—as you can in graded schools. But, when you put eighteen or twenty kids, ages six to sixteen together, you will have plenty of activity. While one class was reciting, the rest were supposed to be studying. You usually listen in, however, to the grades ahead of you because you would be covering the same ground later on."

Glenn R. Durrell, "Homesteading in Colorado"

Community Centers

"During the winter of 1887, school was held in a little one-story one-room building, and one of the popular entertainment[s] during that winter was a spelling school which was always held on Friday night and which not only the school children, but the entire population in and around Springfield attended. They chose up sides, getting everybody into the game."

A. W. McHendrie, "Boyhood Recollections of Springfield, Colorado"

- **How were one-room schools most different from your school?**
- **Was learning in a one-room school easier or more difficult?**

One-room log schoolhouse

Focus Your Reading

- How are territories and states different from each other?
- What branches of government did the new constitution create?
- Whom did the Colorado Constitution not allow to vote?

While You Read

In your notebook, list the steps involved in a territory becoming a state.

STATEHOOD AND STATE GOVERNMENT

August 1, 1876, was a day of celebration in Colorado. On that day, President Ulysses S. Grant proclaimed Colorado a state. This meant that Coloradans were citizens equal to those of other states. They could enact their own laws, vote in presidential elections, and elect their governor and state officials. Since 1861, Colorado had been a territory. Residents of territories could send delegates to Congress, but those delegates could not vote on laws. Delegates are people others elect to act for them. They now were full partners with other states in deciding the nation's future.

Colorado Becomes a State

Colorado's residents had taken the first step toward statehood in December 1875, when they elected delegates to write a state **constitution**. A constitution describes how a government is organized and what powers it has. The new constitution was based on the Constitution of the United States. It created three divisions, or branches, of government. The General Assembly had the power to make laws, the Executive to carry them out, and the Court System to settle disputes. The General Assembly was divided into a Senate and a House of Representatives. The powers of government were separated into different branches to keep any one of them from becoming too powerful. After three months, the delegates completed their work and returned home.

President Ulysses S. Grant

The year 1876 and the nickname the "Centennial State" can be found in many places in Colorado.

The constitution was then submitted to the people for their approval. On July 1, the new constitution was ratified, or approved, by a 15,443-to-4,062 vote. A month later, the people of Colorado received the good news that President Grant had approved their request for statehood. As 1876 was the centennial, or 100th anniversary, of the Declaration of Independence, they called their state the "Centennial State."

Women Cannot Vote

Colorado's new constitution created a democratic form of government but did not give everyone the right to vote. Only men over age twenty-one could vote. Many men in the 1800s believed that women's place was in the home, not in public life and politics. Women were angry that they did not have the right to vote. Only later did Colorado become a leader in giving full political rights to women.

Utes attacked army wagons on their way to the White River Agency.

Focus Your Reading

- Where was the Utes' reservation?
- What happened to Nathan Meeker?
- For what crops is the Grand Valley best known?

THE UTES AND THE WESTERN SLOPE

In 1873, the United States signed another **treaty** with the Utes. The Utes agreed to give up still more land. They kept most of the Western Slope, which was closed to white settlement. This reservation included two government agencies. These were places where the Utes could go for supplies. All went well until 1878, when Nathan Meeker arrived at the White River Agency.

The Meeker Massacre

As the man in charge of the agency, Meeker decided to teach the Utes how to farm. In fact, the Utes hated farming. They preferred to ride horses and hunt bison. When Meeker plowed up the Utes' horse pasture and racetrack, they

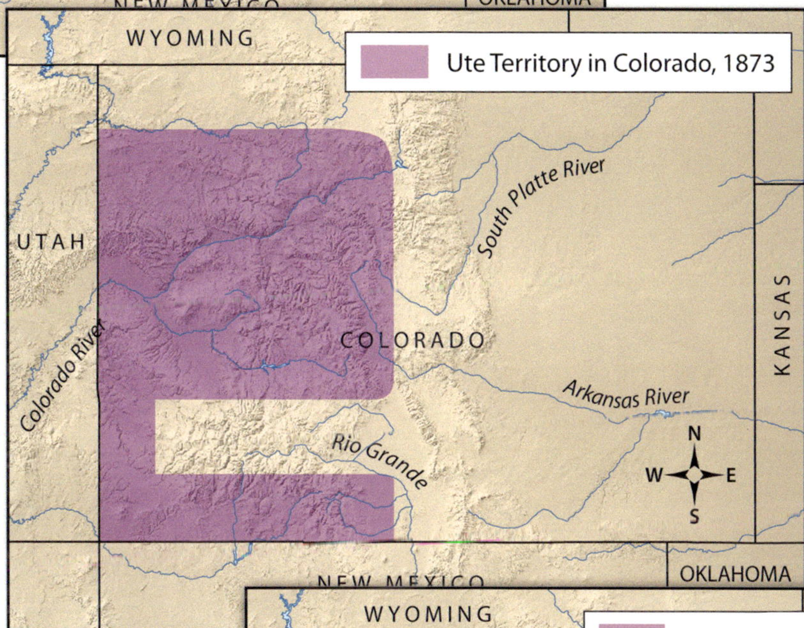

Ute territory in Colorado shrank dramatically between 1868 and 1882.

Schools for Ute Children

At first, the Ute reservations had no schools. The Indian agent sent the children away to boarding schools. These schools forced them to wear non-Indian clothing and to speak English. Boys had to cut their hair short. Several children died trying to run away. After Ute parents refused to send their children away, the government opened schools on the reservations.

While You Read

Find this quote in the text: "The Meeker Massacre, as white people in Colorado called it . . ." What do you know about Nathan Meeker and the Utes that helps you understand what the authors are inferring? Talk about this in your small group.

rebelled. Meeker escaped the first attack unharmed. Then he called in the army, which made the Utes angry. They fought the troops when they arrived, killing fourteen soldiers. Then they attacked the White River Agency, killing Meeker and eleven other men.

The Meeker Massacre, as white people in Colorado called it, was a disaster for the Utes. "The Utes Must Go!" a Denver newspaper demanded. Most people agreed. As a result, the government forced the Utes to sign a new treaty. It removed the Northern Ute bands to Utah. It placed the Southern Utes on a small reservation in the Four Corners area.

Nathan Meeker

Soldiers lead the Utes out of Colorado.

New Settlers Arrive

In September 1881, the Western Slope was opened to settlers. Town builders and farmers rushed into the Grand River (now Colorado River) Valley. They laid out a new town called Grand Junction. A merchant pitched a tent and opened a store. The town soon had a hotel, a schoolhouse, and a jail built of logs. That winter, the settlers dug ditches to irrigate their fields. They planted crops the next spring.

Elam Blaine, an early settler, planted an orchard on his farm. The trees did well in the Grand Valley's mild climate. The valley soon had dozens of apple and peach orchards. At first, the growers sold their fruit to the mining camps. After railroads were built, they shipped fruit to towns and cities along the Front Range. The Grand Valley became well-known throughout Colorado for its fruit.

Peaches

Modern-day peach orchard in Grand Valley

Peach orchard near Grand Junction

While You Read

Make a Venn diagram in your notebook to compare early farming in Colorado with farming today. How are they alike? How are they different?

FARMING TODAY

Farming is still important in Colorado. Half of the state's 31.3 million acres is farmland. Farming is one of the top three businesses in the state. Among the fifty states, Colorado ranks close to the top in the amount of potatoes, sugar beets, and winter wheat its farmers raise. The number of pigs raised has doubled during the past decade or so. Many small cities and towns in eastern Colorado exist mainly to serve nearby farms and ranches.

While farming is still important, it is no longer a growing business. The number of Colorado farms—about 30,000—has changed little during the past forty years. In fact, farming uses less land today than in years past. Since 1992, Colorado has lost an average of 270,000 acres of

farmland and ranchland each year. Most of it was farmland on the edge of cities that was used to build houses. The number of people who live and work on farms has dropped.

Gasoline-powered combines harvest wheat today in a single operation.

How can fewer farmers raise more crops on less land? Irrigation is part of the answer. By drilling deep wells, farmers have turned cattle pasture into cropland. Ranchers once used most of the Eastern Plains to graze cattle. They needed several acres of land to graze one steer or cow. With irrigation, that same land can produce truckloads of corn or sugar beets. Bigger and better machines are also part of the answer. A farmer driving a huge tractor or harvester can do the work of several farmers of years past.

After You Read

1. Skim this chapter again. Then close your book and complete a two-column organizer in your notebook labeled "What's Important" and "What's Interesting." Choose only **big** ideas for "What's Important" and **little** details for "What's Interesting."
2. In your notebook, write five important questions you think your partner should be able to answer after reading this chapter. Then, work with your partner and answer each other's questions. Use the text to check your answers.

Thinking about Colorado Water

Do you know . . .
who has the right to use water in Colorado?

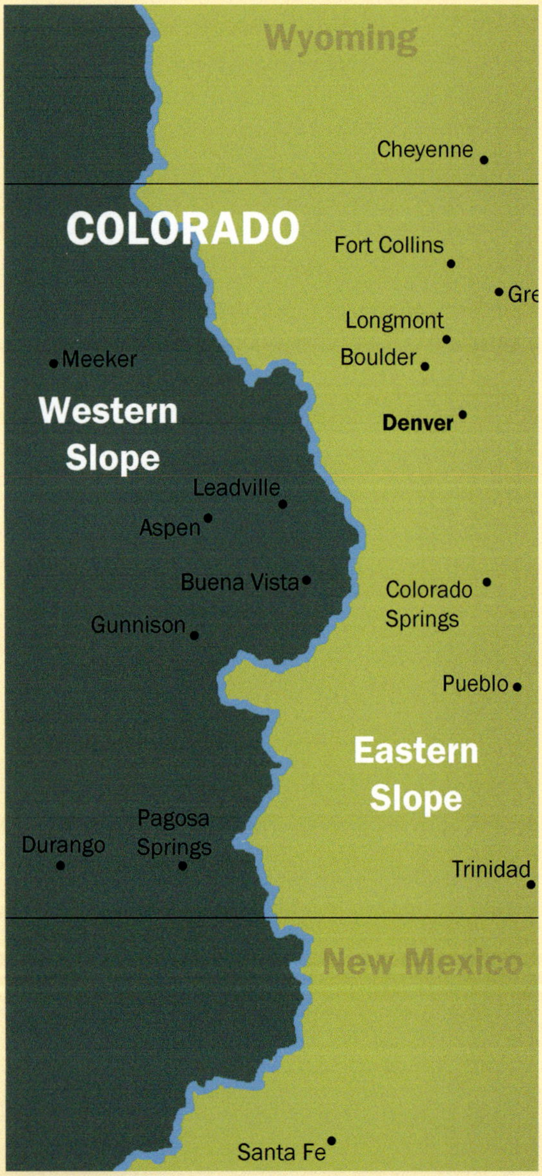

In eastern Colorado, water is scarce. Most of the farms and cities are located there, but most of the rain and snow falls on the Western Slope. The region does not have enough for everyone to have all the water they need.

Have you ever wondered how Colorado decides who gets water and who doesn't?

The rule for using water is part of the 1876 state constitution. It was included because Colorado's water is owned by the people. The constitution decided who has the right to use it.

The Colorado water rule is called "first in time, first in right." It means that the first people to put water to a good use have the right to use all they need. Those who come later can use what they need, if it is not needed by the first users.

In a dry season, the early, or "senior," users can put a "call" or claim on water used by the late-arrivers, or "junior," users.

People with even later claims get to use the water that no one else needs. In dry years, that may be none at all.

Newcomers can buy water rights from people who arrived earlier, but water rights are very expensive.

- Is "first in time, first in right" a good water-use rule?
- Is it a fair rule for using a scarce resource?
- Would you divide it equally, although it might not leave enough water for anyone?
- Can you think of a better rule?

Asking Historical Questions
Your Response

This chapter began with this question:

How and why was farming in eastern Colorado different from farming in the San Luis Valley?

1. **Review**
   Review the information in your notes and in this chapter about why settlers in eastern Colorado sold crops for cash and bought things they needed instead of being self-sufficient.
2. **Reflect**
   With a partner or in a small group, discuss why settlers in eastern Colorado did not become self-sufficient like farmers in southern Colorado.
3. **Respond**
   In your notebook, explain why settlers in eastern Colorado chose this way of life.

UNIT SIX

Colorado in Modern Times

- **1890** Gold discovered at Cripple Creek
- **1893** Colorado women get the right to vote
- **1899** First sugar beet crop
- **1902–1907** President Roosevelt creates National Forests in Colorado
- **1910** Dearfield founded
- **1914** Ludlow Massacre
- **1914–1918** World War I
- **1915** Rocky Mountain National Park created
- **1918** Climax Molybdenum Mine opens
- **1920** First radio station
- **1929** Great Depression begins
- **1929–1941** Great Depression
- **1937** Work begins on Colorado–Big Thompson
- **1941** Pearl Harbor
- **1941–1945** United States involved in World War II
- **1945** World War II ends
- **1948** Uranium discovered

1890 | 1900 | 1910 | 1920 | 1930 | 1940 | 195

People

The people of Colorado have become more diverse than ever before. Since 1890, new immigrants have arrived from Europe, Latin America, and Asia. Among the people of Colorado today are many Ute and Plains Indians.

Places

In modern times, people have found new ways to use Colorado's land. Farmers now grow food where bison herds grazed. Skiers enjoy the mountainsides that once produced gold and silver.

Times

In modern times, the people of Colorado have seen good times and bad times. New inventions have made life easier. Blizzards, dust storms, and the Great Depression brought hard times to many.

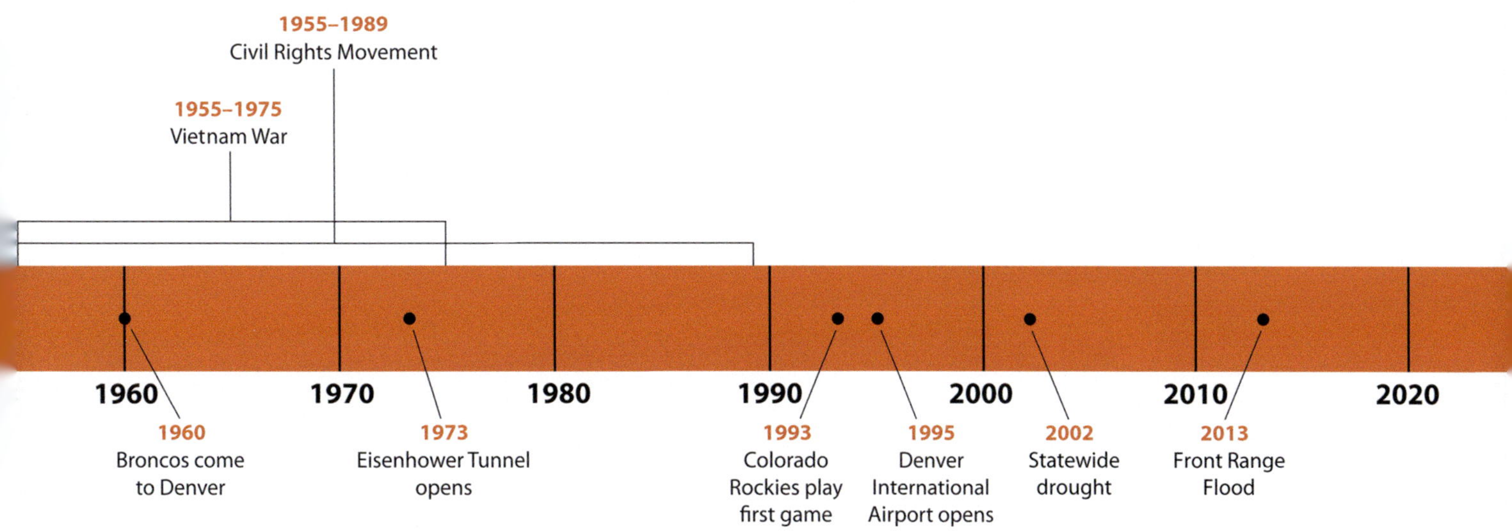

Government and Citizenship

Before You Read

Copy these statements into your notebook. Then, based on what you now know or think, write "Agree" or "Disagree" under each statement. When you have finished reading about government and citizenship, come back to your answers and change them if necessary.

1. The only reason governments exist is to make laws that tell us what we can and cannot do.
2. All governments are democratic, which means that ordinary people are in control.
3. Our right to say whatever we want to say is protected by the US Constitution.
4. As citizens we do not need to know much about important issues, as they are decided by our elected representatives.

KEY-WORDS

- **democracy**
- **constitution**
- **limited government**
- **separation of powers**
- **checks and balances**
- **representative democracies**
- **citizens**
- **citizenship**

WHAT DO GOVERNMENTS DO?

Governments do many things that improve our daily lives. Yet we seldom stop to think about them. What is government? What does it look like? Here are some common scenes that show government at work:

- a police car with its lights flashing
- a school under construction
- a street repair crew at work
- a fighter jet soaring overhead
- a nurse entering a hospital
- a judge leaving a courthouse

Focus Your Reading

- What do governments do that affects you?
- What kind of government does the United States and Colorado have?
- What are your rights and responsibilities as a citizen?

- a state senator voting on a new tax
- a park or a zoo

These everyday scenes describe some of the tasks governments perform. They include:

- enforcing the laws
- building schools and educating children
- providing public services
- defending the nation
- providing health services
- settling disputes
- making new laws
- providing recreation

Reflect for a moment. On a typical day, how does government affect your life? Make a list and share it with a partner.

In the United States, governments make decisions at different levels. The national government in Washington, DC, makes laws for all the people. It also protects the nation, prints money, and decides when to go to war. State governments provide services for citizens of that state. County and town governments make decisions only for the people who live at the local level. School districts are set up to govern a city's schools. Some rural areas have "service districts" that provide a single service. This may be fire protection, public safety, or water treatment. All levels are important, but here we will focus on Colorado's state government.

US Capitol

Our Government at Work

The House of Representatives chamber in the Colorado capitol building, Denver, Colorado

Policeman

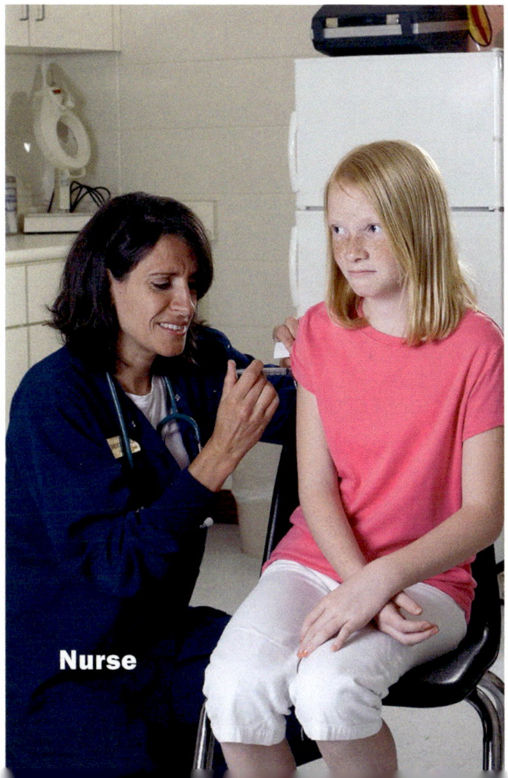

Nurse

Zoo animal

School bus

Street repa

Judge

Fighter jet

Our Government at Work

Mesa Verde National Park

King George III of the United Kingdom

Napoleon Bonaparte, Emperor of France

Joseph Stalin, Soviet dictator

WHAT KIND OF GOVERNMENT DO WE HAVE?

Not all governments are alike. The United States has a democratic form of government. So does Colorado. In a **democracy**, power comes from the people. Not all governments are democratic. In some governments, power is held by a single person. In the past, this person was usually a king, queen, or emperor. This type of government is called a monarchy. A government today that carries out the orders of a single person is called a dictatorship. When a small group of people hold power, the government is called an aristocracy. When these people are army officers, it is a military junta. Those governments do not govern with the consent or agreement of the people.

To create their democracy, Coloradans in 1876 used the US national government as their model. They have the following in common.

While You Read

Read the section "What Kind of Government Do We Have" with a partner. Decide on a stopping point about halfway through. When you reach it, each partner must ask a question or state an opinion about either the government of the United States or the government of Colorado.

A Written Constitution

First, both are based on a written **constitution** or document. Some governments, such as Great Britain's, are based on many documents and court cases. A written constitution makes clear what powers people are giving to the government.

Limited Government

Both governments are **limited governments**. That is, the powers given to the government are limited and clearly spelled out. The governments do not have powers that would violate people's rights, such as freedom of speech.

US Constitution

We the People of the United States, in Order to form a more perfect Union, establish Justice, insure domestic Tranquility, provide for the common defence, promote the general Welfare, and secure the Blessings of Liberty to ourselves and our Posterity, do ordain and establish this Constitution for the United States of America.

Article. I.

Section. 1. All legislative Powers herein granted shall be vested in a Congress of the United States, which shall consist of a Senate and House of Representatives.

Section. 2. The House of Representatives shall be composed of Members chosen every second Year by the People of the several States, and the Electors in each State shall have the Qualifications requisite for Electors of the most numerous Branch of the State Legislature.

No Person shall be a Representative who shall not have attained to the Age of twenty five Years, and been seven Years a Citizen of the United States, and who shall not, when elected, be an Inhabitant of that State in which he shall be chosen.

Representatives and direct Taxes shall be apportioned among the several States which may be included within this Union, according to their respective Numbers, which shall be determined by adding to the whole Number of free Persons, including those bound to Service for a Term of Years, and excluding Indians not taxed, three fifths of all other Persons. The actual Enumeration shall be made within three Years after the first Meeting of the Congress of the United States, and within every subsequent Term of ten Years, in such Manner as they shall by Law direct. The Number of Representatives shall not exceed one for every thirty Thousand, but each State shall have at Least one Representative; and until such enumeration shall be made, the State of New Hampshire shall be entitled to chuse three, Massachusetts eight, Rhode-Island and Providence Plantations one, Connecticut five, New-York six, New Jersey four, Pennsylvania eight, Delaware one, Maryland six, Virginia ten, North Carolina five, South Carolina five, and Georgia three.

When vacancies happen in the Representation from any State, the Executive Authority thereof shall issue Writs of Election to fill such Vacancies.

The House of Representatives shall chuse their Speaker and other Officers; and shall have the sole Power of Impeachment.

Section. 3. The Senate of the United States shall be composed of two Senators from each State, chosen by the Legislature thereof for six Years; and each Senator shall have one Vote.

Immediately after they shall be assembled in Consequence of the first Election, they shall be divided as equally as may be into three Classes. The Seats of the Senators of the first Class shall be vacated at the Expiration of the second Year, of the second Class at the Expiration of the fourth Year, and of the third Class at the Expiration of the sixth Year, so that one third may be chosen every second Year; and if Vacancies happen by Resignation, or otherwise, during the Recess of the Legislature of any State, the Executive thereof may make temporary Appointments until the next Meeting of the Legislature, which shall then fill such Vacancies.

No Person shall be a Senator who shall not have attained to the Age of thirty Years, and been nine Years a Citizen of the United States, and who shall not, when elected, be an Inhabitant of that State for which he shall be chosen.

The Vice President of the United States shall be President of the Senate, but shall have no Vote, unless they be equally divided.

The Senate shall chuse their other Officers, and also a President pro tempore, in the Absence of the Vice President, or when he shall exercise the Office of President of the United States.

The Senate shall have the sole Power to try all Impeachments. When sitting for that Purpose, they shall be on Oath or Affirmation. When the President of the United States is tried, the Chief Justice shall preside: And no Person shall be convicted without the Concurrence of two thirds of the Members present.

Judgment in Cases of Impeachment shall not extend further than to removal from Office, and disqualification to hold and enjoy any Office of honor, Trust or Profit under the United States: but the Party convicted shall nevertheless be liable and subject to Indictment, Trial, Judgment and Punishment, according to Law.

Section. 4. The Times, Places and Manner of holding Elections for Senators and Representatives, shall be prescribed in each State by the Legislature thereof; but the Congress may at any time by Law make or alter such Regulations, except as to the Places of chusing Senators.

The Congress shall assemble at least once in every Year, and such Meeting shall be on the first Monday in December, unless they shall by Law appoint a different Day.

White House

Separation of Powers

A **separation of powers** also helps keep government power in check. This means that power is divided among three divisions, or branches, of government.

- **The Legislature.** At the national level, the legislature is called the US Congress. At the state level, it is known as the State Legislature. The legislative branch of government makes the laws. Congress also approves people the president appoints to important offices.
- **The Executive.** The executive branch of government carries out the laws made by the legislature. The president of the United States is the chief executive at the national level. The governor of Colorado is the head of our state executive branch.
- **The Judiciary.** The judiciary is made up of judges who work in courts to settle conflicts over laws and what they mean. They also decide whether laws

Supreme Court

conflict with the US and the Colorado Constitutions. The highest level of the judiciary is the United States Supreme Court at the national level and the Colorado Supreme Court at the state level.

Checks and Balances

A system of **checks and balances** further limits the government's power. While the legislature can pass a new law, the executive can veto or overturn it. The legislature helps keep the executive in check by voting to override a veto. The judiciary can balance the power of both by throwing out a law the US Constitution does not allow.

Representative Democracy

Colorado and the national government are **representative democracies**. Voters do not go to the State House in Denver or to the nation's Capitol in Washington, DC, to vote on legislation. Instead, they elect representatives to vote for them.

RIGHTS AND RESPONSIBILITIES OF CITIZENS

Citizens of a democracy have both rights and responsibilities. A right is the freedom to do something the government cannot take away. The rights of citizens in all fifty of the United States are protected by the US Constitution. Among the most basic rights are:

- Freedom of speech
- Freedom of religion
- Right to vote (by age eighteen)
- Right to own firearms
- Right to a trial by jury

Rights and responsibilities of citizenship: Bill of Rights

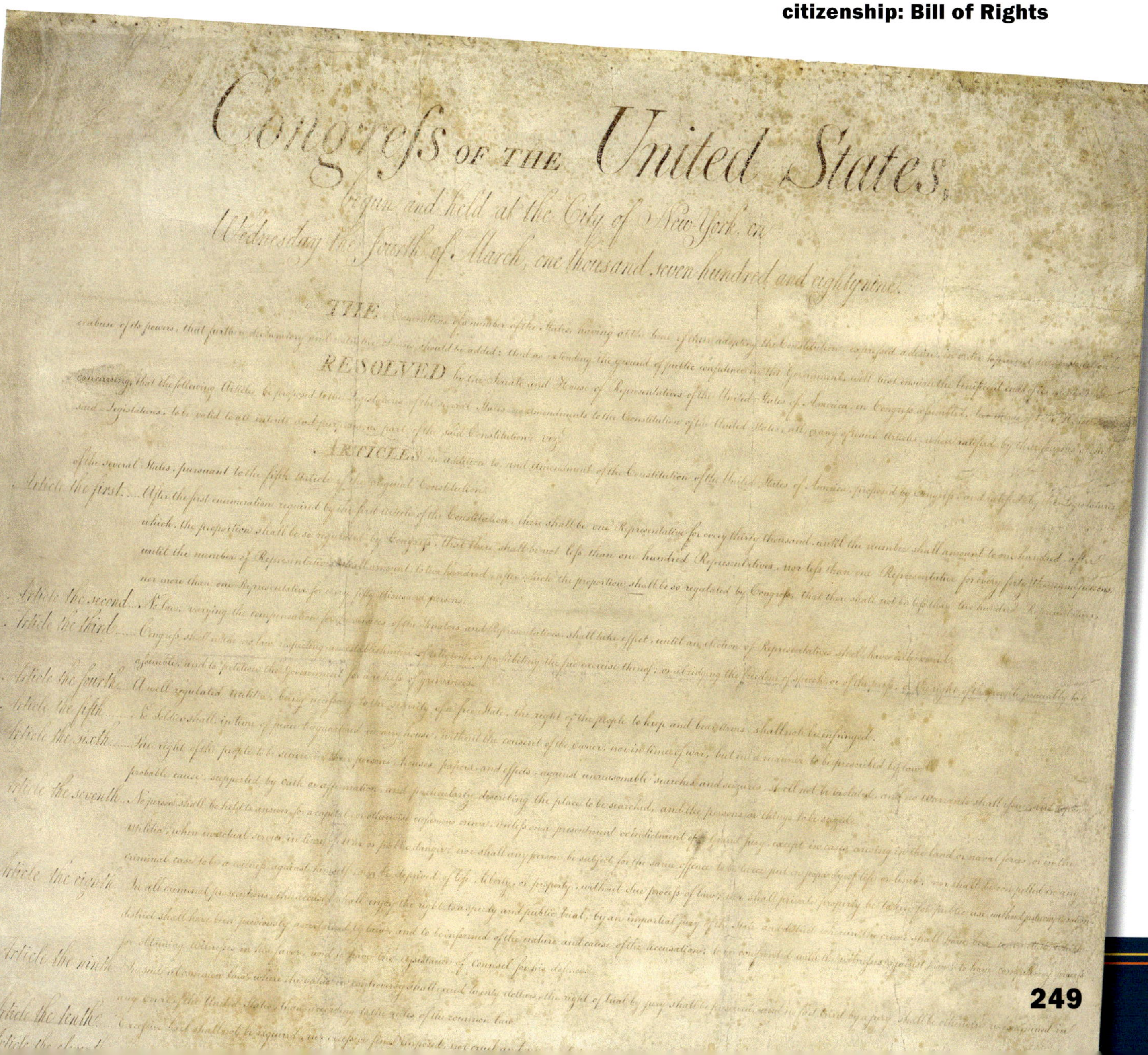
Congress of the United States,
begun and held at the City of New-York, on
Wednesday the fourth of March, one thousand seven hundred and eighty nine.

Rights and responsibilities of citizenship: a Colorado voter drops his election ballot at a ballot drop box

Rights are important, but so are the responsibilities of **citizenship**. Responsibilities of citizenship are what we must do to use our rights wisely and to protect them. They include:

- To know your rights
- To keep informed about public issues
- To be aware of different points of view
- To discuss issues with others
- To listen to other points of view
- To volunteer time to public service
- To vote at election time
- To run for public office

Colorado capitol building with gold-leaf dome

CITIZENSHIP IN A DEMOCRACY

Every citizen should be well informed about public issues. A public issue is a question or proposal that people disagree about. Why is it important to be well informed? Ordinary citizens do not decide most issues. They elect representatives to the US Congress and the State Legislature to do this for them. It is important because voters need to know how individuals running for office stand on public issues. Whether they share or do not share those views should help them decide for whom to vote. They also need to keep their elected representatives informed about issues that matter to them. Well-informed citizens make democratic government good government.

Here are public issues a well-informed citizen today should know about. Select one of these issues and find out as much as you can about it. Then outline your best argument for (Pro) or against it (Con).

School Taxes

Should taxes be increased to provide more money for public schools?

Pro: schools need more money

Con: schools already have all the money they need

Use of Fossil Fuels

Should the state discourage oil and natural gas drilling in Colorado?

Pro: fossil fuels contribute to global warming

Con: we need more oil and gas, which are Colorado's cheapest fuels

Should oil drilling be encouraged?

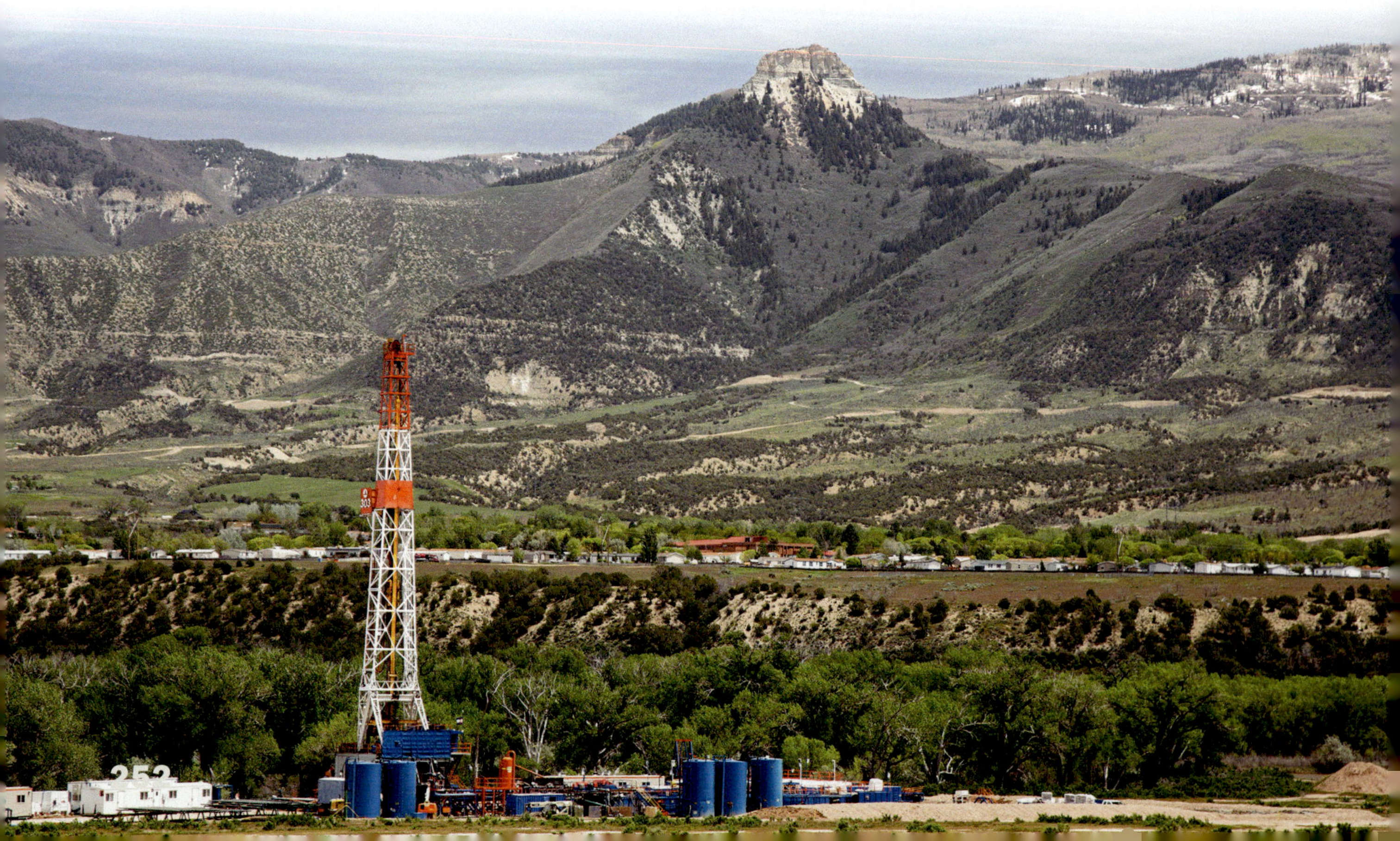

Water Diversion

Should water be diverted from one region to another?

Should Denver and other cities be allowed to divert more water from the Western Slope?

Pro: growing cities need the water more than Western Slope farmers do

Con: taking water from the Western Slope is unfair and threatens fish and wildlife

After You Read

1. Go back to the four statements you copied in your notebook before you read about government and citizenship. Based on what you knew then, you wrote "Agree" or "Disagree" under each statement.
2. Reread the statements and your responses. Do you want to change any of your responses based on what you have learned?

CHAPTER 11

Changing Times, 1890–1945

FOCUS QUESTION

How did mining, farming and ranching, and city life in Colorado change between 1890 and 1945?

Before You Read

Think about the title "Changing Times, 1890–1945." Make a two-column chart in your notebook, and then skim the chapter. In the left column of your chart, list the kinds of changes you think this chapter will describe.

KEY WORDS

- **coal mining**
- **steel mills**
- **referendum**
- **suffrage**
- **amendment**
- **conservationists**
- **Great Depression**
- **Dust Bowl**

The first years of the 1900s were a time of change in Colorado. Gold mining made a comeback. **Coal mining** became a big business. For the first time in the state's history, the majority of people lived in big towns and cities. Farmers found new cash crops. For a time, life was easier for most people. Then came hard times. During those years, life in Colorado was like a roller-coaster ride.

MINING

Most people in 1890 thought Colorado's gold and silver mining days were over. The best placer deposits were mined out. Most of the quartz mines had closed. Even the silver mines were shutting down. In fact, gold mining was ready to rebound.

Focus Your Reading

- Which Colorado mining area produced the most gold?
- What was the Ludlow Massacre?
- What minerals did Colorado produce besides gold and coal?

Cripple Creek Gold

For years, a cowboy named Robert Womack had looked for gold near Pikes Peak. People called him "Crazy Bob." No one had ever found gold at Pikes Peak. In October 1890 he

Fourth of July parade in Cripple Creek, 1898

Cripple Creek Gold

Most miners thought Pikes Peak was the least likely place on Earth to find gold. For thirty years, prospectors panning the mountain's streams had come up empty-handed. Most of Pikes Peak was made up of coarse, pink granite with no trace of gold. The gold seekers had overlooked Cripple Creek, a little stream that flowed down a western spur of the mountain. Under it lay North America's largest concentration of gold ore.

While You Read

Look at the coal mining photo on the next page. How was coal mining like earlier gold and silver mining? How was it different? Talk about this with a partner.

found a rock in Cripple Creek that had tiny flecks of gold. He showed it to people in nearby Colorado Springs. They laughed at him. Gold at Pikes Peak? Not likely. Womack gave up. He sold his claim for a few hundred dollars.

A carpenter named Winfield S. Stratton did take Womack seriously. He set out for Cripple Creek. In 1891 he found the richest vein of gold ever discovered in Colorado. He later sold this mine for $10 million. Miners and town builders rushed in. Ten years later, 50,000 people were living in the Cripple Creek mining region. By then it had produced more gold than all the mines of Colorado since the Gold Rush.

Coal Mining

Colorado also still had coal mines in 1890. The early gold seekers had found coal in the hillsides. The richest veins were south of Pueblo and north of Denver. At first, there was little demand for this fuel. Blacksmiths used it in their forges because coal produced a hot heat. Everyone else burned wood in their stoves and fireplaces.

The demand for coal grew over time. Smelters, stamp mills, **steel mills**, and railroads needed coal. Coal mining companies opened deep underground mines. They hired thousands of workers to dig out the coal.

Portal to a coal mine in Las Animas County, Colorado

Miners digging coal in a mine near Lafayette, Colorado

Immigrant Miners

The coal companies hired immigrants to work in the mines. By 1900, most workers were Italians, Greeks, and eastern Europeans. Miners in southern Colorado had to live in houses owned by the company. They paid high prices for groceries at the company store. The mines were not safe places to work. Fires and explosions killed dozens of miners each year.

In 1913, miners near Trinidad went on strike. That is, they walked away from their jobs in protest. They wanted higher pay and safer mines. The owners locked them out of the company houses. Then they brought in new workers to replace them. That made the strikers angry.

To protect the new workers, the governor of Colorado sent in state guard troops. On April 20, 1914, the soldiers attacked the strikers' tent city at Ludlow Station. Five miners and one soldier were killed. During the attack, the miners' tents were set on fire. The fire killed two women and eleven children. The attack is known as the Ludlow Massacre.

The ruins of the tent city after the Ludlow Massacre

Climax molybdenum mine near Leadville

Molybdenum

Other Minerals

For years, silver miners in Boulder County had cursed the "worthless black iron" that got in their way. In time, they realized that the "black iron" was a mineral called tungsten. Toolmakers used it to strengthen the edges of steel drill bits. Boulder County became the nation's largest producer of tungsten. Miners also discovered molybdenum, another metal used to harden steel. In 1918 the Climax Molybdenum Company opened a mine at Climax, Colorado. The mine became the nation's leading producer of this rare mineral.

While You Read

The authors state that "the railroads were one of the state's biggest employers." How did railroads affect urban growth? Write an explanation in your notebook, and discuss what you have written with a partner.

URBAN GROWTH

By 1900, nearly half of Colorado's people lived in large towns and cities. The state's largest cities in 1900 were Denver, Pueblo, and Colorado Springs. People lived there because that's where they found work. Denver and other cities hired factory and office workers. Immigrants from Europe got jobs in Pueblo's steel mills. Resort towns like Colorado Springs and Estes Park hired people to work in hotels and cafés.

Serving food in a railroad dining car

Focus Your Reading

- What jobs did the railroads provide?
- What work did people do in Colorado's towns and cities?
- What changes took place in long-distance transportation?

Transportation

Denver was Colorado's railroad and airline hub. When they traveled long distances, most people went by train. The Moffat Tunnel, opened in 1927, gave Denver a direct link to Salt Lake City. It was the first railroad tunnel through the Front Range. In 1919 the city got its first airport. It was later named Stapleton Airport, for Benjamin Stapleton, a Denver mayor. The first daily flights between Denver and cities on the East and West Coasts began in 1937. Beginning that year, United Airlines flew two flights each day with twin-engine DC-3 airplanes.

The railroads were one of the state's biggest employers. Men called "section hands" repaired the rails and roadbeds. The railroad shops in Denver hired men to repair locomotives and build railroad cars. African Americans got jobs as sleeping-car porters or attendants and dining-car cooks. They took care of people who traveled long distances.

Denver's Stapleton Airport, 1941

Making tomato juice in a food-canning factory

Factories

The factories in Denver provided thousands of jobs. The Hendrie and Bolthoff Company made mining machinery. In 1899, Denver's ore smelters employed 1,800 men. Hundreds more worked at the Denver stockyards and in food-canning factories. In 1910, Jesse Shwayder opened a factory to make trunks and suitcases. The company still makes Samsonite luggage. Charles and John Gates started the Gates Rubber Company in Denver in 1914. It made auto tires and water hoses.

FARMING AND RANCHING

The early 1900s were good times for farmers. In Colorado, the drought was over. Farmers sold more of their crops.

While You Read

Divide a notebook page in half vertically. Label the left column "Important Points" and the right column "My Responses." As you read, write important words and phrases on the left side that will help you remember this section. When you finish reading, write your personal responses.

Harvesting sugar beets

Potatoes were the biggest cash crop. Each year, farmers shipped millions of bushels of potatoes to market. Colorado farmers also discovered a new cash crop: sugar beets.

Sugar Beets

In 1899, farmers at Grand Junction grew the state's first sugar beets. They found they could make more money growing beets than they could from any other crop. The next year, farmers along the South Platte and Arkansas Rivers began growing sugar beets. Within ten years, Colorado was the nation's leading sugar beet–growing state.

The sugar beet industry helped the state's cattlemen. They found that cattle liked the green beet tops cut from the plants when they were harvested. The pulp from the ground-up beets also made good cattle feed. Feedlots were set up near the sugar beet factories. Fattening cattle in feedlots became a big business.

Sugar beets

Skills and Tools for Learning

Identifying Cause and Effect

Historians try to explain why things happened. To answer *why* questions, they look for **causes** and **effects** or consequences. Why was there a Dust Bowl in eastern Colorado in the 1930s? What effect did it have on people who lived on the plains?

Historians look for multiple (many) causes. They know that most events are too complex to have only a single cause. They also look for immediate and remote causes. The first lead directly to or trigger an event. The second contribute indirectly or are more distant in time.

Select one important event in your own life. Think of an immediate cause or reason it happened. Can you add at least one remote cause? Next, think of a big event that happened in your family. What long-term consequences has it had for you?

When you read about the Dust Bowl of the 1930s later in this chapter, try to explain why it happened. What was the immediate cause of the topsoil blowing away? Try to find one or more remote causes. Was the climate of the plains a factor? How about farming methods used at that time?

A Dust Bowl storm

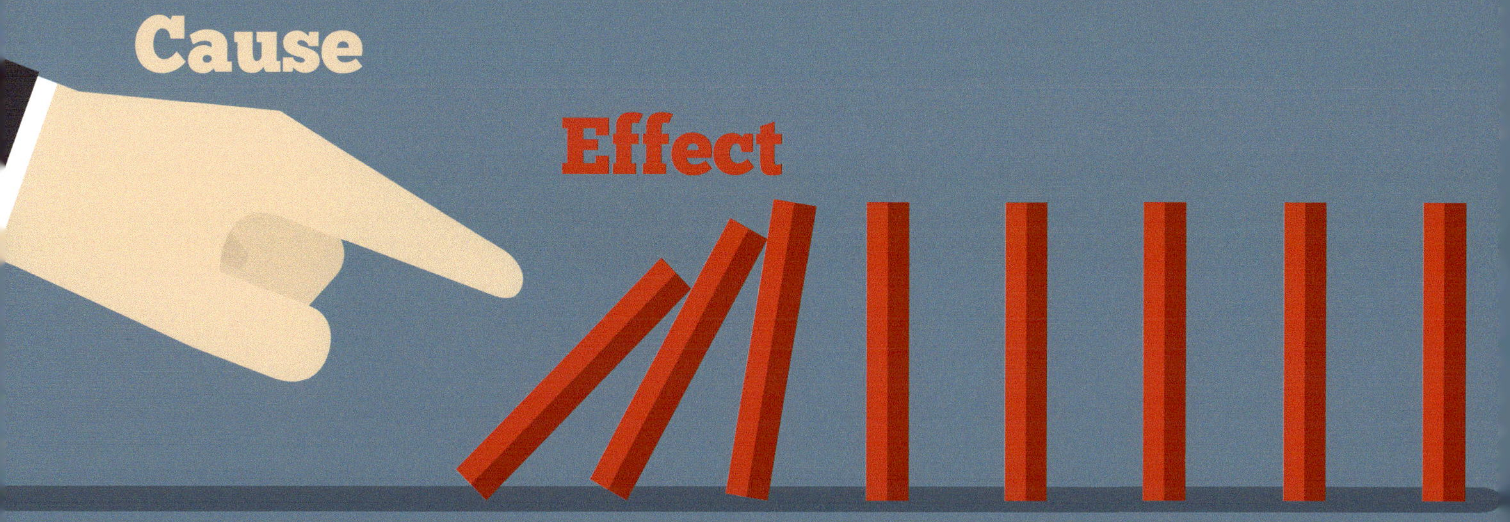

Focus Your Reading

- What new cash crops did farmers grow?
- What new people came to Colorado to help raise sugar beets?
- How did cattle raisers benefit from sugar beets?

Immigrant Farm Workers

Sugar beets brought new people to Colorado. The beets had to be hoed and harvested by hand. Farmers hired immigrants to do this work. Most of them were German Russians. These German farmers had settled in Russia before coming to the United States. Entire families, including young children, worked in the fields. Later, the beet growers brought in Japanese farmworkers from California and workers from Mexico. In some years, as many as 15,000 Spanish-speaking people worked in the fields. Some went home after the harvest. Many stayed to make Colorado their home.

Dearfield

In 1910, O. T. Jackson started a farm settlement near Fort Morgan. He wanted to make it easier for African Americans to become farmers. More than sixty black families settled there. They named the settlement Dearfield, as the land was very dear to them. But it lacked water for irrigation. After years of crop failures, the settlers gave up.

Melon field in Dearfield. The man at the left is probably O. T. Jackson.

A Poor Farm Boy

Not all farm families shared in the good times of these years. Jack Dempsey, a world-champion boxer, grew up in the San Luis Valley. "We never had any 'store' toys," he remembered. "We had to make our own playthings. Chips of wood became boats, sticks became spears, bits of old rope became lariats . . . Looking back at it now, it seems as if I almost always had a good time. The only bad thing was the feeling of being so very poor."
Jack Dempsey, *Round by Round: An Autobiography*

New Farm Machines

After 1920, farmers relied more on farm machines. Tractors replaced workhorses. Combines pulled by tractors took the place of threshing machines. Combines cut wheat and threshed out the grain at the same time. Farmers also bought trucks to haul their crops to market.

Tractors helped farmers plant larger fields with less work.

Focus Your Reading

- How did women in Colorado win the right to vote?
- What did conservationists do to save Colorado's forests?

CIVIC PROGRESS

Women in Colorado finally won the right to vote. In 1876 they were unhappy when the new state constitution did not give them that right (except in school board elections). They demanded that a **referendum**, or statewide vote, be held on the issue of women's **suffrage**. *Suffrage* means "having the right to vote." A referendum held in 1877 failed, with only men allowed to take part. That made women's suffrage leaders work even harder to change men's minds. They set out to win support by writing letters, going door-to-door to talk to voters, and holding public meetings.

Caroline Nichols Churchill was one of those leaders. She edited a Denver suffrage newspaper called *Queen Bee*. In her newspaper she supported an **amendment** to the state constitution to give Colorado women the right to vote. Women would have a good effect on politics and government, she argued. Eventually, men began to agree

Men and women witness as Colorado governor Oliver H. Shoup signs a ratification document for the Nineteenth Amendment, granting women's suffrage, December 12, 1919.

with her. When a second referendum was held in 1893, it passed by a large majority. She was delighted. "Come to Colorado Now. This Shall Be the Land for Women," she wrote in her newspaper. Colorado was the first state to give women the right to vote.

Caroline Nichols Churchill

Saving the Forests

Colorado also made progress in conserving its forests. Settlers and town builders had cut down large areas of forest to build cabins and construct mining towns and to burn as fuel. Many Coloradans worried that too many trees were being lost, leaving too few for future use. The national government owned most of Colorado's forestland. So, to save the forests, **conservationists** needed help from the US Congress and the president.

That help came in 1891, when the national government created the first US federal forest reserve. Forests set aside in these reserves were no longer open to public use. Many Coloradans cheered when President Benjamin Harrison set aside the White River Plateau Reserve in northwestern Colorado. It was the state's first forest reserve.

Creating National Forests

Conservation's best friend was President Theodore Roosevelt. Between 1902 and 1907, he set aside fourteen new forest tracts in Colorado as forest reserves, making the total 15,756,000 acres. This was the beginning of Colorado's system of national forests. These forests continue to provide wildlife protection, miles of hiking and cross-country skiing trails, and beautiful evergreen trees.

While You Read

Read this section about conserving forests with a partner. As you read, take turns making connections to the text. Explain to each other how what people did in the past affects you and other Coloradans today.

Focus Your Reading

- How did life in Colorado's cities change during the 1920s?
- How did entertainment change?
- How did telephones change the way people lived?

WORLD WAR I AND THE 1920S

In 1917, the United States became involved in World War I. This war in Europe broke out in 1914, when Germany and Austria went to war against Russia, France, and Great Britain. The United States favored the latter three nations but kept out of the war for nearly three years. Colorado mine owners and farmers benefited from the war. Weapons makers needed Colorado's tungsten and molybdenum. A shortage of food in Europe drove up crop prices. The acres of wheat planted by Colorado farmers increased 300 percent during the war.

The war also created problems for Coloradans. After the United States declared war against Germany in 1917, nearly 43,000 young Colorado men joined the US Army. That created a shortage of workers for Colorado's farms, mines, and factories. It also cost lives. More than 1,000 Colorado soldiers were killed in battle or died of disease in army camps. Another 1,759 were wounded in battle before the war ended in November 1918.

Secretary of War Newton Baker draws the first draft number on July 20, 1917.

Good Times

The 1920s were good times in Colorado. More workers made good wages. Most families could afford a car. Many city people bought their own houses for the first time. Fewer children worked. More teenagers went to high school.

Life was easier. Most city people had homes wired for electricity for the first time. They used electric lights instead of kerosene lamps. Electric stoves took the place of cookstoves that burned coal. Many people traded their iceboxes for a new electric "fridge." Getting around town was also easier. By 1920, many towns had streetcars. The larger cities bought buses.

While You Read

Think of three questions about the 1920s as you read this section. Write them on sticky notes, and place them in your notebook. When you have finished reading the section, see if your partner or small group can help answer these questions.

Movie theaters on Curtis Street in Denver

Denver's Auto Camp

Many people took automobile vacations during the 1920s. To attract these tourists, Denver developed city parks just for automobile travelers. The largest was Overland Park. It had a campground, grocery store, soda fountain, laundry, auditorium, and auto racetrack. By 1925, around 76,000 tourists visited the city's three auto camps each year.

Telephones

Telephones also changed the way people lived. Phones helped shopkeepers and office workers do business more quickly. At one time, business owners had to write letters or send telegrams to place orders. Now they just picked up the phone. Phones helped people keep in touch, especially rural families.

Phones made cities safer. Police and fire stations could be contacted more quickly by phone. On June 3, 1921, Pueblo's thirteen telephone operators spread the alarm to tell people about the flood sweeping through the city. They kept making calls until the water was twelve feet high on the phone company's building.

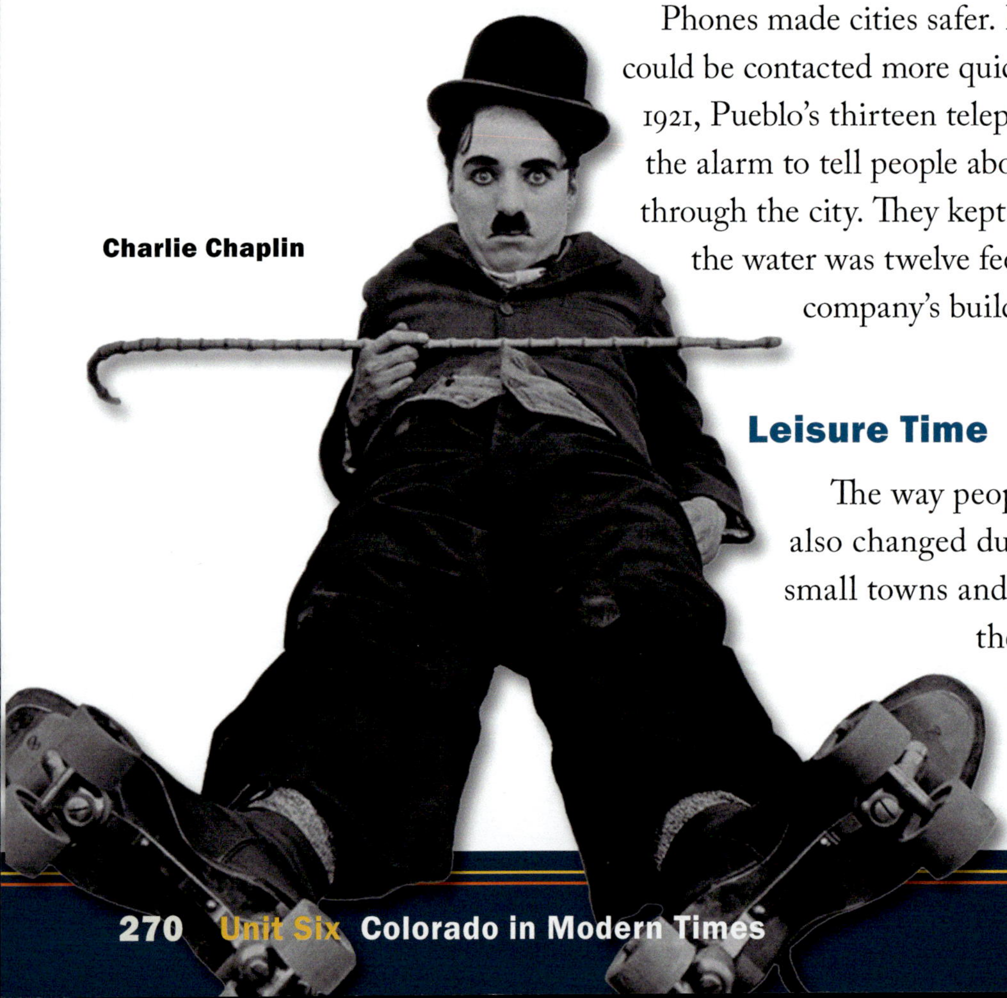

Charlie Chaplin

Leisure Time

The way people spent their free time also changed during the 1920s. Most small towns and all big cities had movie theaters. Tickets cost only a nickel. Comic actors like Charlie Chaplin were very popular.

The auto also affected people's leisure time. They spent less time at home. Cars made it easy to take weekend drives or go camping.

Radios

People also spent time listening to the radio. The state's first radio station began broadcasting in 1920 in Colorado Springs. The owner was William Reynolds, a dentist who liked music. He moved the station to Denver in 1922, where Reynolds entertained his listeners with music over station KLZ. Two years later, Denver added station KOA. It is still one of Colorado's major radio stations. Early radio programs included music, news, coverage of sports events, and political speeches.

Advertisement for radios in a 1922 newspaper

Colorado children during the Great Depression

Focus Your Reading

- What was the Great Depression?
- How did it affect people in Colorado's cities?
- How were farmers affected?
- How did the US government help people in Colorado?

COLORADO DURING THE GREAT DEPRESSION

The **Great Depression** of the 1930s brought the good years to an end. During these hard economic times, mines, steel mills, and factories shut down. Thousands of workers in Colorado lost their jobs. Not able to make their house payments, many also lost their homes. Others lost their savings when banks failed.

Colorado's farmers also faced hard times during the 1930s. The prices of wheat, potatoes, and sugar beets fell. Potatoes had brought $1.40 per bushel basket in 1929. In 1932, a bushel was worth only 24 cents. Some farmers left their crops in the fields to rot. It cost more to harvest them than they were worth. Many farmers lost their farms.

A Depression Gold Rush

Unable to find work, hundreds of men and women in Colorado panned for gold. "With pick and shovel, sluice box and pan, prospectors are seeking gold in the mud flats," wrote a newspaper reporter. "Some average a dollar a day while the best placer mine turns out $7 in gold" (*New York Times,* March 13, 1923). Several Colorado cities offered free lessons on how to use a gold pan.

The Dust Bowl

The 1930s were also the terrible **Dust Bowl** years in eastern Colorado. The stage for this disaster was set during the 1920s by good crop prices and a cycle of wet years. Farmers rushed into eastern Colorado to plow up the plains grassland and plant wheat. When drought returned in the 1930s, their crops died in the fields. With no grass left to protect the soil, dust storms blew it away. Huge clouds of dust turned daylight into night. Many farmers left the Dust Bowl to find farm work in California.

While You Read

In your notebook, sketch two scenes that compare farming in Colorado in the early 1900s with farming during the Great Depression. Write a description beneath each sketch.

Help from the Government

The government tried to help people get through the Depression. Congress passed laws to help people who were out of work. It set up the Civilian Conservation Corps (CCC)

Workers for the Civilian Conservation Corps building a road at Mesa Verde

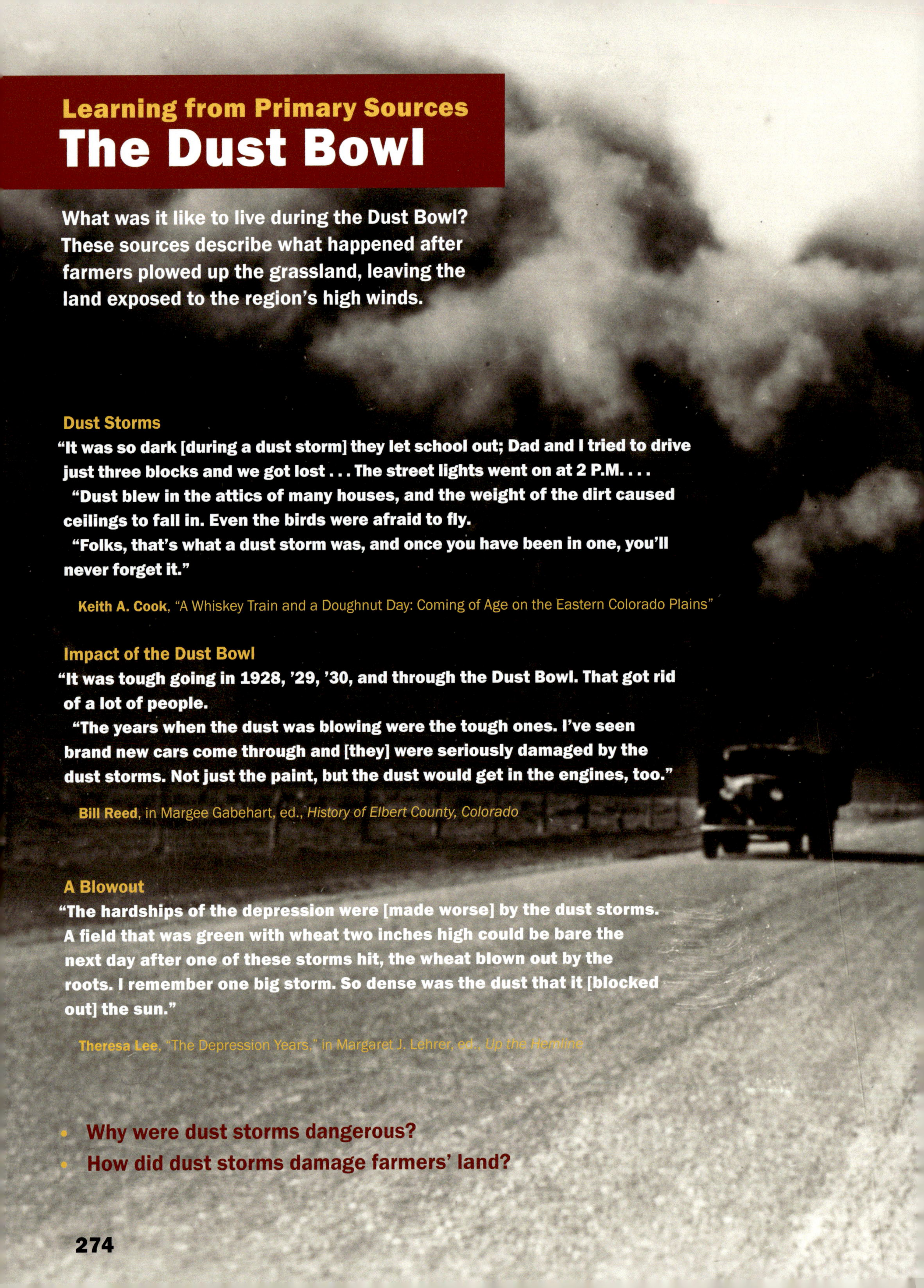

Learning from Primary Sources

The Dust Bowl

What was it like to live during the Dust Bowl? These sources describe what happened after farmers plowed up the grassland, leaving the land exposed to the region's high winds.

Dust Storms

"It was so dark [during a dust storm] they let school out; Dad and I tried to drive just three blocks and we got lost . . . The street lights went on at 2 P.M. . . .

"Dust blew in the attics of many houses, and the weight of the dirt caused ceilings to fall in. Even the birds were afraid to fly.

"Folks, that's what a dust storm was, and once you have been in one, you'll never forget it."

Keith A. Cook, "A Whiskey Train and a Doughnut Day: Coming of Age on the Eastern Colorado Plains"

Impact of the Dust Bowl

"It was tough going in 1928, '29, '30, and through the Dust Bowl. That got rid of a lot of people.

"The years when the dust was blowing were the tough ones. I've seen brand new cars come through and [they] were seriously damaged by the dust storms. Not just the paint, but the dust would get in the engines, too."

Bill Reed, in Margee Gabehart, ed., *History of Elbert County, Colorado*

A Blowout

"The hardships of the depression were [made worse] by the dust storms. A field that was green with wheat two inches high could be bare the next day after one of these storms hit, the wheat blown out by the roots. I remember one big storm. So dense was the dust that it [blocked out] the sun."

Theresa Lee, "The Depression Years," in Margaret J. Lehrer, ed., *Up the Hemline*

- **Why were dust storms dangerous?**
- **How did dust storms damage farmers' land?**

Background: A dust storm rolls across eastern Colorado

An Oklahoma boy during the Dust Bowl era

Dust storm in Baca County, Colorado

Dust storm approaching Stratford, Texas, in 1935

Aftermath of dust storm in Colorado

Focus Your Reading

- How did Colorado help the United States win World War II?
- Why did Japanese Americans come to Colorado during the war?

to put young men to work. They built roads and parks and improved the nation's forests. In Colorado, the CCC workers built Red Rocks Amphitheater west of Denver. Congress also gave Colorado money for new schools and playgrounds.

The federal government also tried to help farmers along the Front Range. They, too, faced a water shortage because of the drought. To provide more water to irrigate their fields, in 1938 Congress approved the Colorado–Big Thompson Project. It would bring water from the Western Slope through a tunnel under the Continental Divide to farms on the Front Range. Congress provided the money to build this project, which took nearly twenty years to complete.

COLORADO IN WORLD WAR II

On December 7, 1941, Japanese planes bombed Pearl Harbor. The attack against this US base in Hawaii killed nearly 2,400 American sailors. The next day, the United States declared war against Japan and its ally, Germany.

US Army mortar crew in training at Camp Carson, Colorado, in 1943

The people of Colorado helped the nation win World War II. More than 138,000 Colorado men and women served in the armed forces. That was one of every eight Coloradans. At least 2,700 were killed.

While You Read

Make four bookmarks by cutting a half-piece of paper into four equal parts. On **Bookmark 1**, write what you find most interesting in this section; on **Bookmark 2**, write what you find confusing; on **Bookmark 3**, write one word you think the whole class needs to discuss; and on **Bookmark 4**, write what you think would have been the most difficult part about living in Colorado during the war.

Army Camps, Factories, and Hospitals

The United States set up several army camps in Colorado. The largest was Camp Carson near Colorado Springs. Soldiers of the Tenth Mountain Division trained near Leadville at Camp Hale. They learned to fight on skis. The army also built air bases in Denver, Colorado Springs, Pueblo, and La Junta.

The government built arms factories in Denver. The largest, called the Denver Ordnance Plant, made artillery shells. It also built the Rocky Mountain Arsenal east of Denver. That factory produced and stored nerve gas.

The government already had an army hospital in Denver. It was called Fitzsimons General Hospital. The doctors there

Soldiers of the Tenth Mountain Division at Camp Hale

The Impact of War

"World War II changed everything," wrote one Colorado historian. The war had a greater impact on Colorado than any single event since the Gold Rush. The army's need for food led to higher crop prices. Land values soared. Factories closed by the Depression opened their doors again. Coal production increased. As the historian concluded, "Most of what constitutes [present-day] Colorado arose from the . . . events of the years from 1940 to 1945" (Carl Ubbelohde, Maxine Benson, and Duane A. Smith, *A Colorado History*).

Japanese Americans were forced to move to Granada. They had to live in buildings like these.

cared for sick and wounded soldiers. By the end of the war, it was one of the largest hospitals in the United States.

Camp Amache

In 1942, 7,500 Japanese Americans arrived in Colorado. They did not come willingly. The United States government forced more than 100,000 Americans who had Japanese ancestors to leave California. The government was afraid these loyal American citizens would help Japan invade California. They were moved to camps in other western states and kept there until the war ended in 1945. The camp in Colorado was located on the plains near the town of Granada. The center was known as Camp Amache, named for the Cheyenne wife of a pioneer settler. In 1988 the United States apologized for the way it had treated the Japanese Americans.

The Depression Ends

A worker at the Denver Ordnance Plant packs machine-gun bullets.

The war brought the Great Depression to an end. Factories opened again to fill orders for military supplies. The Gates Rubber Company made tires for army trucks and jeeps. Other Colorado companies made knives, hand grenades, and ammunition boxes. Wartime orders created new jobs. The Denver Ordnance Plant alone employed 20,000 people.

After You Read

1. Return to the two-column chart in your notebook. Select the change from the left-hand column that most interests you. In the right column, explain what you have found out about this change through your reading.
2. Choose one important idea from this chapter to remember. What is the idea? Why is it worth remembering? What is the best way for you to remember it?

Thinking about Colorado Water

Do you know . . .
how Colorado shares water with other states?

Four major rivers begin in Colorado, but whose water is it? Does Colorado get to keep all the water racing down from its mountain streams? What about the nineteen other states through which rivers flow that begin in Colorado? Farmers and city people in those states also need this water. How much of it belongs to each state?

Have you ever wondered how Colorado and other states share the water from a river?

In 1922, Colorado and other Colorado River states worked out an agreement. It is called the Colorado River Compact. It divided most of the water equally among five upper-river states (Colorado, New Mexico, Arizona, Utah, and Wyoming) and three lower-river states (California, Nevada, and Arizona). Colorado gets about half of the upper states' water. Water that is left over is used by Mexico, where the Colorado River flows through the Gulf of California into the Pacific Ocean. Very little water is left for Mexico, and that water is often very polluted.

Colorado also has compacts with its neighbors for the Arkansas, South Platte, Rio Grande, and some smaller rivers.

- Is sharing water from Colorado's rivers a good idea?
- What are the benefits and costs of this system?
- Have you ever agreed to share things you and others both needed?

Asking Historical Questions
Your Response

This chapter began with this question:

How did mining, farming and ranching, and city life in Colorado change between 1890 and 1945?

1. **Review**
   Review the information in your notes and in this chapter about how mining, farming and ranching, and city life in Colorado changed between 1890 and 1945.
2. **Reflect**
   With a partner or in a small group, discuss the major changes in these areas between 1890 and 1945.
3. **Respond**
   In your notebook, describe these changes and try to explain why they took place.

CHAPTER 12

Modern Times, 1946–Today

How have the ways people live in Colorado changed in recent times?

FOCUS QUESTION

Before You Read

Scan the photos in this chapter. What questions do you think this chapter will answer? What questions do you hope it will answer? Write these questions in your notebook, and list the clues that indicate your questions may be answered.

KEY-WORDS

- **economic incentives**
- **suburbs**
- **diverse**
- **segregated**
- **Civil Rights Movement**
- **national parks**
- **fossils**
- **aquifers**

The number of people living in Colorado grew rapidly after World War II. From a population of 1.1 million in 1940, the state had grown to nearly 5.2 million by 2010. Many of the new people were soldiers who had served here during the war. They returned to live in Colorado.

New factories located in Colorado after the war. Many of the new companies developed computer software. Companies also moved to Colorado to make airplanes, rockets, and space satellites. Eastman Kodak set up a factory at Windsor to make film for cameras. Thousands of people found jobs in hotels, restaurants, advertising companies, hospitals, and other companies that provide services.

Focus Your Reading

- What metal caused Colorado's last mining rush?
- How did farming change after the war?
- What are Denver's major professional sports teams?

MINING, FARMING, AND CITY LIFE

The year 1948 opened a new chapter in the history of Colorado mining. Uranium was discovered on the Western Slope. The United States needed uranium to make atomic bombs and to fuel nuclear power plants. Meeting this demand brought good times to Rifle, Naturita, and other small towns. But the uranium rush did not last long. It was over by the early 1960s.

While You Read

Why do you suppose our state attracts so many new residents? In a small group, use a wall map or an atlas to locate the countries mentioned in this section. Find other geographic information that will help you compare these places with Colorado. Talk about why you think people move to Colorado.

Coal Mining

Coal mining remains an important Colorado industry. This state usually ranks among the top ten states for coal produced. Nearly all of Colorado's mines are located on the Western Slope. They produce "clean coal" that causes less pollution because it is low in sulfur. This coal is in demand in Colorado and other states to produce electricity in coal-fueled power plants.

The years after World War II brought changes to Colorado's farms. Farming became a big business. Many small farmers sold out and moved to town. The farms that remained were bigger than before. Their owners planted and harvested their crops with big tractors and farm machines. They relied even more on irrigation.

Immigrant irrigating a field of lettuce

Farming as Big Business

After World War II, farming in Colorado became a big business. Farmers in the 1920s considered a quarter section of land (160 acres) a big farm. "Today his grandson farms by sections [640 acres]," wrote a Denver newspaper reporter in 1980. "His tractor costs $69,000, can cover 55 acres an hour and is air conditioned. The annual budget of his farm may reach $100,000."

Diverting Water to the Front Range

Farmers along the Front Range had more water to irrigate their crops than before. Much of it came from projects that diverted water from the Western Slope. Tunnels bored through the Continental Divide brought the water to farms on the Front Range.

The Colorado–Big Thompson Project, completed in 1956, provided water to farmers in northern Colorado. Dams built on the Colorado River created two large reservoirs: Lake Granby and Shadow Mountain Reservoir. Large pumps lift water 172 feet from Lake Granby to Shadow Mountain Reservoir. From there it flows into Grand Lake. The water then enters the thirteen-mile-long Alva B. Adams Tunnel bored through the Continental Divide.

Digging the tunnel for the Colorado–Big Thompson Project

Today, plains farmers irrigate crops with sprinklers that draw water from deep wells.

While You Read

Choose five words from this section that you are not certain you understand. List them in your notebook, and, as you read, jot down context clues that help you understand the words. Then find the definitions in the glossary or a dictionary, and copy them in your notebook.

At Estes Park, it enters the Big Thompson River. From there it flows down to reservoirs along the plains that farmers use to irrigate their fields.

The Fryingpan-Arkansas Project provided more water for farmers in southern Colorado. Completed in 1981, it diverted water from the Western Slope to the Arkansas River. Farmers in the Arkansas Valley use this water to irrigate their crops. Many cities use it for drinking water.

Today, farmers on the dry plains of eastern Colorado also irrigate their crops. With no rivers nearby, they drill wells and use pumps to bring water up from deep underground. Sprinklers on long pipes mounted on wheels rotate around the wells. These sprinklers create green circles of cropland in the otherwise dry grassland of the plains.

Skills and Tools for Learning

Scenic mountains

Economic Incentives

The population of Colorado grew rapidly after World War II. People moved here because the state had much to offer. Some of the benefits gained from moving to Colorado are called **economic incentives**.

What is an incentive? Have you ever bought a fast-food meal or a box of cereal because you wanted the toy? The toy was the incentive. A positive incentive is a reward for making a good choice. A negative incentive is the price you pay for making a less desirable choice.

Colorado offered many positive economic incentives. People found jobs in offices, banks, and shops that paid good wages. They could afford to own a house or a new car. Many could afford a vacation. However, the incentives for moving here did not always involve money.

Think of other incentives people might have for moving to Colorado. On a separate sheet of paper, make a list of positive and negative incentives such as the following. Then put a check in either the positive or negative column.

Incentive	Positive	Negative
Scenic mountains		
Snowstorms		
Winter recreation		
State parks		
National forests		
Summer drought		
Wildlife		
Other		

If you were deciding to move to Colorado, which list of incentives would outweigh the other?

Winter recreation

National forests

Wildlife

New houses are under construction in a new subdivision in Golden, Colorado, August 28, 2014.

Living in Cities

More people in Colorado live in cities than ever before. Most of this growth took place along the Front Range urban corridor. While old cities grew larger, people also settled in **suburbs**. These are new communities next to big cities. They especially attracted young families, providing them with new housing, modern schools, and large parks and playgrounds for their children. Growing families added to Colorado's population.

Colorado also attracted out-of-state people and new immigrants from other countries. Most of the latter were Spanish-speaking farmworkers from Mexico. During the 1970s, many Asian immigrants also settled in Colorado. They came from Cambodia, Laos, and Vietnam. More recently, Colorado has attracted immigrants from Russia, India, and Africa. Colorado has a **diverse** society in which people from different parts of the world share their favorite foods, music, and books.

Many aspects of city life also changed after the war. For example, Denver became a big-league sports city in 1960, when it got the Denver Broncos. Since then, the Broncos have won two Super Bowls—in 1998 and 1999.

A Denver Broncos wide receiver catches a pass for a touchdown.

Major League Sports

Denver has acquired other teams since then. In 1967, Denver got a major league basketball team. First called the Denver Rockets, the team later changed its name to the Denver Nuggets. Baseball fans had to wait until 1993 for a major league baseball team. The Colorado Rockies played their first game in Denver that year. The Colorado Avalanche, Denver's National Hockey League team, arrived two years later. The Avalanche have twice won the Stanley Cup, the North American hockey championship.

Transportation

Denver remained Colorado's transportation center. By the 1960s, most visitors arrived by car or plane. Two new interstate highways, I-25 and I-70, brought thousands of cars through Denver each day. Stapleton Airport became one of the nation's busiest airports. Needing a larger airport, in 1995 the city opened the new Denver International Airport.

Denver International Airport

Learning from Primary Sources

Regional Conflict

Water is blood in Colorado.

In 1946, John Gunther wrote *Inside USA*, a book that described life in the United States. This is what he wrote about conflicts over water in Colorado:

> "Colorado is divided down the middle by the sharp and impenetrable spine of the continental divide . . . The west, behind the divide, is mostly mining and livestock country; the east is irrigated and merges into the Great Plains.
>
> "But the chief element of difference between eastern and western Colorado is water. Touch water, and you touch everything . . . Western Colorado has more water than it can use, eastern less than it needs. Hence the east must have irrigation and the problem . . . is to get the water over. This the west resents. It thinks it is being milked of water for the benefit of capitalists [businessmen] in Denver . . . The east replies that the water is 'spare' water and that the west wastes it anyway.
>
> "Water is blood in Colorado."
>
> **John Gunther**, *Inside USA*

- **What did John Gunther think was the main difference between eastern and western Colorado?**
- **What do you think he meant by "water is blood in Colorado"?**

Lake Granby, a reservoir created as part of the Colorado–Big Thompson Project

CIVIL RIGHTS IN COLORADO

In Colorado and elsewhere in the United Staes, people were not treated equally. In the South, African Americans could not vote. In many parts of the country, blacks and Hispanics could only buy homes in neighborhoods **segregated** by race. Schools in many cities were segregated as well. Businesses often refused to hire people of color.

Discriminating against people because of their race violates their civil rights. These are rights that protect one's freedom and equal treatment under the law.

To fight against racial discrimination, leaders such as the Reverend Martin Luther King Jr. organized the **Civil Rights Movement**. They filed court cases against school segregation. In 1952 the US Supreme Court ruled that school segregation had to end because it violated the US Constitution. Congress in 1964 passed a Civil Rights Act, which outlawed many forms of discrimination. The Voting Rights Act of 1965 protected every adult American's right to vote. Civil rights leaders also worked to make sure court decisions and civil rights laws were enforced.

Focus Your Reading

- What are civil rights?
- What was the Civil Rights Movement?
- What groups worked for civil rights in Colorado?

Martin Luther King Jr.

Rodolfo "Corky" Gonzales

While You Read

As you read, make a list of the forms of discrimination minority groups in Colorado have faced.

Denver at the Center

Denver was the center of the Civil Rights Movement in Colorado. In 1961 a group of black and white Denver residents organized a local branch of the Congress on Racial Equality (CORE). Led by James Reynolds, it held peaceful protests against segregated schools and housing. CORE also protested against hiring on the basis of race. Members of CORE marched on the sidewalks in front of department stores that refused to hire black clerks. In time, the stores backed down. CORE also helped integrate Denver's segregated public swimming pools. In 1974, Denver's civil rights leaders won a court battle to integrate the city's schools.

Colorado's Hispanic civil rights leaders worked to improve education for Hispanic youth. Their leader was Rodolfo (Corky) Gonzales, a retired boxer, businessman, and poet. The Crusade for Justice, which he founded in 1966, fought for civil rights for Colorado's Hispanic people. It founded a free school for Hispanic youth, investigated reports of discrimination, and organized protests.

Above: **James Reynolds (*center*) meeting with other civil rights leaders**

Below: **Children carrying signs calling on the birthday of Martin Luther King Jr. to be named a national holiday.**

Focus Your Reading

- How did modern-day skiing get started in Colorado?
- What kinds of summer recreation attract visitors?
- Which national parks and monuments are located in Colorado?

TOURISM AND RECREATION

Colorado has always been a popular place for tourists. The first tourists came during the Gold Rush. They arrived by stagecoach and wagon to visit the mining camps. During the late 1800s, Colorado's healthful climate also attracted visitors. Ever since then, people have come from many parts of the world to spend vacations here.

A few skiers arrived before World War II. Carl Howelsen, an immigrant from Norway, settled in Steamboat Springs in 1914. He was a ski jumper. That winter, he built a ski jump there and held a winter carnival. People came to compete in ski jumps. He later added downhill racing. During the next twenty years, Howelsen helped make skiing a winter sport in Steamboat Springs.

Ski jumping at Howelsen Hill near Steamboat Springs

Skiing in Aspen in the early years

While You Read

With a partner, take turns reading these paragraphs out loud. At the end of each paragraph, put the book down, stop to think, then take turns retelling what you have read. If necessary, use the text to check your retelling.

Colorado's Ski Resorts

Modern-day skiing got its start in Colorado after World War II. Some of the men who had trained at Camp Hale as mountain soldiers returned after the war. They settled in Aspen, where they had skied as soldiers. There they met a wealthy Chicago businessman named Walter Paepcke, who wanted to build a ski resort. Paepcke and the skiers from Camp Hale soon made Aspen a popular place to ski. Later, ski slopes were opened at Vail, Breckenridge, Copper Mountain, and elsewhere. Steamboat Springs, where ski jumping and racing got their start in Colorado, also became a popular ski resort.

Colorado now has twenty-five major ski resorts and a dozen or so smaller ones. People come from all over the world to ski and snowboard on Colorado's slopes. Cross-country skiing is also popular. The state has a system of mountain huts for cross-country skiers. This hut-to-hut trail system is 300 miles long. It connects the ski resorts of Aspen, Leadville, Copper Mountain, and Vail. People can spend days skiing cross-country from one mountain hut to another.

Building the Eisenhower Tunnel

The Eisenhower Tunnel today

The Eisenhower Tunnel

For many years, skiers had to drive their cars over Loveland Pass. The road across the pass was narrow, winding, and dangerous during the winter. This problem was solved in 1973 with the opening of the Eisenhower Tunnel. This tunnel on Interstate 70 is the longest auto tunnel in the United States. It was also one of the most costly. The 8,941-foot-long tunnel cost $1,000 per inch to build.

Hiking, Biking, and Camping

Hiking in Colorado is almost as popular as skiing. Colorado has more than 11,000 miles of hiking trails. The most popular hiking places are state and **national parks**. Experienced hikers enjoy the Colorado Trail, a 469-mile trail from Denver to Durango. People can start hiking at many trailheads along the way and stay on the trail for a day or for up to three or four weeks. The trail has huts as resting places for people who hike long distances.

Biking is also a popular form of recreation. The state has 10,000 miles of bike trails. Most of the state's parks have bike trails. Crested Butte and Durango are well-known for their mountain-bike trails. In summer, many mountain resorts let people take bikes on a ski lift to the top of a mountain and ride the ski trails back down.

Camping, too, is very popular in Colorado. The state has hundreds of public campgrounds. Many are located in state and national parks. The state's many national forests are also popular camping areas.

A Colorado Trail marker

River Sports

River rafting and kayaking attract many visitors to Colorado. Rafters and kayakers love Colorado's rivers. They

Kayaking in Colorado

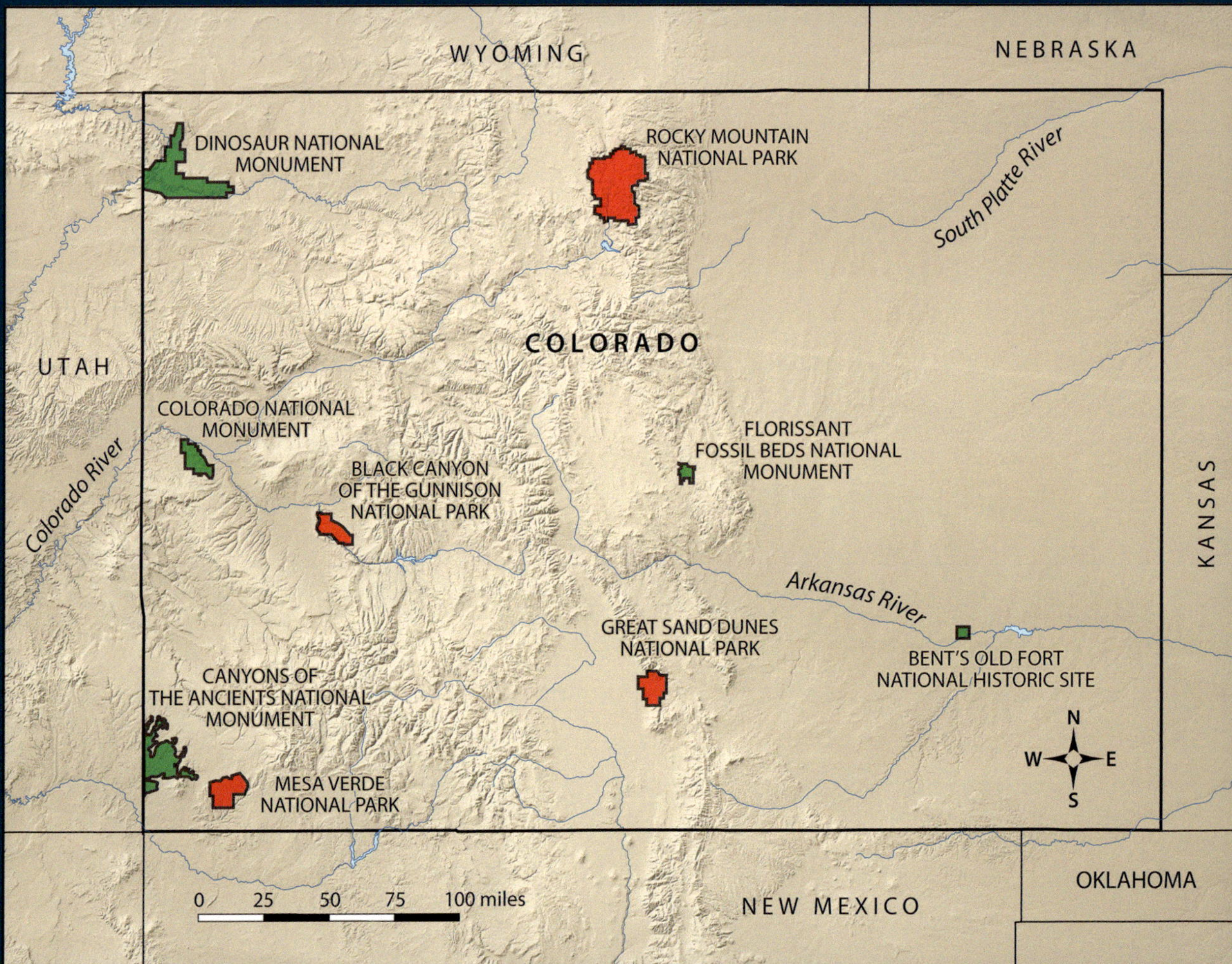

Locations of the national parks and monuments in Colorado

can find calm, lazy streams for floating gently on a rubber raft, wild rapids that only experienced kayakers can run, and everything in between. The most popular rivers for rafting and kayaking are the Green and Yampa Rivers in the northwest, the Arkansas River in the Buena Vista–Salida area, and the Animas and Dolores Rivers in the Four Corners region.

Colorado's National Parks

The Rocky Mountains of Colorado have always been a major tourist attraction. No one loved the mountains more than Enos Mills. As a young man, he worked in a tourist hotel in Estes Park. He spent his spare time hiking in the mountains with his friends. For several years, Enos Mills and other Coloradans worked to have the mountains at Estes Park set aside as a national park. They wrote newspaper articles and sent letters to the US Congress. They finally succeeded in 1915, when Congress set aside 400 square miles as Rocky Mountain National Park.

Colorado now has four national parks. Thousands of visitors each year still visit Rocky Mountain National Park to hike, camp, and fish for trout. The next national park to be created in Colorado was Mesa Verde, located near the town of Cortez. This park preserves the cliff dwellings of the Ancestral Puebloans. More recently, Congress created the Black Canyon of the Gunnison National Park. The narrow canyon has sheer walls of dark gray rock that plunge a half mile into the earth. It probably got the name "Black" Canyon because the bottom of the deep canyon gets very little direct sunlight. The state's newest national park is the Great Sand Dunes National Park. Visitors stop there to photograph and climb the dunes, which rise as high as 700 feet.

Black Canyon of the Gunnison National Park

Dinosaur National Monument

Colorado's National Monuments

Colorado also has several places designated by Congress as national monuments. Western Colorado has the Colorado National Monument. It is famous for its red and yellow canyons, unusual rock formations, dinosaur **fossils**, and Indian rock paintings. Bent's Old Fort National Monument is a rebuilt trading fort located near La Junta. It is a "living history" museum. Visitors can watch people dressed in clothing of the 1830s work as blacksmiths, carpenters, cooks, traders, and makers of adobe bricks. Both monuments are popular tourist stops.

Fossilized dinosaur skull at Dinosaur National Monument

Colorado also has two national monuments that preserve fossils of extinct plants and animals. Dinosaur National Monument in northwestern Colorado is the world's largest Jurassic Period dinosaur quarry. It has fossil bones of many dinosaurs, including stegosaurus, apatosaurus, and allosaurus. Much of the park lies in Utah, just across the state border, where the visitors' center is located. The other monument that has fossils is the Florissant Fossil Beds National Monument near Woodland Park. At Florissant, searchers have found more than 80,000 fossils of extinct insects and plants. The visitors' center has many of them on display.

FACING THE FUTURE

Since the first hunters arrived 12,000 years ago, Colorado has attracted people trying to make a living. That is not likely to change in the future. Over the next 40 years, the state's population of 5.1 million (2010) is expected to double. Many will be newcomers attracted by what this state has to offer. They will find good jobs, fun things to do, and a healthful climate and beautiful mountains. While seeking a better life, Colorado's future citizens will also face problems.

Focus Your Reading

- Why will people move to Colorado in the future?
- What future problems will people in Colorado face?

Global Warming

The slow warming of the Earth's atmosphere may be the most serious problem. Ocean temperatures are rising. The icecaps at the North Pole are melting. How has global warming affected Colorado? Average temperatures are rising. Droughts seem to be getting worse and floods more dangerous. Dry summers also increase the danger of forest fires. What ideas do you have to help Coloradans deal with these problems?

The pika's alpine tundra habitat is affected by global warming.

While You Read

Take a sheet of paper and divide it into five columns. Label each column with one of the five problems facing the people of Colorado. After you read about each problem, talk with a partner about what Colorado's citizens can do to help solve the problem.

Droughts and Rising Temperatures

Colorado has always had periods of drought. They come in cycles, with dry years followed by periods of wet years. However, our droughts may be getting longer and drier. The Dust Bowl years of the 1930s were the longest drought in recent times. Crops failed, and many farmers left their farms. The drought of 2002 was the driest ever. Rising temperatures also mean that farmers will need more water for their crops. Cities, too, will need more water.

After the Dust Bowl, farmers on the plains dealt with the drought by irrigating their crops. They pumped water from **aquifers**, or water deposits deep underground. But these farmers are slowly pumping the aquifers dry. What should the farmers do now?

A drought-stricken Colorado cornfield

An evacuation during the Front Range Flood of 2013

Floods

Colorado has floods as well as droughts. Most are "flash floods" that happen quickly after heavy rainfalls. Flash floods can be deadly, especially when they happen at night. Several days of heavy rain can also cause floods. Global warming seems to make heavy rains and floods more likely.

The Big Thompson Flood of 1976 was the deadliest flash flood in Colorado's history. On the night of July 31, heavy rain brought a nineteen-foot wall of water down the Big Thompson Canyon. It drowned 144 people, destroyed 418 homes, and caused $140 million in damage.

The Front Range Flood of 2013 was Colorado's most costly flood. A slow-moving cold front stalled over the Front Range in September, dumping up to seventeen inches of rain over a weeklong period. That is as much precipitation as the region usually gets in a year. Floodwaters destroyed more than 1,700 homes and drove 11,000 people to temporary shelters. The flood wiped out nearly thirty miles of highway. Eight people were killed.

What can Coloradans do in the future to reduce losses from floods? Most cities have laws that keep people from building homes in high-risk flood zones. Tightening those laws may be one solution. What else can we do?

Forest Fires

Forest fires are another problem Colorado's people face. They are caused both by lightning and by people. The most costly are forest fires near cities where people have built mountain homes. Many Coloradans like to live surrounded by trees in or near the mountains. This can also be a dangerous place to live. Global warming that deprives forests of moisture contributes to the problem. Cycles of drought that turn pine trees into easy-to-burn fuel make the problem worse. Forest fires may be an even bigger problem in the future.

The summer of 2012 was extremely dry. On June 9 a fire broke out in the High Park area west of Fort Collins. This forest area included many mountain homes. The fire burned thousands of acres and destroyed more than 250 houses. Two weeks later the Waldo Canyon Fire in Colorado Springs forced more than 32,000 people to leave their homes. They returned to find 350 homes burned to the ground.

In June 2013 the Black Forest Fire in a Colorado Springs suburb was the most costly fire in Colorado history. A record-setting heat wave and high winds set the stage. Dried-out pine trees in this heavily forested neighborhood provided the fuel. The fire raged for ten days and destroyed more than 500 homes.

Should people be allowed to build homes in these places? Can neighborhoods in dried-out forests be made safer?

The 2013 Black Forest Fire outside Colorado Springs

Fighting the Black Forest Fire

Water Conservation

Water conservation is one solution to the problem of water shortage. Denver and other Colorado cities have reduced water use by urging residents to conserve water. Some cities raise the price of water during the summer months, which cuts down on water use. Still, about one-third of many cities' water is used not for drinking, cooking, and bathing but for watering lawns. Farmers can also conserve water by installing better irrigation systems. Sprinkler systems waste water because much of it evaporates in the hot summer air. A system called "drip irrigation" uses less water by applying drops of water from underground tubes to each plant. But these systems are expensive. How can Colorado's people conserve more water?

What can you do to help Coloradans face the future?

After You Read

1. Think of at least three ways Colorado would be different if it had no mountains. In your notebook, write a descriptive paragraph about this, and illustrate your description. Use this chapter, along with experiences you have had in states where there are no mountains, to support your ideas.
2. In your notebook, make a sketch of the part of this chapter you found to be most important. Then, in a small group, share your sketch and explain why you made a connection to that topic.

Thinking about Colorado Water

Do you know . . .
where the water that you drink comes from?

Where does your drinking water come from? Does it come from the place where you live? Not necessarily. Your drinking water may come from miles away. Farmers are not the only Coloradoans who divert water from the Western Slope.

Have you ever wondered where your city's water comes from? Does it come from underground wells? Does it flow through tunnels from the Western Slope? Is it stored in mountain reservoirs?

City water departments in Colorado provide information about the source of their municipal water. To find this information, do the following:

- Visit the homepage of your local water department or department of public works.
- Look for one of the following links:
    - Water System
    - Water Supply
    - Water Resources
    - Water History

There you will find where the reservoirs, rivers, or wells that provide your city's water are located.

Asking Historical Questions
Your Response

This chapter began with this question:

How have the ways people live in Colorado changed in recent times?

1. **Review**
   Review the information in your notes and in this chapter about how the ways people live in Colorado have changed in recent times.
2. **Reflect**
   With a partner or in a small group, discuss how the ways people live in Colorado have changed in recent times.
3. **Respond**
   In your notebook, explain how the ways people live in Colorado have changed in recent times.

Our State Emblems

Every state has special signs and emblems. They are chosen to represent things that are important to the people who live in the state. Here are the meanings for Colorado's signs and emblems:

THE STATE SEAL

The state seal is used on important state documents and papers. Within the triangle is the eye of God. The Latin words mean "nothing without providence." What are the tools shown on the shield?

THE STATE SONG

The state song, "Where the Columbines Grow," celebrates the majestic mountains, the evergreen trees, the cool summer breezes, and the plains that can be seen rolling out below the mountains.

THE STATE FLAG

The flag is divided into three equal stripes. The two blue stripes stand for Colorado's skies; the white stripe represents the mountain snows. The C is for Colorado, and its red color represents the red soil found in much of the state. The gold circle in the middle of the C is for the metal ore that was so important in the state's history.

THE STATE TREE

The Colorado blue spruce is the state tree. Although it is found wild in only part of the state, it can be planted and will grow everywhere in Colorado. Some trees are almost blue in color; others seem almost silver.

THE STATE FLOWER

The Rocky Mountain columbine has long been the state flower. Like the Colorado flag, columbines have blue for the skies, white for the snows, and gold for the metal. It is against the law to pick wild columbines.

THE STATE BIRD

Schoolchildren chose the lark bunting as the state bird. A little black-and-white bird, the lark bunting sings while it is flying. It is found mainly on the plains.

THE STATE ANIMAL

Not every state has an animal for a symbol. Colorado adopted the Rocky Mountain bighorn sheep because this is one of the few places where it can be found. It is a very strong and brave animal that lives high on the mountain slopes.

THE STATE FOSSIL

In 1982, students from McElwain Elementary School in Thornton were able to get the governor to add a dinosaur fossil to the list of state emblems. The students chose a stegosaurus fossil because the first complete skeleton of the stegosaurus was found in Colorado. The stegosaurus lived in the Colorado area 150 million years ago. It is believed to have weighed ten tons, although its brain only weighed two-and-a-half ounces.

THE STATE DANCE

The square dance is Colorado's official state dance. The square dance is a folk dance that originally came from Europe. American settlers brought it with them when they moved west. Square dancing to country-western-style music is a popular form of entertainment in Colorado.

THE STATE FISH

The greenback cutthroat trout was adopted as the official state fish on May 15, 1994. Greenback cutthroat trout once lived in small creeks, streams, and rivers throughout Colorado, and steps have been taken to protect them and expand their numbers.

THE STATE INSECT

The Colorado hairstreak butterfly was adopted as the official state insect on April 17, 1996. It is two inches wide and has purple wings with black borders, orange accents in the corners, and blue on the underside. Schoolchildren lobbied to have the butterfly adopted.

THE STATE GEMSTONE

The aquamarine was designated Colorado's gemstone on April 12, 1971. Aquamarines are found in Colorado on Mount Antero, one of the state's highest mountains. Colorado has more than 480 types of minerals, more than most other states in the country.

THE STATE GRASS

Blue grama is the state grass of Colorado. This grass is native to Colorado. It was the main source of food for the bison that once roamed the plains. Grama grass grows from 6 inches to 12 inches tall. It is called blue grama because the stems end in a bluish purple spike.

THE STATE TARTAN

Colorado also has a state tartan. It is a pattern on cloth made up of stripes of different widths and colors crossed at right angles. The colors are the Colorado state colors: blue, red, and yellow.

Glossary

acre. A unit for measuring land. A square mile includes 640 acres.

altitude. How high something is above the Earth or above sea level.

amendment. An addition or change made to a law or constitution.

Anasazi. A name the Navajo gave to the Ancestral Puebloan people of the Four Corners area. The word means "ancient enemies" or "ancient people who are not us."

ancestor. A person from whom one is descended, or an earlier relative, such as a grandparent or great-grandparent.

aquifer. An underground layer of rock that contains water.

archaeologist. A person with special training who collects evidence about how people lived in past ages.

artifact. An object produced by a human being, such as a tool, a weapon, or jewelry.

band (Indian). A small group or village of Indians who lived and hunted together. Tribes were made up of many bands.

blacksmith. A person who shapes iron to make horseshoes and other useful items. The individual beats the hot iron on an anvil with a hammer.

brand. An owner's mark burned into the hide of an animal with a hot iron.

canyon. A washed-out area with steep cliff walls. Canyons are formed by fast-running water.

capital cities. Cities where at least the legislative branch of a government is located.

capital resources. Tools and other items used to make goods and services to sell.

causes. People or events that make things happen that are either distant in time (remote causes) or recent in time (immediate causes).

change. To go from one condition or way of living to another.

checks and balances. Ways to keep a balance of power among different branches of government.

citizens. Individuals who owe loyalty to a nation in which they were born or naturalized as citizens.

citizenship. Carrying out the duties and claiming the rights of being a citizen.

Civil Rights Movement. People and organizations who came together to provide minority groups with their basic rights as citizens.

climate. The temperature, moisture, and wind typical of a region or particular area.

coal mining. Digging coal, a black substance composed of fossilized plants used as a fuel, out of the earth.

coniferous. Evergreen trees that produce cones, such as pine and spruce.

consequence. An effect or what happens as a result of an action or event.

conservationists. People who work to protect and preserve natural resources.

constitution. A document or set of laws that creates a government; it describes how the government is organized and what powers it has.

continuity. Things happening as they always have, with little or no change.

corrida de gallo. A sporting event played by riders racing on horseback. They try to reach down and grab the head of a rooster that is buried in the ground up to its neck.

culture. A people's way of life, including their art, beliefs, and religions.

democracy. A government in which power comes from ordinary citizens.

descendants. Persons who are related to ancestors who lived before them.

drought. A long period with no rain.

Dust Bowl. An area on the plains where the topsoil was blown away by strong winds during the 1930s.

economic incentive. Something that encourages people to make or buy things or to invent new products (positive incentive) or that discourages them from doing so (negative incentive).

effect. A consequence or what happens as a result of an action or event.

elevation. The height at which something rises above the ground or above sea level.

European. Something that came from Europe or people who came from there.

expedition. A journey undertaken by a group of people for a particular purpose.

extended family. A family made up of parents, children, and other close relatives, such as grandparents or aunts and uncles.

extinct. Something that has died out.

farmhand. A person (usually a man) who gets paid to work on a farm.

flour mill. A building in which wheat or other grain is ground into flour.

fossil. An imprint on rock left by bones, leaves, or other objects from past ages.

gatherers. People who lived by finding and collecting plants, seeds, and roots.

general store. A store that sold many kinds of products, such as groceries, meat, tools, and clothing.

Great Depression. The economic slump, or hard times, that took place during the 1930s.

hard-rock mining. Removing gold, silver, or other minerals from quartz rock.

high plains. The central plains of eastern Colorado, which are higher in elevation than the lower river valleys.

historical period. A length of time in the past known for a particular kind of change or way of life.

human resources. The people who produce goods and services.

immigrant. A person who leaves one country to settle in another country.

irrigate. To bring water by ditches or pipes to land that otherwise would be too dry to farm.

landscape. The surface of the land that can be viewed from any one place.

latitude. The distance on the Earth's surface measured north and south from the Equator.

limited government. A government that has only those powers listed in its constitution or basic laws.

livestock. Animals such as cattle, horses, or pigs raised for home use or to sell.

location. Where a place is situated or can be found on a map.

longitude. The distance on the Earth's surface measured in degrees from the prime meridian at Greenwich, England.

Los Pastores. A play about the birth of Christ performed on Christmas Eve in Hispanic communities.

merchant. A person who sells goods to customers, such as a shop owner or storekeeper.

mesas. High places or landforms that have a flat top and cliff-like sides.

mine tailings. The waste rock taken from a mine that is left on the mountainside.

mules. Animals that are a hybrid of a horse (mother) and a donkey (father).

national park. An area of land set aside by the national government for public use.

native culture. A people's way of life before newcomers arrive.

natural resources. Objects found in nature that can be used to produce goods and services, such as land, water, and minerals.

Navajo. An Indian tribe that lives in New Mexico, Arizona, and Utah.

nuclear power. Using atomic energy to generate power, usually by heating water to create steam.

open range. Unfenced grassland owned by the federal government on which cattle grazed.

opportunity cost. Giving up the next-best choice when you choose one thing over another.

ore. A natural substance such as rock that contains gold, silver, or other valuable minerals.

oxen. Male cattle trained to pull wagons and plows.

pathfinder. A person who discovers or finds his or her way into an unexplored region.

patron saint. A holy person whose spirit guards a nation, place, or person.

piedmont. The region that lies between the Front Range of the Rocky Mountains and the high plains of eastern Colorado.

pithouse. A shelter built of poles and dried mud with a floor just below the level of the ground.

place. The space at which something is located, such as a town or city.

placer mining. Using moving water to separate flakes or nuggets of gold from gravel and soil taken from the bed or bank of a stream.

plateau. An elevated, generally flat area of land; a tableland.

plaza. An open area where people gather. In early Spanish American settlements, the plaza was surrounded on all four sides by rooms or walls.

pottery. Pots, bowls, or plates made from moist clay and hardened by heat.

powwow. A meeting or gathering of American Indians.

precious metals. Metals such as gold and silver that have a high value.

precipitation. Moisture that falls in the form of rain or snow.

primary source. A firsthand or eyewitness account by someone who lived at the time.

pueblo. A village or large community dwelling (up to five stories in height) built by Indians of the American Southwest.

Pueblo Indians. Indian people who live in New Mexico and Arizona, related to the Ancestral Puebloans.

raid. A surprise attack against an enemy camp, village, or fort.

rawhide. The untanned hide of animals.

referendum. A vote directly by the people on an issue or whether a measure will become a law.

region. A geographic area in which places or landforms have much in common.

rendezvous. A meeting place and time arranged beforehand.

representative democracies. Governments in which people elect others to represent them in a legislature.

reservation. Land set aside by the United States government as living space for American Indian tribes.

reservoir. A body of water stored in a natural or human-made lake.

resort. A place to which people go to relax and have fun.

roundup. Herding together cattle that range on the open plains so calves can be branded and older cattle shipped to market.

rural. Having to do with the country rather than the city, or related to farming.

scarcity. Not having enough resources to satisfy people's needs and wants.

sea level. The level of the ocean's surface, used as the base to measure the elevation of land or the depth of the sea.

secondary source. An account based on primary sources written by someone who lived at a later time.

segregated. Providing separate schools, housing, or services based on race.

semiarid. Having too little snow and rainfall (10–20 inches per year) to grow crops without irrigation.

separation of powers. Dividing power among different branches of government.

significance. Being important, having an impact, or being valuable.

sod house. A house made of grass-covered soil held together by roots.

sorghum. A plant grown for its grain or as animal feed; also a source of syrup.

spatially. How places are located in relation to each other.

statehood. Being a state rather than a territory of the United States.

steel mill. A building where iron ore is heated in blast furnaces to be made into steel.

suburbs. Small towns and communities where people live close to the larger cities where they work.

suffrage. Having the right to vote.

territory. A part of the United States that has not been admitted as a state. A territorial government has a legislature elected by the people but no senators or members of Congress. The governor and other top officials are appointed by the president of the United States.

trading post. A store where traders from the outside come to exchange goods for furs or other local products.

trappers. People who trap wild animals for their skins.

travois. A frame made of poles pulled by a horse. The Plains Indians used it to carry their belongings from one place to another.

treaty. A written agreement between two or more states or between Indian tribes and the United States concerning trade, peace, or ownership of land.

tribal government. The elected officials who make and enforce laws for Indian tribes.

tribes. The large groups to which villages or bands of Indians belong.

tundra. The area of a mountain above tree line. Only low-growing plants and shrubs can survive because of the tundra's cold climate, frozen subsoil, and harsh winds.

uranium. A silver-white metal that is radioactive. It is used for fuel for nuclear weapons and power plants.

urban corridor. The area in Colorado along the Front Range of the Rocky Mountains where the largest cities and most of the population are located.

vein. A long, narrow deposit of ore that contains gold, silver, or other minerals.

village. A small town or cluster of shelters.

World War I. A war in Europe from 1914 to 1918 in which the United States and its allies fought Germany, Austria, Hungary, and Turkey.

World War II. A war in Europe, Africa, and Asia from 1939 to 1945 in which the United States and its allies fought Germany, Italy, and Japan.

Bibliography

TEACHER RESOURCES

Bachus, Harriet Fish. *Tomboy Bride.* Boulder: Pruett, 1969.

Coel, Margaret. *Chief Left Hand.* Norman: University of Oklahoma Press, 1981.

Crum, Sally. *People of the Red Earth.* Santa Fe, NM: Ancient City, 1996.

Crutchfield, James. *It Happened in Colorado.* Guilford, CT: Globe Pequot, 1993.

Ellis, Anne. *The Life of an Ordinary Woman.* Lincoln: University of Nebraska Press, 1980.

Krudwig, Vickie Leigh. *Searching for Chipeta.* Golden, CO: Fulcrum, 2004.

Lamb, Susan. *Mesa Verde National Park.* Mariposa, CA: Sierra, 1999.

Marsh, Charla. *People of the Shining Mountains.* Boulder: Pruett, 1982.

Mutel, Cornelia, and John Emerick. *From Grassland to Glacier.* Boulder: Johnson Books, 1992.

Ubbelohde, Carl, Maxine Benson, and Duane Smith. *A Colorado History.* Boulder: Pruett, 2001.

Wills, Charles A. *An Historical Album of Colorado.* Brookfield, CT: Millbrook, 1996.

Yue, Charlotte, and David Yue. *The Pueblo.* Wilmington, MA: Houghton Mifflin, 1986.

STUDENT RESOURCES

Arnold, Caroline. *The Ancient Cliff Dwellers of Mesa Verde.* Wilmington, MA: Clarion Books, 1992.

Avi. *The Secret School.* New York: Scholastic, 2001.

Ayer, Eleanor. *The Colorado Chronicles.* Frederick, CO: Jende-Hagan Bookcorp, 1980–84.

Ayer, Eleanor H. *Colorado*. Celebrate the States. New York: Benchmark Books, 1997.

Bacon, Melvin, and Daniel Blegen. *Bent's Fort.* Brookfield, CT: Millbrook, 1995.

Baylor, Byrd. *When Clay Sings.* New York: Aladdin Paperbacks, 1987.
Bouchard, David. *If You're Not from the Prairie . . .* New York: Aladdin Paperbacks, 1998.
Bunting, Eve. *Cheyenne Again.* Wilmington, MA: Clarion Books, 1995.
Downing, Sybil, and Jane Valentine. *Colorado Heritage Series.* Boulder: Pruett.
Elias, Megan. *World Almanac: Colorado.* Strongsville, OH: World Almanac Library, 2005.
Finley, Mary Peace. *Little Fox's Secret: The Mystery of Bent's Fort.* Palmer Lake, CO: Filter, 1999.
Finley, Mary Peace. *Meadow Lark.* Palmer Lake, CO: Filter, 2003.
Finley, Mary Peace. *Soaring Eagle.* Palmer Lake, CO: Filter, 1998.
Finley, Mary Peace. *White Grizzly.* Palmer Lake, CO: Filter, 2000.
Flanagan, Alice. *The Pueblos.* True Books: American Indians. Danbury, CT: Children's Press, 1998.
Fradin, Dennis Brindell. *Colorado.* From Sea to Shining Sea. Danbury, CT: Children's Press, 1995.
Freedman, Russell. *Cowboys of the Wild West.* Wilmington, MA: Clarion Books, 1985.
Friggins, Myriam. *Tales, Trails and Tommyknockers.* Boulder: Johnson Books, 1979.
Goble, Paul. *The Return of the Buffaloes.* Westchester, OH: National Geographic, 1996.
Hobbs, Will. *Beardance.* New York: Aladdin Paperbacks, 1993.
Hobbs, Will. *Bearstone.* New York: Aladdin Paperbacks, 2004.
Hobbs, Will. *Kokopelli's Flute.* New York: Aladdin Paperbacks, 1995.
Hoyt-Goldsmith, Diane. *Pueblo Storyteller.* New York: Holiday House, 1991.
Kalman, Bobbie. *Boomtowns of the West.* Life in the Old West. New York: Crabtree, 1999.
Kalman, Bobbie. *The Gold Rush.* Life in the Old West. New York: Crabtree, 1999.
Kalman, Bobbie. *Homes of the West.* Life in the Old West. New York: Crabtree, 1999.

Kalman, Bobbie. *Life in a Plains Camp.* New York: Crabtree, 2001.

Kalman, Bobbie. *Life in a Pueblo.* New York: Crabtree, 2003.

Kalman, Bobbie. *Life on the Ranch.* Life in the Old West. New York: Crabtree, 1999.

Kalman, Bobbie. *Life on the Trail.* Life in the Old West. New York: Crabtree, 1999.

Kalman, Bobbie. *Nations of the Plains.* New York: Crabtree, 2001.

Kalman, Bobbie. *Nations of the Southwest.* New York: Crabtree, 2003.

Kalman, Bobbie. *A One-Room School.* Historic Communities. New York: Crabtree, 1994.

Kalman, Bobbie. *The Wagon Train.* Life in the Old West. New York: Crabtree, 1999.

Kalman, Bobbie. *Who Settles the West?* Life in the Old West. New York: Crabtree, 1999.

Keegan, Marcia. *Pueblo Boy: Growing Up in Two Worlds.* New York: Cobblehill Books, 1991.

Keegan, Marcia. *Pueblo Girls: Growing Up in Two Worlds.* Santa Fe, NM: Clear Light, 1999.

Kehoe, Stasia Ward. *I Live in the Mountains.* New York: Rosen, 2000.

Krudwig, Vickie Leigh. *Hiking through Colorado History.* Englewood, CO: Westcliffe, 1998.

la Pierre, Yvette. *Welcome to Josefina's World:* 1824. The American Girls Collection. Middleton, WI: Pleasant Company, 1999.

Lawlor, Laurie. *Crossing the Colorado Rockies* 1864. American Sisters. New York: Minstrel Book Pocket Books, 1999.

McCluskey, Krista. *Colorado.* A Kid's Guide to American States. New York: Weigl, 2001.

Moody, Ralph. *Little Britches.* Lincoln: University of Nebraska Press, 1991.

Osborne, Mary Pope. *Adaline Falling Star.* New York: Scholastic, 2000.

Patent, Dorothy Hinshaw. *Homesteading—Settling America's Heartland.* New York: Walker, 1998.

Petersen, David. *The Anasazi.* New True Books. Danbury, CT: Children's Press, 1995.

Petersen, David. *Dinosaur National Monument.* New True Books. Danbury, CT: Children's Press, 1991.

Rennicke, Jeff. *Colorado Wildlife.* Denver: Falcon, 1996.

Russell, Marion. Adapted by Ginger Wadsworth. *Along the Santa Fe Trail: Marion Russell's Own Story*. Morton Grove, IL: Albert Whitman, 1993.

Schlissel, Lillian. *Black Frontiers.* New York: Simon and Schuster Books for Young Readers, 1995.

Shaughnessy, Diane, and Jack Carpenter. *Chief Ouray: Ute Peacemaker.* New York: Rosen, 1997.

Simmons, Marc. *Friday the Arapaho Boy.* Albuquerque: University of New Mexico Press, 2004.

Thompson, Kathleen. *Portrait of America: Colorado.* Orlando, FL: Steck-Vaughn, 1991.

Trimble, Stephen. *The Village of Blue Stone.* New York: Macmillan, 1990.

Warren, Scott. *Cities in the Sand.* San Francisco: Chronicle Books, 1992.

Wroble, Lisa A. *Kids in Pioneer Times.* New York: Rosen, 1997.

Young, Mary Taylor. *On the Trail of Colorado Critters.* Denver: Denver Museum of Natural History, 2000.

WEBSITES

http://geography.unco.edu/mapco/

http://memory.loc.gov/ammem/award/codhtml/hawphome.html

http://wildlife.state.co.us/WildlifeSpecies/Profiles

http://www.coloradohistory.com

http://www.cpluhna.nau.edu/People/ute_indians.htm

http://www.desertusa.com

http://www.hewit.unco.edu/dohist/

http://www.historycolorado.org/kids-students/kids-students

http://www.nps.gov/beol/index.htm

http://www.nps.gov/meve/index.htm

http://www.state.co.us/kids/history.htm

Credits

FIGURES

Alamy: Action Plus Sports/Alamy Live News, 289 (*top*); age footstock, back cover (*center right*), iii (*right inset*), vii (*bottom*), 238–39 (*top*); Amar and Isabelle Guillen—Guillen Photo LLC, vi (*center*), 48–49 (*top*), 82, 218; epa european pressphoto agency b.v., 250; Everett Collection Historical, 266; Ian Dagnall, 85; Jim West, ii (*bottom left inset*), 243 (*top*), 252, 253; Keystone Pictures USA, 291; North Wind Picture Archives, ii (*bottom right inset*), 140

Bailey Library and Archives, Denver Museum of Nature & Science: 51, 53, 211 (*bottom*)

Carlson, Eric: 50, 56, 57, 58, 62 (*top*), 72 (*bottom*), 78 (*right*), 131 (*background and inset*)

City of Greeley Museums, Permanent Collection: #C1_3015.0001.2d, 264

Collector, Steve: ii–iii (*background*), 17, 20 (*background*), 21, 22, 23, 40 (*background*), 41, 43

Colorado Bureau of Land Management: 59 (*bottom*)

Colorado Clouds Blog, Kevin Udy: 147 (*background*)

Corbis: Marilyn Angel Wynn/Nativestock Pictures, 76; RICK WILKING/Reuters, 288

Cripple Creek & Victor Gold Mining Company, Gaylon Wampler Photography: 211 (*top*)

Cushman, Ruth Carol: 44 (*bottom*)

Denver Public Library, San Luis Museum and Cultural Center: i, 97 (*center inset*)

Denver Public Library, Western History Collection: 272; CHS-B1026, 214; CHS-X4629, 201 (*top*); Con88Box8FF9_Peck, 97 (*top background*); F-22692, 141; GB-8294, 9 (*center left*), 257 (*background*), 260; H-461, 92, 119 (*right*); MCC-1348, ii (*bottom center*), 284; OP-8600, 205 (*left*); TMD-469, ii (*top right inset*), 277; WH1089, 97 (*right inset*); X-246, 207 (*top*); X-760, 201 (*bottom right*); X-809, 256; X-6158, 295 (*top*); X-6559, 278 (*bottom*); X-7531, 172 (*background*); X-7685, 261; X-21803, 192; X-22622, 269; X-27668, 270 (*top left*);

X-30351, 105 (*bottom left*), 108 (*bottom*); X-31282, 123; X-32191, 118 (*right*); X-32366, back cover (*bottom left*), 119 (*left*); X-32649, 126 (*bottom*); X-33850, 127; X-62343, 204 (*right*); X-276623, 270 (*top right*); Z-99, 273 (*bottom*), 279; Z-102, 254; Z-103, 294; Z-104, 265 (*bottom*); Z-108, 296 (*top*); Z-114, 262 (*top*); Z-117, 260; Z-128, 207 (*bottom*); Z-152, viii–ix, 227 (*bottom*); Z-6673, 224; Z-10811, front cover (*bottom left*), 289 (*bottom*)

Flickr: John Morgan, 129 (*background*); US Department of Agriculture, 263 (*top*)

Getty: Dave Buresh/The Denver Post, 293 (*bottom*); George Crouter/The Denver Post via Getty Images, 293 (*top*)

Hayden, Nikki: 2, 20 (*inset*), 173 (*right*)

History Colorado, Denver, Colorado: front cover (*center left*), iii (*left inset*), 74 (*left*), 232 (*bottom*), 292; 73.28.1, 97 (*left inset*); 76.58.1, 151 (*top right*); 81.132.24, Z0009191, 170; 84.37.1, 10037041, 210; 84.192.1003, 10028086, 196; 84.211.7.A, 83 (*top*), 97 (*bottom*); 86.70.124, 10025298, 190; 86.200.20000, 10048000, 219 (*bottom*); 86.200.2612, 10024607, 110 (*right*); 86.296.5450, 10027865, front cover (*top center*), vii (*center*), 178–79 (*top*), 219 (*top*); 86.298.1, 172 (*inset*); 88.189.39, 20101000, 221 (*bottom*); 88.318.16, 10034865, 274–75; 89.451.279, 10027307, 204 (*left*); 90.156.570, 20030443, 100, 109; 91.234.1, 10036106, 105 (*bottom right*), 111; 91.237.17, 10046581, 217; 91.342.12, 10025847, 206; 91.429.451, 10037181, 152; 91.537.34, 10028392, 200 (*bottom*); 93.84.1, 10030609, 163 (*top*); 94.367.4, 10045242, ii (*top left inset*); 108 (*top*); 95.200.933, 10047763, 194; 95.200.919, 10027902, 202 (*top*); 99.270.41, 20006593, 198; 99.270.2877, 10035507, 202 (*bottom*); 99.270.4207, 10024607, 197; 2000.129.234, 10046479, 234 (*right*); 2000.129.839, 10037003, iii (*center left inset*), 110 (*left*); 2004.24.177.B, 125 (*left*); 10027731, 267; 10036893, vii (*top*), 138–39 (*top*), 155 (*top*); 10041183, 259 (*top*); 10044477, 74; 10044478, 166; 3001383, 154 (*bottom inset, center left inset*); AA.2011.12.07.177, 157 (*top*); D.H.278.1, 40000334, 151 (*top left*); E.1327.1, 20020026, 106 (*left*); E.1697.1, 20020009, 124 (*top*); E.1894.99, 10037003, 106 (*right*); H.6130.2, 154 (*background and top inset*); H.6130.37, 10025804, 208 (*top*), 208–9 (*background*); H.6130.39, 20020088, 230; H.6131.14, iii (*center right inset*), 147 (*right inset*); H.6131.30, 10035995, 147 (*left inset*); H.6670, 40000484, 151 (*bottom*); PH.00057, 90.156.555, 112; PH.00168, 20006087, 201 (*bottom left*); PH.00422, 10027185, 160; PH.00422, 10028665, 165 (*bottom*); PH.00493, 20005548, back cover (*top left*), 285 (*bottom*); PH.PROP.269, 10029364, 223; PH.PROP.633, 10029692, 168 (*top*); PH.PROP.864, 10025996, 233 (*top*); PH.PROP.1390, 10030367, 167; PH.PROP.1548, 10030554, 148; PH.PROP.1556, 10030564, 149 (*bottom*); PH.PROP.1869, 10030889, 222; PH.PROP.2057, 10028698, 150; PH.PROP.3009, 10027263, 120 (*bottom*); PH.PROP.3242, 10028241, 128; PH.PROP.3242, 10036029, 122; PH.PROP.4999, 10037181, 156

IKONOS: 7

Library of Congress: 42 (*left*); Geography and Map Division, 205 (*right*); Prints and Photographs Division, 154 (*center right*), 275 (*top center and bottom*)

Macys, Sonya, courtesy of www.yampatika.org: 103 (*left and right*)

Massey, Tony: 229 (*top left*)

McBeth, Sally, PhD: vi (*bottom*), 90–91 (*top*), 113

National Park Services: 28, 38 (*inset*); Mesa Verde National Park, x–1, vi (*top*), 69, 72 (*top*), 77 (*bottom*), 79 (*top and inset*), 81 (*top*), 83 (*bottom*), 87, 244 (*bottom*)

Nelson, Bill: 5, 6 (*top*), 8 (*inset*), 14, 19, 30, 46, 48–49 (*bottom*), 52, 55 (*top*), 70, 77 (*top*), 84 (*bottom*), 90–91 (*bottom*), 102 (*top*), 118 (*left*), 138–39 (*bottom*), 142, 145, 153, 165 (*top*), 178–79 (*bottom*), 218, 203, 231, 298

Pratt, Daniel: back cover (*center left*)

Salazar, Ken: 173 (*left*)

Shutterstock: Andrea Izzotti, 63; arek_malang, 185 (*top*); AridOcean, 15 (*bottom inset*); Arina P Habich, 33 (*bottom inset*), 182 (*bottom*), 282; Asillem (164); bikeriderlondon, 240, 244 (*center left*); Bonnie Taylor Barry, 221 (*top*); Brandon Bourdages, 248; Brian Eichhorn, 243 (*bottom center*); Brian Gerber, 301; Charles Butzin III, 129 (*inset*); Chris Bianco, 42 (*right*); Christopher Boswell, 62 (*bottom*), 187 (*bottom inset*); Chursina Viktoriia, 102 (*bottom*); Colwell Photography, 11 (*bottom left*); Cora Reed, 189; cristi180884, 96; cvm, 11 (*bottom left*); Dasha Rosato, 244 (*top left*); Dmitry Kalinovsky, 183 (*top*); EdgeOfReason, 302; Eric Isselee, 29; farbled, 180, 187; Fer Gregory, 199 (*top*); Frances A. Miller, 244 (*top right*); Fredlyfish4, 9 (*left*), 162 (*bottom*); gashgeron, 84 (*top*); Globe Turner, 15 (*top inset*); Graceson, 37 (*left*); Gyvafoto 306 (*right*); Hammon Photography, 126 (*top right*); Henryk Sadura, 9 (*center right*), 299; Igor Kovalenko, 25 (*top right inset*); Images by Dr. Alan Lipkin, 37 (*right*); Ingka D. Jiw, 263 (*bottom*); iofoto, 183 (*bottom left*); Jeffrey M. Frank, 88 (*bottom*);

Jen duMoulin, 107 (*top inset*); Jim Harris 287 (*bottom center*); John De Bord, 11 (*bottom center left*); John Hoffman, front cover (*bottom right*); John R. Mcnair, 36 (*top right inset*); Juli Scalzi, 11 (*center left*); Kane513, 40 (*inset*); Krasowit 107 (*center inset*); Lane V. Erickson, 26 (*bottom inset*); Lester Balajadia, 185 (*bottom center*); Lilac Mountain, 244 (*center right*); Linda Armstrong, 24 (*left inset*); Luis Carlos Jimenez del rio, 78 (*left*), 262 (*bottom*); M. Ali Khan, 185 (*bottom left*); MarcelClemens, 195 (*bottom*); Marc Venema, 251; marekuliasz, 32 (*bottom inset*), 306 (*left*); Marzolino, 130; Mauro Rodrigues, 193; Mike Monahan, 4; Monkey Business Images, 183 (*bottom right*); Nagel Photography, 174 (*bottom right inset*); Natalia Pushchina, 247; ndoeljindoel, 188; Nicole Paton, 26 (*bottom center inset*); Pagina, 107 (*background and bottom inset*); Patrick Poendl, 297 (*inset*); Patsy Michaud, 33 (*center inset*); Paul Gana, 11 (*top left*); pio3, 243 (*bottom left*); Pixel Embargo, 6 (*bottom*); Positive thinker, 105 (*top*); pzAxe, 182 (*top left*); Rawpixel, 182 (*top right*); rCarner, 9 (*right*), 26 (*top center inset*), 36 (*bottom left inset*), 285 (*top*); Rimgaudas Budrys, 185 (*bottom right*); robert cicchetti, 32 (*top inset*); Robert Gubbins, 273 (*top*); ronstik, 295 (*bottom*); Samot, front cover (*top right*), 11 (*top right*); SCOTTCHAN, 55 (*bottom*); Seita, 121; Sharon Day, 11 (*top center*), 24 (*top right*), 33 (*top inset*); Shebeko, 124 (*bottom*); sjgh, 193; Sopotnicki, 88 (*top*); steve estvanik 132; Svetlana Larina, 287 (*top center inset*); Teri Virbickis, 234 (*left*); ThelmaElaine, 136; 3Dstock, 287 (*background*); Timberlakephoto, 297 (*bottom*); Tim Pleasant, 290 (*top*); Tim UR 233 (*bottom*); Tom Potter, 243 (*bottom right*); Tupungato, 25 (*center right inset*); Volt Collection, 286; WorldPictures, 25 (*bottom center inset*); Zack Frank, back cover (*bottom right*), 25 (*bottom right inset*), 174 (*top left inset*), 300 (*top and bottom*)

Stampsbook.org: image 1111, 229 (*bottom right*)

Tipis.org: 126 (*top left*)

US Army: 26 (*top inset*)

US Department of Agriculture: 31; Gary Kramer, National Resources Conservation Service, USDA NRCSCO01095, 38 (*background*); Irv Cole, NRCSCO68004, USDA National Resources Conservation Service, 35 (*background*); Jack Dykinga, Agricultural Research Service, USDA K3912-1, 35 (*inset*)

US Department of the Interior, Bureau of Reclamation: 36 (*bottom right inset*), 280

US Government: front cover (*top left*),16, 34, 45, 104, 157 (*inset*), 171, 235, 246, 249, 286

Wikimedia: 133, 134, 144 (*background*), 208 (*bottom left*), 209 (*bottom*), 229 (*bottom left*); Adam Baker, 59 (*top*); Adrian Pingstone, 73 (*center*); Ahodges7, 304; Allan Ramsay, 245 (*left*); Andreas F. Borchert, 32 (*top center inset*); The Athenaeum, 146; Arturo de Frias Marques, 54; Asbestos, 75; Benjamin Clark, 296 (*bottom*); Carptrash, 208 (*bottom right*); Daniel Mayer, 60; Daniel Schwen, 24–25 (*background*), 174 (*center inset*); DEMIS Mapserver, 18; Edward S. Curtis, 120 (*top left*); George V. Allen, 209 (*top right*); Gift of Mrs. Sidney T. Miller, 116; Hans Hillewaert, 66; HJPD, 71, 143; Hoggs555, 290 (*bottom*); Intel Free Press, 73 (*bottom*); Isaak Brodsky, 245 (*right*); Jacques-Louis David, 245 (*center*); James G. Howes, 135; Jeffrey Beall, 225; JimIrwin, 15 (*bottom center inset*); Jimmy Thomas, 32 (*bottom center inset*); Joe Haupt, 271; John Fowler, 12; Jurii, 259 (*bottom*); Karol M., 86; Library of Congress, 94–95, 195 (*top*); Library of Congress Prints and Photographs Division, 212 (*bottom*), 226, 227 (*top*), 232 (*top*) 258, 265 (*top left and right*), 275 (*top*); Library of Congress Prints and Photographs Division, Brady-Handy Photograph Collection, 169 (*top inset*), 228; Marduk, 229 (*top right*); MPF, 39; NASA, 8 (*background*), 15 (*background*); National Archives and Records Administration, ARC Identifier 165-WW-420(P379), 268; National Park Service Digital Image Archives, 174 (*background*); Newell Post, 81 (*bottom*); Nez Perce National Historical Park, NEPE 8894, 155 (*bottom*); NOAA George E. Marsh Album, 275 (*bottom center*); Ra'ike, 125 (*right*); Robert N. Dennis collection of stereoscopic views, 199 (*inset*), 200 (*top*); Sebastian Wallroth, 242; Tomia, Licenced GFDL and CC-BY-2.5, 212 (*top*); Tourbillon, 73 (*top*); Travis Leland, 305; US National Archives and Records Administration, back cover (*center*), 257 (*inset*), 276; Ulrich Egert, 68; US Department of Defense, 303; US Government, 15 (*top center inset*); Uyvsdi, 120 (*top right*); Vmenkov, 169 (*bottom inset and background*); William Henry Jackson, 98

Wilson Pratt, Christy: 44 (*top*)

TEXT

Page 83: Frey Angelico Chavez (translator), *Diary and Itinerary by Silvestre Velez de Escalante* (Madison: Wisconsin Historical Society Digital Library and Archives, 2003), p. 148

Page 107: Warren Angus Ferris, *Life in the Rocky Mountains* (Denver: Old West, 1940), p. 212; Isabel Kent (1985), quoted in Jan Pettit, *Utes: The Mountain People* (Boulder: Johnson, 1990), p. 28

Page 129: Althea Bass, *The Arapaho Way: A Memoir of an Indian Boyhood* (as told by Carl Sweezy) (New York: C. N. Potter, 1966), pp. 30–31

Page 144: Frey Angelico Chavez (translator), *Diary and Itinerary by Silvestre Velez de Escalante* (Madison: Wisconsin Historical

Society Digital Library and Archives, 2003), p. 149; Hubert Howe Bancroft, *The Works of Hubert Howe Bancroft*, volume 25: *History of Nevada, Colorado, and Wyoming, 1540–1888* (San Francisco: History Company, 1890), p. 340

Page 147: Zebulon M. Pike, *Account of Expeditions to the Sources of the Mississippi and through the Western Parts of Louisiana* (Philadelphia: 1810), appendix to part 2, p. 11; Edwin James, *Account of an Expedition from Pittsburgh to the Rocky Mountains* (Philadelphia: H. C. Carey and I. Lee, 1823)

Page 152: From Kit Carson, *Memoirs, 1809–1856* (1856)

Page 169: "Nathaniel P. Hill Inspects Colorado: Letters Written in 1864," *Colorado Magazine* 33 (October 1956): 267

Page 200: Horace Greeley, *An Overland Journey* (New York: C. M. Saxton, Barker, and Co., 1860); James F. Meline, *Two Thousand Miles on Horseback* (New York: Hurd and Houghton, 1868); Bayard Taylor, *Colorado: A Summer Trip* (New York: G. P. Putnam and Son, 1867)

Page 209: George E. Hyde, *Life of George Bent* (Norman: University of Oklahoma Press, 1968), p. 162

Page 222: Clara Hilderman Ehrlich, "My Childhood on the Prairie," *Colorado Magazine* 51, no. 2 (1973): 120; Thomas Sisk, Colorado Historical Society, CWA Interviews, document 44, p. 350

Page 227: Mrs. Jennie Lucas, "Pioneer Education" (1941), WPA, Box 5, Denver Public Library; Glenn R. Durrell, "Homesteading in Colorado," *Colorado Magazine* 51 (1974): 102–3; A. W. McHendrie, "Boyhood Recollections of Springfield, Colorado," *Colorado Magazine* 11 (May 1944): 99

Page 265: Jack Dempsey, *Round by Round: An Autobiography* (New York: Whittlesey House, 1940), p. 12

Page 274: Keith A. Cook, "A Whiskey Train and a Doughnut Day: Coming of Age on the Eastern Colorado Plains," *Colorado Heritage* (Spring 1998): 4; Recollections of Bill Reed, in Margee Gabehart, ed., *History of Elbert County, Colorado* (Dallas: Curtis Media Corp., 1989), p. 17; Theresa Lee, "The Depression Years," in Margaret J. Lehrer, ed., *Up the Hemline* (Colorado Springs: Delta Kappa Gamma Society, 1975), p. 133

Page 278: Carl Ubbelohde, Maxine Benson, and Duane A. Smith, *A Colorado History* (Boulder: Pruett, 1995), p. 321

Page 290: John Gunther, *Inside USA* (New York: Harper and Brothers, 1947), pp. 214–15

Index

Bold type indicates illustrations

D

E

F

Q

R

S

T

U

V

W

Y